DISNEY AND HIS WORLDS

Disney and his Worlds is a thorough overview of what is by now quite a large literature on the Disney organization, in particular the theme parks and their significance for contemporary culture.

The author looks at Walt Disney's life and how his biography has been constructed; the Walt Disney Company in the years after his death; and the writings of various commentators on the Disney theme parks. He raises important issues about the parks: whether they are harbingers of postmodernism; the significance of consumption at the parks; the nature of the parks as tourism; and the representation of past and future. The discussion of theme parks is central but links with the presentation of Walt Disney's biography and his organization by showing how central economic and business considerations have been in their development, and how the significance of these considerations is typically marginalized in order to place an emphasis on fantasy and magic. In the process, the book questions the assumption that the parks are sites of postmodern sensibility.

Disney films, merchandizing and theme parks are one of the defining features of our times and one of the more effective elements in American cultural imperialism. It is impossible to imagine an encyclopedic sociology of contemporary culture that did not devote at least a chapter to Disney and his Worlds. In particular the parks are often employed as examples in areas like cultural studies, the sociology of postmodernism, tourism and leisure studies, while Walt Disney and his organization are important to the area of organization studies. All will welcome Bryman's clear and judicious overview of literature on the man, the organization, the theme parks and their significance to contemporary culture.

Alan Bryman is Professor of Social Research, Loughborough University.

DISNEY AND HIS WORLDS

Alan Bryman

London and New York

First published 1995
by Routledge
11 New Fetter Lane, London EC4P 4EE

Simultaneously published in the USA and Canada
by Routledge
29 West 35th Street, New York, NY 10001

Typeset in Palatino by LaserScript, Mitcham, Surrey
Printed and bound in Great Britain by
Mackays of Chatham PLC, Chatham, Kent

British Library Cataloguing in Publication Data
A catalogue record for this book is available from the British Library

Library of Congress Cataloguing in Publication Data
A catalogue record for this book has been requested

ISBN 0–415–10375–4 (hbk)
ISBN 0–415–10376–2 (pbk)

For Sue and Sarah,
my partners-in-Disney

'We just try to make a good picture. And then the
professors come along and tell us what we do.'
(Walt Disney)

CONTENTS

PREFACE

This book's origins derive from a realization some time ago, following a trip to Disney World, that various people had written about the Disney theme parks. They had apparently found them significant. It struck me that it would be a good idea to examine these writings to see what the various authors made of the parks, and to produce a short article on my findings. I saw it very much as a sideline interest, which would not divert me too much from the kinds of book that I normally write (in areas such as leadership theory, research methodology and quantitative data analysis for social scientists). But I soon became aware that there was a sizeable literature on Walt Disney, on his organization, and on the theme parks as well, and that it would be useful to consider the three in tandem. Moreover, the parks in particular seemed to be everyone's favourite example when it came to specifying the characteristics of postmodernity or contemporary tourism. I was also struck by the huge variety of people who had written on Disney issues, encapsulating such notables as Jean Baudrillard, E. L. Doctorow, Umberto Eco, and Stephen J. Gould. When I raised the possibility of writing a book on Disney and his worlds, after my colleague Mike Gane had put the idea into my head, my then editor at Routledge, Chris Rojek, announced that he had just had an article on Disney culture accepted in a journal. Moreover, the interest in Disney matters seems to be growing, as indicated by Susan Willis's comment in her introduction to a special issue of *South Atlantic Quarterly* (volume 92, number 1, 1993) on 'The World According to Disney': 'From what I hear on the cultural studies grapevine, the floodgate of Disney criticism is about to open.'

Part I of this book is concerned with Walt Disney and his

organization after his death. In the chapter on Walt Disney, I am concerned to show how his biography was constructed, while in the chapter on the Walt Disney Company (formerly Walt Disney Productions) the various phases of the post-Walt years are examined. Part II, which represents the bulk of the book, discusses the numerous writings on the theme parks. The two parts are related because a major theme of the book is the way in which the creation of an appearance of fantasy and magic, in which harsh economic considerations are sidelined, permeates the construction of Walt's biography, the organization after his death, and the theme parks. It might seem that such a structure neglects the Disney films, but in fact they pervade virtually every page, since they are at the heart of the Disney enterprise.

In discussing what the many writers on the Disney theme parks have made of the parks, I will be extracting the main ingredients of their explorations. Inevitably, my own observations intrude on many occasions. My aim has been to provide a text that will be useful to lecturers, students and others with an interest in areas like cultural studies, leisure and tourism studies, organization studies, and the sociology of postmodernism. Too often people use the Disney parks as illustrations of pet ideas, but do not proceed much further. I hope that this book will provide them with the resources for more informed analyses. I have tried to write it in such a way that it is not too drenched in the terminology of the debates which are touched on. However, I am likely to be a poor judge of whether I have succeeded in this regard and some people will possibly suggest that I should stick to statistics texts.

I have had no assistance from the Walt Disney Company and this work is entirely independent of the company. My request to visit the Disney Archives in California to examine their repository of writings on the theme parks was firmly rebuffed by someone in 'paralegal'. This is not in the least an uncommon experience among writers on Disney issues. As a result, I have had to maintain a constantly watchful eye for references to ensure that I did not miss anything, though some items will undoubtedly have slipped through the net. Nor are there any photographs in this book due to the tight hold kept not just on the cartoon characters but also the buildings in the theme parks. However, I have not allowed their general attitude to diminish my enthusiasm for the parks, which I still enjoy greatly. In this respect, I also differ from many of the commentators whose writings I examine in this book. Many of them exhibit a disdain of Disney products which is common among intellectuals but which I have never been able to understand. On the other hand, I have tried not to allow my enthusiasm to deflect the critical analysis that follows.

I have received assistance from many people. I want to thank Robin Allan for his tremendous help with material on Walt Disney and the organization. The staff in Inter-Library Loans in the Pilkington Library have been a constant source of help and good humour with respect to my search for often quite obscure items. The following have read all or parts of the manuscript and have offered valuable support and comments: Robin Allan, Mike Gane, Chris Rojek, Graham Murdock, and Mike Pickering. Many others have been helpful in providing me with snippets of information, press cuttings, and their thoughts. None of these people, however, can be blamed for the book's deficiencies. Sue and Sarah have put up with my usual absorption when writing a book, and even I have to admit that I have been worse than usual while writing this one. I know that they share my love of Disney cartoons and the parks and I hope that I have allowed this to show through sufficiently in this book.

ALAN BRYMAN

Part I

DISNEY AND HIS ORGANIZATION

1

THE LIFE OF WALT DISNEY

What follows is a brief biography of the life of Walt Disney. This is undertaken in order to provide, along with the analysis in the next chapter of his company in the years after his death in 1966, a background to an appreciation of the Disney theme parks which are the chief focus of this book. There is no absolute necessity to undertake an examination of Walt Disney's life, since the theme parks could logically be analysed in their own right or with little recourse to his biography. However, an examination of his life, and most especially the writings on his life, form an important backcloth to a number of observations which will be extracted in the context of the analysis of the theme parks.

In this biography and in subsequent chapters, Walt Disney will be referred to as Walt, rather than as Disney. There are two reasons for this, aside from parsimony. First, 'Disney' is often used to refer to the Walt Disney Company (formerly Walt Disney Productions) and in some writings it is not always obvious which is meant. Second, the biography of Walt Disney is also the biography of Roy O. Disney, his brother and business partner from Walt's arrival in Hollywood in the 1920s onwards. Stanley (1993) has noted that biographies often subsume the biographies of other people, albeit in shorter form. Nowhere is this a more appropriate observation than in the case of Walt Disney's biography, where the figure of his brother looms extremely large. Roy Disney will be referred to as Roy. 'Disney' will be used to refer to the company that Walt and Roy created.

In the next section, Walt's life will be presented in largely neutral terms in order to allow a number of points to be made about the biography which will be presented. Most of these basic facts are well known and can be found in a number of standard works on which the following account is based. Probably the best of the 'factual' accounts is Thomas's (1976) biography, which strongly influenced the present résumé, but a more detailed discussion of the sources of Walt's biography will follow.

THE LIFE OF WALT DISNEY: A FACTUAL ACCOUNT

Walter Elias Disney was born in Chicago on 5 December 1901 to Elias and Flora Disney. Elias Disney, both before and after Walt's birth, was a serially unsuccessful businessman who was continually seeking to improve his and his family's lot by moving on, both geographically and from business to business. Walt was their fourth son and he was followed by their only daughter, Ruth, in 1903. Roy was the third child and was born in 1893. Elias and Flora were unhappy about bringing Walt and the other children up in the disorder of a modern city, and they moved in 1906 to a farm in Marceline, Missouri, which many writers have viewed as the inspiration for the Main Street, USA attraction in Disneyland (e.g. Francaviglia, 1981). It was here that Walt spent his formative years and it is often regarded as the source of the interest in animals which was to be so evident in his animated cartoons. Most biographers depict him as not a strong school pupil, who tended to concentrate on his interests, like the movie house. The family left Marceline in 1910, after Elias was forced to sell the farm following financial problems and illness. Elias is depicted by many of Walt's biographers as a hard, humourless taskmaster who regularly beat his sons, and at around this time the two eldest sons deserted him. The family moved to Kansas City, Missouri, where Walt and Roy delivered newspapers for their father who had taken out a distributorship. Roy left home in 1912 to help his uncle on a farm. Walt's record at school continued to be undistinguished and he is often described as letting his attention wander too much. During these years, Walt's interest in drawing developed but was frowned on by his father who saw it as a frivolous activity. Walt remained close to Roy, who periodically returned to see him. In his mid-teens, Walt developed an interest in gags used by burlesque comedians and others and kept a file of them; he also took a correspondence course in art, which his father was prepared to pay for because Walt contributed to the family finances by working in a jelly factory. Walt joined the

4

Red Cross Ambulance Corps at the end of the war and was sent to France for a year.

On his return in 1919, Walt sought work as a cartoonist in Kansas City, and eventually was employed at a commercial art studio where he met and became friendly with another recently hired cartoonist, Ubbe Iwwerks (who later shortened his name to Ub Iwerks). Walt's job was short-lived and he teamed up with Iwerks to go into business. But Walt soon got a job as a cartoonist with the Kansas City Film Ad Company. Iwerks followed him shortly afterwards when their company went bankrupt in 1920. Although Iwerks is recognized as a brilliant draughtsman, he was a shy, diffident person, and it is generally reckoned that his personal traits contributed to a lack of ability at selling or generating interest in their products. At Film Ad, Walt began working on moving cartoons in the form of short advertising films. The method that he used was crude and Walt was dissatisfied with these films. He began to study animation and to experiment on his own at night. He found an outlet for his experiments in the Newman Laugh-O-Grams, which were brief cartoons based on simple gags made for the Newman Theater. In order to develop his experimental work further, Walt left his job and incorporated Laugh-O-Gram Films. Iwerks joined him, as did a number of other animators, and together they began work on fairy-tales. But the enterprise ran into difficulties and the cartoonists, including Iwerks, gradually left. At one point, Walt was telephoned by a local dentist who was interested in commissioning a film for the promotion of dental hygiene. When the dentist asked Walt to come over to finalize the deal, Walt had to admit that he did not have the $1.50 to recover his shoes from the local cobbler. The dentist not only came to Walt to hand over $500 for the deal, but also gave him the cobbler's fee. Walt then began work on *Alice's Wonderland*, in which a child was placed against a cartoon background, but this stream of activity also went bankrupt. In 1923, Walt decided he was getting nowhere and left for Hollywood to work in the movies with just $40 in his pocket.

Having failed to get a number of jobs, Walt was encouraged by Roy, who was living in Los Angeles at the time, to go back into cartoons. Roy managed to secure some financial backing and a distributor, Margaret Winkler, who had been sent *Alice's Wonderland*, expressed interest in the work and provided further financial backing. A series of Alice adventures began. Walt moved into offices whose front window bore the inscription 'Disney Bros. Studio', and in February 1924 he hired his first animator. By May 1924, the series was complete, although profit margins for each cartoon had deteriorated, due to the rising costs of making technical improvements. Walt decided to cease work on drawing and to concentrate on story-lines, and he persuaded Iwerks to join him. The Alice series then re-started. During this period Walt's romance began with one of the women working at the Studio – Lillian Bounds – whom he married in July 1925. Roy continued to oversee the business side of the Studio. Negotiations with their distributor became increasingly difficult when Margaret Winkler retired following her marriage to Charles Mintz, who took over the running of the company. However, in 1926, on the strength of a new agreement with Mintz, the brothers moved into a new studio premises on Hyperion Avenue close to downtown Los Angeles, but it was by then known as the Walt Disney Studio. Thomas (1976) suggests that the name-change occurred because Walt felt that the association of the studio with a single name would both appeal more to audiences and give it a stronger identity.

By the end of 1926, the Alice series had exhausted the range of possibilities open to it. The head of Universal Pictures had suggested to Mintz that he would like a cartoon series based on a rabbit. Following Mintz's encouragement, Walt began work on Oswald the Lucky Rabbit, but the initial offerings were not well received by the distributor. The cartoons were revised (in particular, improvements in quality and comedy situations) and the series began to receive great plaudits. Merchandise bearing Oswald's name and image appeared but the Disneys received no income or fee for their use. When the initial contract for the Oswalds came to an end, Walt took Lillian to New York to negotiate a new contract. Due to the success of Oswald, Walt and Roy fully expected to be able to secure better fees for their work. Instead, Walt was offered a much-reduced fee coupled with the threat that, if he did not sign, Mintz would sign all of the Disneys' animators. Moreover, the rights to using the Oswald name and character belonged to Universal so Walt had no further claim to it. Walt declined and on the train journey home he dreamed up a cartoon character based on a mouse named Mortimer. Lillian disliked the name and suggested the name Mickey.

Walt and Roy saw through their remaining contractual

obligations to produce Oswalds, but worked with Iwerks, who had remained loyal, on developing Mickey Mouse secretly at night (since they did not want the animators who had been signed by Mintz to know about the new character). Most writers agree that it was almost certainly Iwerks who developed and drew Mickey. Walt generated little interest in the first Mickey shorts, but at around the same time sound came to Hollywood. Walt felt that he needed not just to add sound, but that it should be fully synchronized with the action. Walt searched out a number of sound systems until he found what he felt was the best – Cinephone, a system owned by Pat Powers, which was based on a number of pirated designs. Walt applied Cinephone to *Steamboat Willie*, a Mickey Mouse animated cartoon short, and after some difficulty getting it shown, managed to secure a position on the bill of the Colony Theater, New York, on 18 November 1928. The cartoon was a sensational success and many distributors vied for a contract, but Walt's insistence on owning the films and on controlling character merchandising deterred most of them. Powers, however, entered into a contract with Walt to promote and sell future Mickey cartoons, so that he could promote his Cinephone system, in return for 10 per cent of gross receipts and a fee for the use of Cinephone. Roy felt that the contract gave too much away to Powers.

In order to build up the Mickey Mouse series, many new animators were hired. At the same time, Walt worked on a non-Mickey cartoon, *The Skeleton Dance*, which was to be the first of the Silly Symphonies series. This cartoon gave him and the Studio greater opportunity to experiment with their art. Mickey Mouse became a great success in 1929 but the cost of each new short escalated as Walt sought to improve quality. However, receipts seemed to have dried up. Walt hired a lawyer, Gunther Lessing, who had once advised Pancho Villa, and went to Powers to confront him about the lack of income. Powers refused to show them the books detailing receipts from the Mickeys but still tried to get them to sign a further deal. Powers felt that Walt could be convinced to sign when he played his trump card – he had a telegram showing that Iwerks had agreed to work with Powers to produce a cartoon series. Although shaken by this news, Walt refused to sign. Iwerks developed a number of series on his own, such as Flip the Frog, but these did not develop into major characters and his attempts to strike out on his own largely failed.

7

In 1940 Iwerks returned to Disney, where he stayed for the rest of his working life, playing a major role in developing a number of technological innovations.

In February 1930, Walt signed an agreement with Columbia to distribute the cartoons. Columbia also agreed to buy the Disneys out of their contract with Powers. The following year Walt suffered a breakdown from running what was still a hand-to-mouth operation, due to the rising costs of animation. Their financial problems would have been worse were it not for merchandising. Initially, agreements to use manufactured items with Mickey on them were haphazard but in February 1930 they signed a licensing agreement with the George Borgfeldt Company of New York. The Disneys were not entirely satisfied with Borgfeldt's efforts and in July 1932, following overtures made to them by Kay Kamen, who offered a greater emphasis on quality and a wider range of products, a new deal was signed with Kamen, with whom the Disneys enjoyed a highly successful relationship until his death in 1949.

Shortly after leaving Columbia and striking a new deal with United Artists, Walt decided to improve the quality of the Studio's output with colour. Despite Roy's reservations, Walt struck a deal with Technicolor for the exclusive use for two years of its new three-strip colour system. Walt felt that colour would give a great boost to the Silly Symphonies series and he used it for a short that was already in production, *Flowers and Trees*, which became the first cartoon to receive an award from the Academy of Motion Picture Arts and Sciences and was a huge success when it opened in July 1932. At around this time, Walt decided that the quality of cartoons could be enhanced by providing more training for his staff. This began in 1931, and from November 1932, classes in the Studio itself were conducted. A further boost to Walt's and the Studio's reputation was *The Three Little Pigs*, which was a great success for a number of reasons: its catchy tunes; its apparently optimistic message about the work ethic in the midst of the Great Depression; and most importantly, its investment of the three pigs with clear, identifiable personalities that brought animation to new heights.

By 1934 the staff had grown from six in 1928 to 187. During the early 1930s, the Studio's stable of characters grew, as Pluto, Donald Duck and Goofy gradually emerged in their own right. But by around 1934 Walt came to the view that he needed to make a feature film. One of the main reasons was that it was becoming increasingly difficult to combine the growing costs of animation, due to improvements stemming from sound, colour and technique, with the inherently limited returns that could accrue from shorts. Roy had very great reservations about the project but Walt went ahead and decided that *Snow White and the Seven Dwarfs* would provide a suitable story for treatment. The biographies and reminiscences about Walt invariably tell of an occasion shortly after his decision to make *Snow White* when he called many of the top animators to a late-night session at which he delivered a spell-binding narrative of the story and characters that he had envisioned. The Studio continued to make shorts after the decision was taken but the feature film was the source of everyone's enthusiasm. Walt allocated the main animators to specific tasks according to his perception of each of their strengths. The film received much adverse advance publicity and was dubbed 'Disney's folly', because of its escalating costs and because many commentators doubted the capacity of audiences to sit through a long animated cartoon. At one point it was apparent that the film needed further financing and Walt was persuaded to give a presentation to their bankers, Bank of America, so that they could see what they would be loaning the money for. After the showing and as he was leaving, the Bank's taciturn representative turned to Walt and said: 'That thing is going to make a hatful of money.' When it opened on 21 December 1937 it was an immense critical success, and subsequently an immense commercial success, earning $8 million on its initial release.

Largely as a result of *Snow White*'s success, Walt realised that feature film production had to become the Studio's main focus, and soon afterwards work began on *Pinnochio*, *Fantasia*, and *Bambi*. In order to accomplish this level of production effort, the Studio clearly needed to expand, but since the existing Hyperion buildings limited the extent to which much further expansion would be possible, the brothers decided to build a new studio. In the summer of 1938, they placed a deposit for a new purpose-built studio in Burbank. In effect, the new studio building would consume the bulk of the profits from *Snow White*. The move was completed in May 1940, by which time the Studio had about 1,100 employees. The Studio's financial position began to deteriorate around the beginning of World War II. Both *Fantasia* and *Pinnochio* performed poorly at the box office and produced sizeable losses, the former especially so, since they had proved very costly to produce. Also, Disney's European market had all but dried up as a result of the war. Walt and Roy tried to redeem the situation by producing two cheap feature films: *The Reluctant Dragon* (which included some live action) and *Dumbo*. The latter provided a much-needed injection of money at a time when so much was being spent on the new studio. Even so, the Studio was heavily in debt and was forced to issue shares to the public in April 1940, a move to which the brothers had always been opposed.

There is little doubt that the camaraderie that existed in the Hyperion studio was dissipated after the move to the large, rather antiseptic studio at Burbank and this almost certainly contributed to a lengthy strike at the Studio which began on 29 May 1941. The strike is a fascinating event, not least because most commentators agree that the work atmosphere was never the same again after the strike and because it pushed Walt's politics into a decidedly rightward direction, since he saw it as a product of the work of communists. It is also said that Walt never again felt the same about the bulk of those who worked for the company. Most biographers depict the strike as the product of a jurisdictional dispute as a result of the efforts by the Screen Cartoonists Guild, under the leadership of Herb Sorrell, to unionize the Studio. Walt refused to recognize the Guild and tried to appeal directly to his staff by outlining all that he and Roy had done in creating the company and its current parlous financial state. This was to no avail and the strike lasted nine weeks with approximately half the staff joining it. Walt seems to have become increasingly intransigent and vehement in his condemnation of the strikers, the Guild and the organizers. Indeed, it seemed that the only way that the strike could be settled would be to get Walt out of the way, and that is exactly what happened. Just at the point that both sides were becoming more and more obdurate, Walt received an invitation to go on a goodwill tour of South America, which would offer the opportunity for making films and developing ideas. He accepted, and the strike was settled by conciliators in his absence. The settlement was largely unfavourable to the Studio.

In December 1941, the Studio was commandeered by the US army and Walt spent the rest of the war making films to help the US war effort and health films for the State Department. During this period the company continued to experience financial setbacks. *Victory Through Air Power* lost $436,000 and the response to *Bambi* was disappointing, while *Saludos Amigos*, a product of the South America trip, fared quite well. By the end of the war, Walt Disney Productions was deeply in debt to Bank of America. Work began slowly on a number of cartoon shorts and then on feature films, including *Make Mine Music* and *Song of the South*, both of which included a great deal of live action in order to keep costs down. These films were moderately successful, but also constituted an important transitional point between the days when the company was (with the exception of *The Reluctant Dragon*) purely a cartoon studio and a period in which the company diversified gradually into non-cartoon films. One strand in this trend was the hiring of a couple who had experience of making travel and educational films to spend a year filming wild-life in Alaska, a project to which Roy was opposed. The result was *Seal Island*, a half-hour film which was well received. However, various other immediate post-war offerings were not well received by critics or the box office. The second strand of the shift away from cartoons was *Treasure Island*, a live-action adventure film which was made in England to secure access to millions of dollars in revenue that the company had built up, but which had been frozen. This film, along with *Cinderella* and *Beaver Valley*, another true-life short, greatly improved the company's financial position in 1950. It also marked the beginning of a period which continues to today, in which the balance of film production shifted away from cartoons to live-action adventures. This trend occurred side-by-side with a sharp decline in the number of cartoon shorts produced.

In 1951 *Alice in Wonderland* was neither a critical nor a financial success. Walt and his company were still in a situation where the company's position could be substantially affected by a single success or failure. In 1953 the company's fortunes were con-solidated by *Peter Pan* and *The Living Desert*. The latter marked an important turning-point for the company: because of their dist-ributor's lack of interest in this true-life feature film, Roy formed Disney's own distribution channel, called Buena Vista, which thereafter distributed all their films.

Some time in the late 1940s, Walt had become interested in the idea of an amusement park in which the cartoon characters would figure strongly, but which would also be a tribute to America's past and provide a vision of its future. When he had taken his daughters, Diane and Sharon, to such parks, he had been taken aback by their vulgarity and grime. He felt that he

11

could create a park that would be a place that adults and children would enjoy. However, Roy was implacably opposed to the idea. Walt created an organization to plan, design and administer the park, which was to be called Disneyland, and at the end of 1952, he founded Walt Disney, Incorporated, which later became WED Enterprises (WED is an acronym based on his initials), since shareholders might object to his use of the Walt Disney name. In fact, Roy threatened to sue Walt on behalf of the shareholders if he did not change the name. Walt also set up Retlaw (Walter spelt backwards) through which he controlled the merchandising rights to his name. Retlaw received 5 per cent of income from merchandising deals with Walt Disney Productions. Roy's opposition to Disneyland meant that he was unwilling to risk company money on the venture and bankers were similarly unenthusiastic about it. Walt raised the money through a variety of channels, of which the most frequently referred to are borrowing on his life insurance policies and forming a liaison with television. In essence, Disney offered a weekly television show in return for capital put up to help with the financing of Disneyland. An agreement was reached with the then up-and-coming American Broadcasting Company (ABC). The *Disneyland* series proved very important to the park's success in that it acted as a regular advertising medium both before and after the park's completion. It also gave the company the opportunity to advertise its forthcoming films such as the expensive *20,000 Leagues Under the Sea*, which was a major box-office success in 1954–5. In 1955 the television series was also the springboard for the successful *Davy Crockett* film, which had originally been made for television as a serial. On 17 July 1955, Disneyland, which had been sited in Anaheim in southern California, opened to the public. The opening day was a fiasco for a number of reasons: due to a large number of forged tickets, too many people got into the park; the water fountains failed to work on a blisteringly hot day, leading to accusations that it was a strategy to get people to buy drinks; and many attractions were incomplete or failed to work, while the asphalt melted in the heat. None the less, Disneyland proved a tremendous financial success.

Following the success of Disneyland, for the first time the brothers and their company were placed on a stable financial footing. In 1952 the profits of Walt Disney Productions were approximately $0.5 million; in 1959 they were $3.4 million; and by

1965 they were $11 million. Disneyland had changed not just the company's profile, with a growing percentage of profits deriving from the theme parks, but its profitability. The television series continued to be popular, and in 1961 the company moved from ABC to the National Broadcasting Company (NBC) in order to develop a new series in colour, which became *Walt Disney's Wonderful World of Color*. During the late 1950s and early 1960s, there was a steady flow of successful films, though the costs of *Sleeping Beauty* resulted in a small loss in 1960. Disneyland continued to be developed though Walt expressed disappointment with the way in which its environs had become populated with sleazy motels, diners, and attractions. He took the view that if he were to build Disneyland again, he would buy much more land in order to be able to control its periphery.

This possibility, along with a few other concerns, preoccupied him during the 1960s. One of these was the World's Fair in New York in 1964–5. For some time, Walt had been developing an interest in what he called 'Audio-Animatronic' figures – in essence, electronic robots which could move and speak. These had been under development for some time at WED, but the Fair acted as a catalyst since he persuaded major corporations to sponsor attractions for the Fair. These attractions were subsequently incorporated into Disneyland. The attractions and their sponsors were: Progressland (General Electric); It's a Small World (Pepsi-Cola); Magic Skyway (Ford); and Great Moments with Mr Lincoln (the World's Fair Committee). A second preoccupation was securing the rights to *Mary Poppins*, which proved to be the most successful Disney film when it opened in 1964. A third preoccupation was the idea of building a second theme park, this time in the east and with sufficient land to control the park's perimeter. In 1964, having chosen an area of land in Orange County, Florida, near Orlando, a clandestine operation was set up and implemented to purchase large tracts of land anonymously in order not to push up the cost of that land. The fourth preoccupation was the idea of building a city of tomorrow, a controlled urban Utopia, which he dubbed 'EPCOT' (Experimental Prototype Community of Tomorrow) and which led him to read widely in the area of urban planning. Walt expressed his vision for EPCOT by depicting it as 'like the city of tomorrow ought to be, a city that caters to the people as a service function' (cited in Mosley, 1986: 275). He continued:

13

It will be a planned, controlled community, a showcase for American industry and research, schools, cultural and educational opportunities. In EPCOT there will be no slum areas because we won't let them develop; there will be no landowners and therefore no voting control. People will rent houses instead of buying them, and at modest rentals. There will be no retirees, because everyone must be employed. One of our requirements is that the people who live in EPCOT must help keep it alive.

(Ibid.)

However, Walt was not to see this project or the Florida theme park come to fruition. After steadily worsening health in 1966, he died on 15 December of that year. It is sometimes suggested that he was in fact frozen, since a fifth preoccupation in his last years was the science of cryogenesis, but this is disputed by most commentators.

WALT DISNEY AS A CHARISMATIC LEADER

Walt Disney can be viewed as a member of a fairly select band of individuals who have not simply built up organizations, but who inculcate high levels of enthusiasm in themselves and in their goals among those who work for them. Steve Jobs of Apple Computer, Don Burr of People Express, Mary Kay Ash of Mary Kay Cosmetics, and Anita Roddick of Body Shop belong to a category of charismatic leaders/entrepreneurs who dream up a vision about the need for a product, attract others to that vision and build the organization into an enthusiastic group of adherents. By the term 'charismatic leader', is not meant someone who possesses glitz, sparkle and a spellbinding oratorical style – the common view of charisma. Instead, following Weber's (1968 [1925]) writings, by charismatic leadership I mean a relationship between leader and led

in which, by virtue of both the extraordinary qualities that followers attribute to the leader and the latter's mission, the charismatic leader is regarded by his or her followers with a mixture of reverence, unflinching dedication and awe.

(Bryman, 1992: 41)

Three elements are central to this definition. First, the charismatic leader is someone with a mission or vision of the future to which he or she wishes to attract others. Second, the charismatic leader, possibly by dint of the vision, is believed to be extraordinary by those followers. Third, the followers of charismatic leaders evince a high level of commitment to themselves and their cause. Walt Disney seems to conform to these three criteria quite well, along with the other previously mentioned figures.

First, Walt was certainly a visionary individual, but it is hard to say that he was possessed of a single vision. At a very general level, it could be said that his mission was 'to bring happiness to millions' (Schickel, 1986: 9), but this is not very illuminating. In similar vein, Snyder *et al.* (1994: 217) suggest that his vision 'was to bring warmth, laughter, and amusement to audiences around the world; his medium of communication would be an enterprise known for its quality, attention to detail, and constant striving for improvement'. This gets us a bit further but seems to concentrate too much on the organization he built and not enough on the products. Thomas and Johnston (1981: 186) suggest that he did not have what they refer to as 'a big overall dream' but developed dreams in the course of his work. This seems much closer to the mark. Walt was a 'serial visionary', someone who had big dreams about new ways of doing many things, whether it was making animated cartoons, designing amusement parks, or creating new approaches to urban living, rather than someone with a single all-consuming vision.

Second, he was seen by many of those who worked for him as exceptional. He was viewed as a brilliant story-teller who had changed the face of animated cartoons (Eisen, 1975: 40–1; Thomas and Johnston, 1981: 37, 97, 380) by giving them clear narrative structures. His development of true animation – investing cartoon characters with distinctive personalities – was greatly admired (for example, Culhane, 1986: 32; Merritt and Kaufman, 1992: 20; Thomas and Johnston, 1981: 35). Walt was known as a spell-binding actor, who often acted out the movements and words of characters in the films, though his *Snow White* performance is probably the best known (for example, Allan, 1985: 157; Culhane, 1986: 149; Thomas and Johnston, 1981: 41, 97). His relentless and uncompromising pursuit of quality earned him tremendous admiration among his workforce, who were often envied by animators at other studios (for example, Hand, n.d.: 71; Jones, 1991: 65; Solomon, 1989: 50, 143, 149; Thomas and Johnston, 1981:

86–7). He was known as a brave risk-taker (Culhane, 1976: 34; Thomas and Johnston, 1981: 25) and was admired for his desire for constant experimentation (Brophy, 1991: 75; Thomas and Johnston, 1981: 25) and for his ability to recognize talent and to get the best out of people (Cabarga, 1988: 52). As a result of these abilities, he was seen by many of his employees as exceptional and extraordinary. Solomon quotes one of his animators, Dick Huemer: 'You couldn't help feeling awe in the presence of genius' (1989: 56). Thomas and Johnston quote an inker, Mary Tebb: 'Walt had something, that power. It was just his personality, his genius, I guess' (1981: 145).

There is also ample evidence of the third aspect of charismatic leadership – a high level of commitment to charismatic leaders and their visions. Eisen quotes one of the top Disney animators, Marc Davis:

> It wasn't that you *had* to do these things – you *wanted* to do them. You were so proud. . . . What we were in on, really, was the invention of animation. Animation had been done before, but stories were never told.
>
> (Eisen, 1975: 41)

Fessier quotes a Disney writer: 'You'd do anything to get his approval' (Fessier, 1967: 17). Thomas and Johnston indicate that Walt was greatly supported by his workers whose 'loyalty and dedication' motivated them to make great sacrifices on his behalf (1981: 23). Culhane (1986) and various other animators have written of their dedication to Walt's cause during the last weeks of working on *Snow White*, when many of them were working for nothing or next to nothing. To a very large extent, this level of commitment changed during the period immediately before and in the years after the strike of 1941, but it is also true to say that as many as half the workforce remained loyal to Walt (especially those of longer standing, according to Allen and Denning, 1993), though Walt's relationship with even the loyal staff was changed forever.

Of course, charismatic leaders often possess a decidedly negative side (Calás, 1993; Conger, 1989; Howell and Avolio, 1992) and there is a great deal to suggest that Walt is no exception. He became increasingly remote after the move to the Burbank studio. Thomas and Johnston (1981) indicate that Walt's obsession with quality made him extremely impatient with employees who failed to achieve what he wanted. He could be brutal towards staff when this occurred, as David Hand reports, when he was vilified at a discussion following a showing of his first effort as a director:

> It would be impossible for me to describe the abuse I took from Walt during that meeting. His anger developed until he at times became incoherent. I sat quietly, listened, and said nothing. I remember that he said (among other degrading things) 'You should never have become a director. You don't know what it's all about.' 'You're hopeless.' 'Anybody could have done a better job than you did.'
>
> (Hand, n.d.: 74)

Kinney (1988) also reports incidents of this kind and notes that Walt used 'scare tactics' to keep people on their toes. He also notes, as have a number of others (for example, Merritt and Kaufman, 1992), that Walt was hugely inconsistent with people, and that his treatment of them was profoundly affected by his mood at the time. Friz Freleng, who became one of the top animation directors at Warner Bros., reports that when he arrived at Disney Studios in the 1920s, his predecessor had left because of the abuse he had taken from Walt and that Freleng himself left for similar reasons (Crafton, 1982). Freleng is also reported as saying that he was told that the Disney staff deserted him for Mintz because they were tired of the abuse meted out to them (Lenburg, 1993). When Richard Fleischer, son of Walt's great rival Max, went to work as a director on *20,000 Leagues Under the Sea*, he was surprised to learn 'that the employees didn't like Walt and lived in terror of him' (1993: 104). To many staff there seemed to be more than one Walt Disney. It has also been pointed out by many commentators that Walt often exerted excessive control and supervision of others' work, especially in comparison with other studios like Warner Bros. (Ford, 1975).

To a very large extent, Walt Disney fits the picture of the charismatic leader/entrepreneur well. For their part, his employees benefited from the relationship that is inherent in charismatic leadership by being part of a very important enterprise that would change the face of animation. In the years after the Studio's 'golden age' (early 1930s to early 1940s), the loyalty of many staff was retained by their recognition of their participation in the only studio to have a programme of feature-length cartoons and in its expansion into new areas, although it is clear that their feelings about him and the company changed after the move to Burbank and the strike (Adamson, 1975: 26). The image of Walt as a charismatic figure, and particularly the perception of him as a genius, was substantially enhanced by his often strident self-promotion and the persona that was created by biographical accounts from the early 1930s onwards. Maltin (1987) sees this capacity for self-promotion as important and has suggested that one of the main reasons for the failure of Max Fleischer's studio was that, unlike Walt, he was not adept at self-promotion. Maltin points to the 'better publicity staff' as an illustration. Walt refused to be photographed with a drink, and a number of people have pointed out that the smiling figure who was photographed right from the beginning of the interest in him rarely smiled or laughed and was often moody and grumpy (Davidson, 1964; Eddy, 1955; Schickel, 1986). In later years, the Walt who appeared on the television series created a new persona in later age of a favourite uncle (Apple, 1983). Of course, Walt's reputation for animation of the highest quality cannot be disputed, but Walt made sure that as many people as possible knew that this was his goal, and in this and a number of other respects he was assisted by biographers and journalists.

CONSTRUCTING WALT DISNEY: BIOGRAPHIES

There are no truly official biographies of Walt but two come close to deserving such an attribution. The first was Diane Disney Miller's (1956) book about her father which was originally published in the *Saturday Evening Post* in a serial form.[1] The book was described as 'an intimate biography . . . as told to Pete Martin' and according to Thomas was based on a series of long interviews with Walt. The second is Thomas's (1976) own book which derived from an excellent level of co-operation from individuals (including relatives and employees) and the Disney Archives, a repository of a large collection of materials, such as letters, interview transcripts, transcripts of meetings about stories, and company documents. Access to the Archives is closely guarded and controlled by the company rather than by the Archive staff. For his analytical biography of Walt Disney, Schickel (1986 [1968]) was refused co-operation by both the Disney family and the company. His book is part biography and part analysis of Walt's influence. Jackson (1993) has produced a 'bio-bibliography' of

Walt Disney, which contains a quite detailed biography plus a great deal of bibliographical information for scholars.

Two other prominent biographies have been of the 'dark side' genre which draw attention to the less savoury features of their target. This style of biography has become increasingly popular in recent years, especially in the context of movie personalities and rock stars. Mosley's (1986) biography draws attention to a variety of frailties – Walt's anti-Semitism, his persecution of Iwerks, his drinking habit, and so on. Mosley enjoyed the co-operation of the company and the Archives for this work, as well as many employees, so that the less than favourable portrayal may have made the company wary of future approaches. Eliot is the author of the other 'dark side' book (1993), but his goes much further than Mosley's which looks quite mild by comparison. Walt emerges as an FBI spy who may not have been born to Elias and Flora Disney after all and perhaps not even in the USA, but in Mojacar in Spain. He suggests that the FBI used Walt's uncertainty about his origins to their own ends. Walt also emerges as a womanizer (an affair with Dolores del Rio), an anti-Semite, a heavy drinker, a compulsive-obsessive (hand-washing), and as possessing sundry other foibles and frailties. Eliot was initially rebuffed by the company, which then experienced a change of mind provided he allowed them to approve the manuscript before publication, a condition with which Eliot was not prepared to comply. He was forced to rely on various generally available documents and on interviews with present and former employees.

There are also a number of biographies which seem to have been written primarily for older children or teenagers. Two of the most recent are Ford (1989) and Greene and Greene (1991). The former's sources are not at all clear, but Greene and Greene had excellent access to the Archives, to relatives, and to past and current employees, including Michael Eisner, the current Chief Executive Officer.

Quite detailed biographies can also be found in histories of the studio or of animation at Disney. The most prominent examples of this kind of work are the books by Bailey (1982), Finch (1973), Holliss and Sibley (1988), Maltin (1973), Thomas (1991), and Tietyen (1990). General histories of animation, such as Bendazzi (1994), Maltin (1987) and Solomon (1989), invariably contain quite detailed biographical information. The studio histories and books on animation, along with the books written for the teen market and Thomas's (1976) biography, tend to be the most unmistakably hagiographic in tone and approach.

While discussing his fraught dealings with Disney, Eliot notes a feature of the biographies that are striking to anyone who has ploughed through them – their incredible similarity. The majority of the facts are reproduced from book to book with very little added in each case, in spite of different informants being interviewed. There seems to be a constant recycling of the same anecdotes which are referred to in book after book. Indeed, once a number of biographies of Walt Disney are read, it becomes apparent that much of the narrative structure of his life is transmitted through vignettes (some of which are probably apocryphal) which are constantly recycled and create a coherence to his life (arriving in Hollywood with $40, the dentist story, losing Oswald, dreaming up Mortimer on the train, the *Snow White* 'hatful of money' story, etc.). They can be found in all or most of the biographies (especially the longer ones) and often in short magazine articles. It is as though writers have so little information to go on that they are forced time and time again to reproduce these pithy, partially illuminating stories to help make sense of the life they are seeking to lay bare. Even Eliot (1993), who tries to provide the most deviant of the biographies, repeats some of the basic motifs of Walt's life (Mortimer, hatful of money). But Eliot also provides the beginnings of an explanation of the similarities in the biographies, when reporting a conversation with a Disney public relations representative:

> [S]he told me off the record that I really didn't need the archives at all. Laughing softly on the phone, she explained that no one had ever been given information by the studio it didn't want them to have, the reason all the other Disney biographies were so alike. If I wanted to see what I would have learned had I been given access to the archives, all I had to do was read Bob Thomas's [1976] book. I did. She was right.
>
> (Eliot, 1993: xiii)

This statement is consistent with Schultz's view, after he had visited the Archives twice, that they contain 'little beyond Disney publicity puff' (1988: 277).

These reflections imply that, in spite of the often lavish praise heaped on the Archives by various writers (e.g. Jackson, 1993;

Mosley, 1986), the basic biography of Walt Disney is tightly controlled by the company. As Wiener (1993) has pointed out, the culture industries seem to be especially prone to seeking to control their image and to ward off scholarly interest in their operations. Even when various individuals (family and friends and past and present employees) are interviewed, the basic elements of the story seem to remain the same. Even the two dark side biographies have stayed with the basic elements of the story, but have emphasized aspects of his biography or personality which cast him in a less favourable light. Sometimes this approach turns into exaggeration and can most clearly be discerned in Eliot's treatment of Walt's FBI connections which become the focal point for much speculation about how these affected Walt. For example, Eliot suggests that Walt's uncertainty about his parentage was used by the FBI to entice him to hand over information about people in Hollywood in exchange for an FBI investigation about his origins. However, there is no evidence that Walt actually acted as an FBI spy, and two former FBI special agents have submitted affidavits saying that he never acted in this capacity (Solomon, 1993). Smoodin (1993), in the course of writing about Hollywood cartoons, seems quite separately to have uncovered a great deal of information about Walt's dealings with the FBI. However, Smoodin makes much less of the connections from the point of view of understanding Walt's concerns and preoccupations, and views the Walt–FBI relationship as much more ambiguous than the way in which it is depicted in Eliot's book.

We find, then, that biographies of Walt Disney are remarkably similar, drawing on similar linear sequences and similar renditions of key events which collectively provide a narrative structure for his life. These similarities are in large part a product of the company's tight control of these biographical details so that even interviews with often quite different groups of people have not resulted in substantially different accounts of his life. Those writers who have dwelt on his darker side have kept the basic narrative structure intact and have tacked on to that structure details of the less salubrious aspects of his life. But relatively few people read biographies and histories of animation. Much more significant in the creation of an understanding of Walt's biography and persona have been a large number of magazine articles about him which started to be published relatively soon after the success of *Steamboat Willie*. These articles contain, albeit

21

summarily, details of Walt's life and speculations about the reasons for his success. But they have also been instrumental in creating a particular form of his biography that began to take shape in the early 1930s.

CONSTRUCTING WALT DISNEY: POPULAR ARTICLES

Smoodin (1993) has shown that during the 1940s, *Time, Saturday Review, Commonweal,* and *Popular Science* ran many articles on Walt (to the virtual exclusion of other animation studios) and that in so doing they constructed a view of him for their readers. But these articles of the 1940s had been preceded in the previous decade by an approach to writing about Walt that presaged many of the later preoccupations and themes. These 1930s articles invariably included sketchy biographical details, an outline of the animation process and its technological wonders, and some speculations about what made Walt so special. In fact, as early as 1934, a *Fortune* writer felt that Walt's biographical details barely needed repetition:

> Enough has been written about Disney's life and hard times already to stamp the bald Algeresque outlines of his career as familiarly on the minds of many Americans as the career of Henry Ford or Abraham Lincoln. It need not be told again here.
>
> (Anon., 1934: 146)

However, the *Fortune* writer did proceed to provide an outline of his career to date.

To a certain extent, Walt himself had set the trend for this kind of article, when he published two articles in *Windsor*, an English periodical (Disney, 1931, 1934). It is unlikely that two articles in an obscure English journal would have had much of an effect on the public perception of Walt, but as Waller (1980) has observed, the information in the 1931 article is very similar to that contained in one of the earliest pieces on Walt – an article in *American Magazine* by Carr (1931) based on an interview with the man himself. An early article on Walt in the *New Yorker* by Seldes, published at the end of 1931, also contains a great deal of information found in Walt's (1931) article and in Carr (1931), coupled with what appear to be observations based on a visit to the

Studio. Waller observes that a constant recycling of Carr's facts seems to have then occurred, as a host of articles on Walt and the Studio were published in popular journals, using almost the same information (though obviously updated) and with the same fixations, until the early 1940s.

One discrepancy between Disney (1931) and Carr's article of the same year concerns the origins of Mickey Mouse. In the latter article, Walt seemed uncertain about where the idea came from and is quoted as saying:

I can't say just how the idea came. We wanted another animal. We had had a cat; a mouse naturally came to mind. We felt that the public – especially children – like animals that are 'cute' and little. I think we were rather indebted to Charlie Chaplin for the idea. We wanted something appealing, and we thought of a tiny bit of a mouse that would have something of the wistfulness of Chaplin . . . a little fellow trying to do the best he could.

(Quoted in Carr, 1931: 57)

However, in his own article of the same year he wrote:

Why did I choose a mouse for my principal character? Principally because I needed a small animal. I couldn't use a rabbit, because there already was a rabbit on the screen. So I decided upon a mouse, as I have always thought they were very interesting little creatures. At first I decided to call him Mortimer Mouse, but changed his name to Mickey as the name has a more friendly sound, and Mickey really is a friendly sort of character. . . . While returning from a visit to New York, I plotted out the first story.

(Disney, 1931: 642)

Here, then, we have one of the earliest published versions of the genesis myth of Mickey Mouse. It becomes embellished in the second early Disney article:

Thirteen years ago a young, obscure commercial artist used to work late at night in a studio where a company of mice scratched around for any stray crumbs. The young man made friends with those mice, adopted a family of ten in a cage, and even tamed one sufficiently to sit on his drawing-board. [Walt refers to his return train journey from New

York to Los Angeles and how the idea of a mouse character gradually dawned on him.] The idea completely engulfed me. The wheels turned to the tune of it. *'Chug, chug, mouse, chug, chug, mouse,'* the train seemed to say. The whistle screeched it. *'A m-m-m owa-ouse,'* it wailed.

(Disney, 1934: 259, 261)

By the time of the publication of Miller (1956), we are simply told about the original naming of the mouse as Mortimer and the preference of Mrs Disney, who is missing from the Disney (1931) account above, for Mickey. But is there any significance to the contrast between Walt's equivocality about Mickey's origins in Carr's article and the greater certainty that is found in his own article of the same year which presents a story that has been reused in countless accounts of Walt's early years? One possibility is that Walt had hit on the advantages of mythologizing both himself and his characters. There is little doubt that the story made very good publicity copy; for example, the story of the mouse walking on his drawing-board was used by RKO in a biographical sketch of Walt in the early 1930s (Crafton, 1982: 295). It is also just the kind of myth or legend with which charismatic leaders are inclined to surround themselves (Bryman, 1992). There are a number of incidents in Walt's life that are shrouded in mystery and legend, and Mickey's genesis is definitely one of them.

By and large, however, the popular articles on Walt told a common tale. They usually contained information about his early life, the animation process and some of its technological wonders, the work of the Studio staff, Walt's latest project(s), speculations about his personality and life-style, and so on. Walt was invariably depicted through the biographical details as the embodiment of the American dream, a farm-boy made good in a new art medium. The allusion to Horatio Alger in the *Fortune* quotation above is typical, as is the following quotation from the *New York Times Magazine* of the same year:

Walt Disney, the Horatio Alger of the cinema. . . . There is, perhaps, no more accurate way of summing up the life story of the farm youth, later newsboy, who through industry, courage, and all the other Algerian virtues attained international recognition.

(Churchill, 1934: 12)

This portrayal of Walt is consistent with Lowenthal's (1944) analysis of biographies in popular American magazines in the 1901–41 period, in which he noted that the successful hero of the piece was with remarkable frequency depicted as achieving that success through industry and as having to go through considerable discomfort and hardship on the way.[2] Lowenthal also noted that over the period he covered there was a shift in attention from 'heroes of production' to 'heroes of consumption' (including entertainment). Part of Walt's appeal may have been that he was a hero of both spheres. The tone of the popular articles on Walt was invariably hagiographic, with frequent allusion to him as a genius, while simultaneously acknowledging his reluctance to view himself in such terms and his unease about those writers and critics prone to seeing in his work a new art form (for example, Churchill, 1938).

Smoodin (1993) argues that by the mid-1940s Walt's work was being less well received by the critics in the popular press and magazines. However, in articles he was still widely revered at the very least for his earlier work. A eulogizing piece in *Collier's* by Wallace (1949) takes the reader through an account of Walt's life on the occasion of Mickey's twenty-first birthday. At the time of the release of *Cinderella* in 1950, a *Newsweek* contributor gave a brief account of Walt's life up to that point (as well as sundry other details about animation and the Studio):

> Once again the man who has probably given more theatrical joy to more people than any other living human had reverted to his formula of filming a story of mice and girls, and had produced pure delight . . . . 'Cinderella' provides ample evidence that his artistic sensibilities have survived unscathed both the war and the often more lethal effects of Hollywood success.
>
> (Anon., 1950: 84, 88)

A two-part article in 1953 for *Saturday Evening Post*, one of the most detailed biographies of Walt to appear in a popular medium, recycled the old and some more recent vignettes and was every bit as hagiographic as the early magazines, referring to him as 'the greatest of the Hollywood magicians' (Alexander, 1953b: 26). Thus, Smoodin's observation about Walt's loss of support in the 1940s probably applies primarily to the film critics; the wider constituency of writers were still producing the same kind of

25

broadly adulatory article that first made its appearance in the early 1930s. This eulogizing tone continued after the mid-1950s and even intensified after a string of hit films in a wider range of cinematic forms than in his earlier work (live-action, nature), the popular television series, and the opening of Disneyland. This can be seen in articles in *Time* (Anon., 1954), *Business Week* (Anon., 1965), *National Geographic* (de Roos, 1963), *Newsweek* (Anon., 1962), *Fortune* (McDonald, 1966), and *American* (Eddy, 1955).

These popular articles from the early 1930s on, together with the teenager books and biographies such as Thomas (1976) and Miller (1956), which was itself serialized in a popular magazine, built an image of Walt Disney and his life in the popular imagination. The distinctly hagiographic tone of most of this writing played an important part in the building of an image of Walt as a genius, though this is not to suggest that the designation is inappropriate. Thus, Walt's reputation was substantially boosted by a variety of people who created for the public the persona of a genius. As writers such as Lang and Lang (1988), Kapsis (1989), and Mulkay and Chaplin (1982) have shown, the support of artists and film personalities by critics can be crucial to the acceptance and the subsequent elevation of their work. Self-promotion also plays a role, and it is not irrelevant that Maltin (1987) suggests that this is one of the reasons for Walt's success over one of his main competitors, Max Fleischer, quoting an animator as saying: 'I guess Disney had a better publicity staff and Max just cared about what he did rather than a lot of personal glory' (Myron Waldman, quoted in Maltin, 1987: 83).

The popular articles and, in some respects, the biographies are also interesting because of certain omissions or equivocations, four of which will be examined. First, the popular articles invariably make little mention of Roy in spite of the recognition in more substantial biographies of his immense contribution to sustaining the company's financial and organizational health. The animators themselves are also a faceless mass, whistling while they work in order to realize Walt's dreams, and even the early popular biographies make little mention of Iwerks's importance in the creation of Mickey Mouse. The book biographies tend to be much better in this regard and are often very explicit about the contribution of Iwerks and other animators. However, a Harvard art professor, Robert Feild, who spent a year at the Studio, wrote a book, *The Art of Walt Disney* (1942), which attracted considerable attention. This item also contains virtually no discussion of Roy or of individual animators. The effect of these omissions was to concentrate the public's focus even more on Walt and to under-score his credentials as a genius.

Second, the popular biographies and to a large degree the full biographies give scant recognition to pre-Disney animation, giving an impression that it represents a kind of pre-history, with Walt and his Studio as a turning-point. Disney animation does represent a watershed in the history of animation, but the signifi-cance of early animation should not be ignored, since many of the basic concepts and modes of organization had been forged before Walt's arrival on the scene. For his part, Walt never suggested that he invented the animated cartoon, as his daughter's book testifies (Miller, 1956). However, simply drawing attention to some of his artistic forebears (such as McCay and Bray), as Miller does, fails to give full recognition to the significance of pre-Disney animation. The following five points seem especially significant.

First, up until around 1912 animated films were viewed by studios and audiences as 'trick' films, that is, films in which the animator's wizardry made the near-impossible, if not the im-possible, happen. The best-known example of this is Blackton's *The Haunted Hotel* (1907). In the 1910s, animated cartoons gradu-ally included story-lines, rather than merely presenting marvels of movement for the delectation of audiences. Walt took the emphasis on story much further, insisting on strong stories with clearly articulated characters, and thereby bringing the cartoon much closer to a conventional cinema form.

Second, the comedic nature of both stories and characters had been established during this period.

Third, the idea of continuity series of cartoons, with recurring focal characters, had been established by such popular characters as Felix the Cat (1920–8), Colonel Heeza Liar (1913–24), Bobby Bumps (1915–25), The Katzenjammer Kids (1916–18), Krazy Kat (1916–29), and Mutt and Jeff (1913–26). Moreover, while the earlier of these series characters tended to derive from syndicated car-toon strips, the later ones, such as Felix, were created for the screen, as would be the case with Oswald and Mickey.

Fourth, the most critical technical development in cartoon ani-mation, which Halas and Manvell refer to as 'fundamental to all advanced cartoon film technique' (1959: 27), had been invented by Earl Hurd and patented by 1915. This technique is 'cel animation' which allows characters and objects that move to be drawn on celluloid sheets which can then be superimposed on backgrounds. The two or more sheets can then be photographed to give an impression of a character against a background, and obviates the time-consuming work of constantly redrawing backgrounds for each minute piece of action. It was the constant need to redraw backgrounds which slowed down early, though astonishingly fast, animators like Winsor McCay and which meant that their animation was not commercially viable (see, for example, Barrier, 1974). The patent expired in 1932 (Bendazzi, 1994).

Finally, before Walt's arrival, specialization of labour within a studio system had been established by early animators such as Bray. The different phases of animation production that were consequent on, and even necessitated by, cel animation could be done by different people. As a result, the whole process of animation could be speeded up and made commercially viable. This Fordist organization had been established by 1920 and had been codified in an early treatise on animation by Lutz (1920), which had influenced Walt (Merritt and Kaufman, 1992: 56).

In fact, animation had developed to such a degree that Miller says that when her father arrived in Hollywood he looked for work as a director, because he felt that 'he'd got into cartoons too late' and that he should have got into them six years earlier (Miller, 1956: 75). Thus, animation was substantially developed by the time of Walt's arrival and the exclusion of these details, even in the most sketchy form, has the effect of magnifying his contribution. Walt may even have been advantaged by his slightly late arrival, because he could exploit the basic existing technical, artistic and organizational achievements and take stock of their products. Out of this he could recognize deficiencies and areas for improvement which would be his hallmarks in later years (such as high quality animation, strong stories, and character animation), so that it may have been beneficial not to be a 'first mover' in this fledgling industry. This discussion should not be taken to imply that Walt Disney's significance to the history of animation has been exaggerated by writers. In fact, his impact on the industry has been incalculable. Animators at other studios were invariably in awe of Walt and his work (Adamson, 1975), and as Chuck Jones, one of the great animation directors at Warner Bros. in the 1940s, has said: 'Practically every tool we use today was originated at the Disney studio – not necessarily by Walt, but his men couldn't have originated them unless he had encouraged them to exist' (quoted in Barrier, 1979: 6). Instead, the point that is being made is that the tendency in many biographies to pay little attention to pre-Disney animation has had the effect of inflating his innovativeness to a degree that is not entirely warranted.

The third example of omission or equivocation is that the strike of 1941 is either ignored, treated very cursorily, or Walt's definition of events – that it was a jurisdictional dispute organized by communists – is given in most of the articles in popular magazines and to a large extent in biographies. Even Feild's (1942) book, which contains a detailed examination of the new plant, portrays the workforce as blissfully happy in its willingness to do Walt's bidding, while Leyda's (1942) review of it in the *Saturday Review* makes no mention of the strike and contains the following passage which seems at the very least disingenuous just nine months after the strike:

> At the Disney Studios a group of imaginative, disciplined artists give their work an amount of time and concentration that make them the envy of the motion picture industry.
>
> (Leyda, 1942: 5)

There can be little doubt that the strike represents a problem for the more hagiographic accounts of Walt for two reasons. One is that he personally came out of it badly. He became increasingly unreasonable, vindictive and entrenched towards the strikers, and it was fortunate that he was whisked away to South America. Second, the treatment of the strike as jurisdictional and as 'a Communist group trying to take over my artists', as he put it in his testimony before the House Committee on Un-American Activities,[3] fails to give adequate recognition to grievances at the plant in that period, which have been examined by Allen and Denning (1993). Although the top animators could earn substantial sums, wages were often poor for most of the workforce, although articles in popular magazines often seemed concerned to establish that they were well paid (e.g. Hollister, 1940). Moreover, pay differences were arbitrary and there was little pay for overtime. Bonuses promised for overtime during the making of *Snow White* had not been paid and in 1940 Walt had proposed layoffs and wage cuts. The animators did not receive screen credits, because of Walt's insistence on the priority his own name should receive. Moe Goolub, a Disney cartoonist, says of the atmosphere just prior to the strike:

> All we knew is that they were hassling us, playing one element against the other. Every time we tried to get a raise they actually tried to cut us back a few notches here and there. If we didn't receive a raise [you would think] that we would at least be permitted to continue as we were, but that wasn't always the case. I lost a few dollars and I never got a lot of overtime.
>
> (Massie, 1992: 15)

The neglect or benign treatment of the strike by various writers has the effect of minimizing the impact of a distasteful episode in Walt's and the company's history.

Finally, there has been an ambivalence about discussions of Walt as a successful businessman and about the nature of many of his actions as the products of business decisions. Schickel (1986) takes a distinctively different line, arguing that Walt was first and foremost an entrepreneur, driven far more by a quest for success in business than in art. When Walt was asked to name his most rewarding experience, he replied: 'The whole damn thing. The fact that I was able to build an organization and hold it' (Schickel, 1986: 37). This remark chimes well with Schickel's alternative view. Generally, in popular writings about him he was depicted from the early 1930s as someone who made next to nothing from cartoons because, in his relentless pursuit of quality, everything was ploughed back into the firm to fund the necessary technical and artistic innovations. Indeed, some commentators depicted Walt as uninterested in making money (e.g. Anon., 1962: 49; Jacobs, 1939: 505; Miller 1956). There is little doubt that Walt and Roy made little money from animation in the 1930s and did not make substantial profits until after the opening of Disneyland.

However, the constant need for ploughing money back into the company in order to enhance quality was not based entirely on the grounds of quality. The decision to apply the expensive innovations of sound and then colour to the early cartoons can be viewed as a strategy of product differentiation – a strategy to steal a march on competitors like Fleischer, Bray, Terry, and Mintz by making cartoons distinctively different from the efforts of these studios (Gomery, 1994). It should not be forgotten that there was virtually no interest in the early silent Mickey Mouse cartoons and that sound, in spite of the problems it presented, saved the Studio. Even the much-heralded multiplane camera, a cumbersome device used in the late 1930s for a few years to give a greater illusion of depth, was used much less than is often suggested because of the time taken to set up each shot; it largely served as publicity for drawing attention to technological improvements (Hulett, 1992; Solomon, 1989: 59; Thomas and Johnston, 1981: 309). Langer (1992), for example, views the multiplane camera as a strategy of product differentiation by technological innovation. The decision in the mid-1930s to make an animated feature film was almost certainly as much to do with a strategy of diversification in order to reduce the company's reliance on animated cartoon shorts which would be unlikely to generate substantial profits. The move in the 1940s into films which mixed animation and live action was motivated by the escalating costs of cartoon animation and permitted greater diversification, which would act as a bridge to the growth of live action in the 1950s. During this decade we see a strategy of ever-growing diversification – into live-action films, nature films, television, and theme parks. In other words, many of the key developments at Disney can be interpreted as motivated by decisions stemming from financial considerations and business strategies and not simply in terms of the relentless pursuit of quality and of experiment which tends to pervade most interpretations.

A further area which tends to be given minimal attention in many accounts of the Studio in the early and later years is merchandising. It was nearly always mentioned in the Disney biographies, but was invariably depicted as a simple adjunct to the making of animated cartoons. Some articles dwelt on the Disney merchandise (e.g. Anon., 1932; Bristol, 1938; Anon., 1948), but these were largely descriptive and rarely analysed their significance in depth. Mickey Mouse arrived on the scene at a time when interest in movie-related merchandise was growing and Felix the Cat had spawned a sizeable range of such items. The Disneys moved very quickly to sign up merchandising and licensing deals through Borgfeldt and were keen to improve the quality and range of the products of such agreements, which Kamen offered to do and was in fact successful in achieving. Such deals were central to the Studio in the 1930s and about half of the profits came from these areas, according to Klein (1993), while Merritt and Kaufman (1992: 144) have suggested that it was merchandise that kept the brothers afloat in the 1930s. Cartoon shorts were not very profitable, due to the small and frequently late advances that were often forthcoming. It is possible that the development of merchandise was therefore much more central to the Disneys' business strategy than is commonly suggested. For example, it might be that cartoon characters were being developed with their potential for marketing as a much more central feature than is commonly implied by the biographies. Feild (1942) suggested that Mickey's 'Gang' simply evolved, but there may have been far greater intent involved which allowed new series to be produced and new lines of merchandise to be produced.

The idea of merchandise having a role in the creation of characters, while speculative, is not entirely fanciful. In 1934, Churchill interviewed Walt for the *New York Times Magazine* and wrote on his notepad: 'Fifteen people work in the New York office handling royalties on articles manufactured in Mickey's name. That's where the big profit is' (1934: 13). Forgacs (1992) has noted that in the 1930s there was a growing emphasis at the Studio in the importance of characters possessing the attribute of 'cuteness' and suggests that this may have been motivated by the greater merchandising and licensing potential of such characters.[4] In an interview, a Disney animator, Bill Dover, ventured the view that one of the main reasons why Walt was keen on doing *The Jungle Book* in spite of difficulties of bringing it off was 'it has a little boy in it, Mowgli, and a lot of animals and both are great for merchandising' (in Fessier, 1967: 19). A *Wall Street Journal* article in 1958 was unusual in its attention to merchandising and used for its title Walt's summary of his business philosophy, which fits well with much of the present discussion: 'dream, diversify – and never miss an angle' (Gordon, 1958). A detailed account of the significance of merchandising at Disney needs to be written, but in the meantime it is being suggested here that accounts of Walt and the Studio tended to play down the importance of merchandising and licensing and that they were much more central to their business strategy than is often recognized. It is also suggested that the Disneys may have encouraged that view to retain an ambiguity about Walt's status as a businessman. This ambiguity was underscored by giving the impression that Roy was the brother who was concerned about business, while Walt concentrated on the artistic side of the organization. As late as 1962, a *Newsweek* journalist wrote about Walt that he was 'a hugely successful businessman, but he can't be bothered with financial details' (Anon., 1962: 48). The cloaking of financial and business considerations is interesting partly because it represents an area of equivocality in treatments of Walt and the company, and because it is a powerful device which will provide an interesting focus when we come to the theme parks.

CONCLUSION

A biography of Walt Disney has been presented because it will form an important backcloth to the preoccupations and predilections that are manifested in the theme parks. But equally, I have been at pains to suggest that 'Walt Disney' is also in a sense a social construction – a product of his own and others' efforts at creating a public face and a personal biography that would serve his business's aims. Attention has been drawn to the equivocality of the treatment of Walt as a businessman. While the business press was full of encomia for his business success, though often without probing into his business strategies and financial machinations, the popular accounts of Walt and his Studio tended to be silent about such issues. This was almost certainly helpful to a company which manufactured fantasy, since widespread discussion of its business side might diminish the dream. In suggesting that Walt Disney's public face was socially constructed, does this mean that the present discussion is meant to join forces with those who seek to probe his 'dark side' and thereby cast doubt on his genius? The answer to this is an unequivocal negative. It would be absurd to suggest, for example, that because he and others fostered a public persona that there was nothing behind that image, that it was a mere façade. The biography and public face that he created and which was fabricated for him merely helped to oil the wheels of his genius. Whether he could have achieved what he did without such lubrication can only be a matter of conjecture.

2

DISNEY AFTER WALT

The death or departure of the founder of an organization always heralds a period of uncertainty and concern for those left behind (Schein, 1985). But the effect of the death of someone like Walt Disney, who was both a national institution and the fount of new ideas for the organization, was bound to be traumatic for the organization he created.[1] Walt claimed that he was preparing for his departure by giving others 'more responsibility' and by 'trying to organize them more strongly' (de Roos, 1963: 207). But the strategy did not result in anyone emerging as an obvious successor. In July 1967, a *Forbes* journalist wrote:

> Walt, toward the end of his career, was encouraging others to take on more responsibility. He had given his seven top producers an opportunity to share financially in the success of their projects. He hoped that one of them would emerge as his clear successor. But it didn't work. It couldn't. As long as he was around, the force of his personality and his stormy insistence on perfection inhibited would-be successors from asserting themselves fully.
>
> (Anon., 1967: 39)

This view is to some extent contradicted by a statement by Roy in an interview in 1969: 'Walt was preparing for the day when he would be gone. He began grooming *a team* to take up the reins' (Weber, 1969: 7 – emphasis added). Roy's comment suggests that Walt did not expect an individual to succeed him and that his company would have a group at the helm. In the event, no successor emerged and a team did take over.

THE THREE MAIN PHASES AT DISNEY AFTER WALT

The history of Walt Disney Productions after Walt's death lends itself to being broken down into three main periods:

1 the period of the 'Disney troika' when a three-man team, which included Roy, ran the company. This period lasted until Roy's death on 20 December 1971;
2 the second period from the time of Roy's death until the arrival of a new management team in October 1984. The final six months of this period almost constitute a distinct period as the company went into a limbo when it was the subject of two take-over attempts;
3 the third period until the present time. During this period the company has been led by Michael Eisner and Frank Wells (who died in a helicopter crash in April 1994).

Clearly, periods like these overlap in certain respects, but this three-fold division represents a simple and fairly uncontentious framework for examining the key events at Disney after Walt.

The reign of the Disney troika, 1966–71

Almost immediately after Walt's death, Roy issued a statement reassuring 4,000 employees that 'we will continue operating Walt Disney's company in the way that he has established and guided it' (quoted in Zehnder, 1975: 75). The overall direction of the company was to be guided by the 'Disney troika', as it was often referred to (e.g. Weber, 1969), which was made up of Roy as chairman, Donn B. Tatum, formerly executive vice-president of administration, as president, and E. Cardon (Card) Walker, formerly head of marketing, as vice-president of operations. Tatum had worked on the company's financial side and Walker, who had been with the company since 1938, had been more concerned with marketing. During the 1966–71 period, a division within the company became more evident than it had been during Walt's days. Many commentators refer to a division between 'Walt men' and 'Roy men'. This division reflected a feud between Walt and Roy which is barely mentioned in many, if not most, of the biographical accounts referred to in the previous chapter, namely, the creation of Retlaw, which effectively diverted revenue away

35

from the company into the pockets of Walt and his heirs. The dispute divided the loyalties of many within the company. They became known as Roy and Walt men: the former tended to be in financial, legal, accounting and administration departments and the latter in marketing, sales, films and the parks (Taylor, 1987). Walt and Roy made up in the 1960s, but the division between the two sides of the company remained. The presence of Tatum (a Roy man) and Walker (a Walt man) as members of the trium-virate was probably a tactic by Roy to ensure that neither side felt left out and possibly to enable some degree of reconciliation.

During this period, the company's fortunes were greatly enhanced. There were a number of box office successes, most notably *The Jungle Book* (1967), *Winnie the Pooh and the Blustery Day* (1968), *The Love Bug* (1969), and *The Aristocats* (1970). Disneyland continued to be developed, with a number of new attractions in 1967 in particular. But most notably, on 1 October 1971 Walt Disney World in Florida opened its gates. Most of the successes of the period derived directly or indirectly from projects which Walt had put in train before his death. The three men and their Board of Directors saw themselves as custodians of a tradition estab-lished by Walt. Tatum wrote in the 1969 President's Letter to shareholders: 'We have a deeply ingrained and clearcut philosophy of constructive and wholesome entertainment for the entire family, in keeping with the traditions set by Walt Disney, for which we know there is a substantial market.' But equally, under the troika's supervision the company was increasingly changing its profile and, in the words of one financial commentator, 'was being diversified into a broad-scale recreation-entertainment enterprise' (Thomas, 1969: 36). Walt Disney World became not just a Disneyland-style theme park, but a vacation resort, compris-ing hotels, camp-sites, and various related recreational facilities. Film production did not increase in scale, because Roy agreed with Walt's view that 'when you try to make more than five or six pictures a year, you begin to lose control of the quality' (in Thomas, 1969: 37). Under the troika's leadership, profits soared from $12.4 million in 1966 to $26.7 million in 1971.

The period of the custodianship of the Disney troika essentially came to an end on 20 December 1971 with the death of Roy O. Disney, just a few months after he had presided over the opening of the Florida theme park. With Walt, he had built up Walt Disney Productions into a major US corporation. His role had been that of handling the business side – giving rein to and sometimes reining in Walt's flights of fantasy.[2] As noted above, the brothers often argued and over some issues the disputes were very damaging to their relationship, but Walt was sometimes quoted as saying that the company could not have been created without Roy, whose contribution he felt often went unrecognized. Roy left a son, Roy E. Disney, who had worked for the company for a number of years and who would play an important role in the company's future in the early 1980s and thereafter. In the following discussion, Roy E. Disney will be simply referred to as Roy Disney.

The years of languish, 1972–1984

Following Roy's death, Tatum became chairman and Walker became president. In 1976, Walker made Walt's son-in-law, Ron Miller, head of production at the Studio, a move that consolidated Walker's own position and gave a boost to the Walt side of the company. During the troika years, Miller had already been made a member of the company's executive committee, where he was joined by Roy Disney in 1972. The executive committee essentially ran the company during the 1970s. Roy Disney and Miller did not get on, and in March 1977 the former resigned as an executive, though he remained on the board, citing in his resignation letter a number of ominous reasons which were signals of problems in the company. His letter referred to 'deep and irreconcilable differences with present management', to a belief that 'the creative atmosphere for which the Company has so long been famous and on which it prides itself has . . . become stagnant', and to a criticism that 'present management continues to make and remake the same kind of motion pictures with less and less critical and box-office success' (in Taylor, 1987: 15, 16). He left and formed Shamrock Holdings, through which he became a major and highly successful stock market investor.

Ostensibly, Roy Disney had good reason to be concerned. Profitability had increased substantially since his father's death, with net income up from $40.3 million in 1972 to $74.6 million in 1976, but revenues from film rentals were not keeping pace with the other areas of activity. They increased from $78.3 million in 1972 to $119.1 million in 1976, while revenues from other areas of the company were increasing at a much faster rate. In fact, worse was to come, and in 1977 revenue from film rentals was slightly lower than in 1976. The 1978 figures were considerably better, but the 1979 figures for the motion pictures division posted an 11 per cent decline in profits and a 26 per cent decline in operating income over the preceding year. In itself, the decline in one division might not appear too problematic to a company experiencing substantial increases in its other divisions, namely, entertainment and recreation (essentially the theme parks and related activities), and consumer products and other activities (merchandise, licensing, publishing). However, motion pictures had considerable symbolic importance to the company which was still called Walt Disney Productions and they had the potential to provide new ranges of merchandise and new rides for the theme parks. Walt and Roy had long realized the importance of inter-referential products and the films were very much the centre of that notion. If the films continued to disappoint, there was the risk that the enterprise as a whole would begin to suffer.

But why were the films suffering at all? Virtually all of the commentators on Disney in this period portray the company as caught in the grips of a paralysis in which a 'what would Walt have done?' litmus test was constantly applied. Even Roy admitted that his brother's presence lingered when he wrote: 'Every time we show a new picture, or open a new attraction at Disneyland, someone is bound to say, "I wonder how Walt would like it?"' (Disney, 1969: 133). The paralysis affected the Studio by engendering in the 1970s and the early 1980s a series of bland comedies, few of which met with critical or box-office favour. Commentators saw the company as not wanting to take risks for fear of breaking with the traditions that Walt was seen as having set. One of these was a tradition of producing films for family entertainment. However, teenagers increasingly wanted somewhat spicier fare than the Studio was offering and were increasingly taking the view that they would not be seen dead at the showing of a Disney film. Walker, who exerted considerable influence over the kind of film Disney made, was set firmly against an R-rated movie for fear of its possible damage to the company's reputation.

Even the company's animation seemed to be in decline. A *New York Times Magazine* article described the Disney animators as disenchanted with the quality of animation that was expected of them and with the style of story-telling; they were depicted as wanting to return to the golden days of *Snow White* and *Bambi*

38

(Culhane, 1976). This article identified a new group of ambitious Disney animators under the informal leadership of Don Bluth, their most experienced member, who had their sights set on new horizons for their art. However, in September 1979 Bluth left, taking many of the best young animators with him, a move that damaged the company's reputation and pride. The company's lack of success at the box office was exacerbated by the fact that teenagers were trooping in large numbers to a variety of films like *Jaws*, *Star Wars*, and *Raiders of the Lost Ark*, which met with success without sacrificing the commitment to family entertainment that concerned the Disney executives. The film division would have been in a considerably more parlous state were it not for successful re-runs of such classics as *Snow White*, *Fantasia*, and *Pinnochio* in the late 1970s and early 1980s. In an interview in *Fortune*, Walker recognized that teenagers want 'a more sophisticated point of view, with more sex and violence' but added 'we don't ever want to go that far' (Ross, 1982: 66). In 1979, Disney released *The Black Hole*, a film that it hoped would recapture the lost teen market, and which would be able to take on films like *Star Wars* and *Star Trek*, but it did far less well than had been hoped. In October of the same year, work began on the EPCOT Center, a new project in which Walt's vision of a new type of community was turned into a theme park. In the late 1970s and the very beginning of the 1980s, Disney still looked to many commentators as being in good shape. An article in *Financial World* described Walt's successors as preparing for 'a journey that could carry Disney to new heights of growth and profitability . . . Disney's prospects . . . have rarely looked better' (Goff, 1979: 14). Meanwhile the company was included in Peters and Waterman's (1982) influential management text as an example of an 'excellent' company. But there were clear signs that the position was not as bright as these prognostications implied.

In 1980, Tatum retired and his position as chairman was taken over by Walker; Miller became president and chief operating officer. In the same year, work began on Tokyo Disneyland. The 1981 annual report presented a worrying set of figures to shareholders. Net income was down 10 per cent on the previous year to $121.5 million. The downturn was attributed to start-up costs associated with the EPCOT Center, which opened in October 1982, and to poor returns on live-action films. In 1983, the motion pictures division made a loss of $33.4 million. This loss was by no means entirely due to the poor box-office showing of the year's films. A more significant cause was the Disney Channel, a new cable television channel, which in a 1981 interview Walker had described as 'The greatest opportunity we've had since we opened Disneyland' (in Chamberlain, 1981: 28). In fact, reality was very far from this optimistic assessment and the channel lost money heavily due to a low level of subscription. In order not to compete with its own cable TV channel, the company's *Wonderful World of Disney* network television programme had been cancelled, but as a result the company lost the opportunity to advertise its products, including the parks. Moreover, receipts from the theme parks were declining due to a decline in their physical maintenance. In 1983, Walker stepped down and Miller became chief executive. Ray Watson, a rich real-estate developer whom Walt had consulted about his EPCOT plans, was persuaded by Walker to become vice-chairman. Grover writes that Walker enlisted Watson because he 'didn't trust Ron Miller to run the company by himself' (1991: 15). At the time, Walker and Miller had fought over the latter's desire to release less family-orientated entertainment under a different label. Walker had relented and Touchstone Pictures was created. The new company released its first film, *Splash*, in March 1984 to provide Disney with its first big hit in years.

But this hit and a number of other measures to restore Disney's position were too late, and when Roy Disney resigned from the board in March 1984, Saul Steinberg, a corporate raider, began buying Disney shares. Steinberg felt that the company had excellent asset strength but was poorly led. Roy Disney had also been buying shares because they represented good value. He and his advisor, Stan Gold, had approached Frank Wells, a lawyer with a strong track record in the motion picture industry, to determine if he would be interested in a top position at Disney, if the existing management could be deposed. Wells expressed interest, but advised them to approach Michael Eisner, a successful Paramount executive.

Watson and Miller had realized they were vulnerable to a take-over and had increased their line of credit with their bank. In April 1984, Steinberg gave notice of his intentions to buy 25 per cent of stock through his company Reliance Group Holdings. Following financial advice, Watson and Miller agreed on a counter-strategy of acquisitions. They agreed to buy a Florida real-estate and development company, Arvida, from the Bass brothers who owned a wide range of companies (mainly oil and gas). The deal was struck for $200 million of Disney shares, the effect of which was to dilute Steinberg's holding, though much to Roy Disney's chagrin the deal also diluted his own holding and that of all other shareholders. In order to appease him, Roy Disney and his advisor were invited to return to the board.

Watson and Miller also began to explore a further acquisition – Gibson Greetings, a greetings card company with the rights to such characters as Garfield and Big Bird. The move was agreed by the board and by early June 1984, Watson and Miller had committed the company to investments of over $500 million in the area of real estate and greetings cards in the space of just three weeks. Shortly afterwards Steinberg had found partners who could join him in launching a full-scale offer, although he had to offer inducements in the form of commitment fees to attract support. He and his partners formed a shell company which they called MM (Mickey Mouse) Acquisition and on 11 June announced an offer of $67.50 per share ($2.50 a share above the market value). Steinberg was frightened off by a threat by Disney to leave him with massive debts if his tender offer for the shares was successful. Miller and Watson then offered to buy back Steinberg's shares – a strategy known as 'greenmail', whereby a company essentially pays a predator to go away. The amount paid to Steinberg by Disney allowed him to pay off his legal bills and commitment fees and left him $31.7 million better off. One of Steinberg's equity partners, Irwin Jacobs, held on to his holding and continued to add to it and by 30 July had accumulated 6 per cent of the stock. He soon increased it to 8 per cent.

Opposition to the Gibson Greetings deal continued, most especially over the price that had been mooted. Equally, criticism was mounting of the company's senior executives and, most particularly, Miller was singled out as lacking leadership. Watson seems gradually to have come round to recognizing that Miller represented a problem. In August, a committee was formed to examine among other things problems with current management. As it became increasingly apparent that there would be changes at the top, active interest began to be taken in Eisner and Wells. Watson decided on Eisner because he felt that he understood and his views were consistent with the Disney company culture. Grover has written: 'Eisner's mixture of creative inspiration and tight-fisted practices [at Paramount] won the approval of the

41

shell-shocked Disney board. So too, did his track record at ABC and Paramount' (1991: 32). Wells was seen as someone who could act as a deal maker and strategist. On 7 September, the board asked Miller to resign and soon afterwards Eisner was made chairman and chief executive officer and Wells became president and chief operating officer, replacing Watson who had himself proposed Wells to the board. Shortly after their appointment, Eisner and Wells visited Sid Bass, one of the two brothers still holding stock from the Arvida deal, in order to persuade him not to sell his holdings. Bass was convinced by the new management's plans. Jacobs asked Bass if he wanted to join forces to make a bid for Disney. Bass quickly bought out one of Steinberg's other partners and then refused to sell to Jacobs, who felt compelled to sell out to Bass. By the end of September, Bass owned nearly 25 per cent of Disney's stock. A second take-over attempt had been rebuffed.

Disney under new management, 1984 to the present

The accounts of Eisner and Wells's arrival convey the impression of a whirlwind hitting a sleepy town. There appear to be two aspects of this stirring: a sudden escalation of activity in a variety of directions and more intensive levels of work activity. The latter was evident in much longer working days and weeks expected of senior executives than were the case in the Tatum–Walker–Miller years. The surge in work effort expected was given a substantial boost by one of the duo's most important early decisions, which was to lure Jeffrey Katzenberg, with whom Eisner had worked at Paramount, to head the Studio. Katzenberg was known as a phenomenally hard worker and he immediately raised executives' and others' perceptions of a working day to unprecedented levels. As to the second aspect, Flower has written: 'Eisner's overall strategy was to expand in all directions at once' (1991: 182). Much needed to be done. In spite of *Splash* the movie division was at an all-time low, the cable channel was losing money and subscribers, and EPCOT had come in way over budget at $1.2 billion and attendances had fallen after an initial flurry of interest. Not everything was seen as needing transformation: for example, the theme parks and the Disney University, an institution set up in Walt's days to train new recruits in the Disney culture and way of doing things, were seen as basically sound.

Eisner and Wells examined a host of different projects to which the company was committed and closed down those that they felt were consuming too much money and time. In the process, within nine or so months of their arrival hundreds of Disney employees lost their jobs. Much of the new management's attention focused on movie production which was the area most symbolic of the company's malaise. Eisner and Katzenberg recognized the need for Disney to have a hit and for a film that would signal a change of direction for the company. Their aim was to apply principles which they had used to good effect at Paramount, namely, to concentrate on scripts with strong stories, to recruit stars who would not be expensive, and to exercise tight control of costs and of production. These principles were in many ways consistent with Walt's approach. He too had always recognized the importance of a strong story and had a reputation for securing the services of rising stars or those whose reputation had waned (Holliss and Sibley, 1988).

These various principles were applied to a script which was turned into *Down and Out in Beverly Hills*, whose stars, Bette Midler and Richard Dreyfus, had become less popular in Hollywood. It was the first R-rated Disney film and as such provided the kind of signal Eisner and Katzenberg intended. It was also a considerable box-office success when it opened in early 1986 and was soon to be followed by a series of successes in more adult movies in 1986 and 1987, such as *Ruthless People, The Color of Money, Outrageous Fortune, Three Men and a Baby,* and *Good Morning, Vietnam*. Moreover, the number of films being released annually was stepped up greatly from three in both 1983 and 1984 to ten in 1987 and twelve the following year. In 1988, Disney had a 20 per cent share of the box office in the USA compared to just 4 per cent in 1979. The 1988 figures were boosted by the widely acclaimed *Who Framed Roger Rabbit*. The following year was not as good, but the success of *Pretty Woman* in 1990 brought a return to the success of earlier years. A new film division was created – Hollywood Pictures – which released its first film, *Arachnophobia*, in 1990. In 1993, the company bought Miramar Pictures, a successful independent film company which had been responsible for a number of relatively inexpensive hits, including *Sex, Lies and Videotape* and *The Crying Game*. The deal gave the Studio access to a library of over 200 films and presented it with another label for film releases. Eisner and Katzenberg also created a new framework for film production, showing a greater preparedness than their predecessors to go outside the company to acquire talent, and secured the services of a large core of scriptwriters and producers on long-term flexible contracts.

Also symbolically and financially important for the company has been the resurgence of animation after Eisner's arrival and his appointment of Roy Disney as head of the animation studio. The studio was responsible for a number of critical and box-office successes, including *The Great Mouse Detective, Oliver & Company, The Rescuers Down Under, The Little Mermaid,* and the enormously successful *Beauty and the Beast* (1991), which was seen as heralding a return to traditional Disney animation. Moreover, by this time the company had committed itself to producing one animated feature a year. The resurgence of animation at Disney, coupled with a growing number of animation feature films in the 1980s, prompted Solomon (1990) to write about 'the new toon boom'. Grover (1994) described animation as 'fabulously profitable' for Disney, citing the in excess of $500 million brought in from the film, video and licensing of *Beauty and the Beast*. In May 1994, Twentieth-Century Fox announced that it planned to spend $100 million on a new animation studio under Don Bluth. Thus, the revival of animation at Disney coincided with, and may even have stimulated, a revival of animation more generally. A factor in this renaissance is that the economics of film production became increasingly favourable to animation due to the high fees that actors are often able to command for live-action films. This represents a reversal of the economic considerations prevailing in the late 1940s and the 1950s which resulted in live-action films having a cost advantage over animation, as a result of which Walt moved further away from animation, as did many of the other studios at the time.

Walker had begun to release Disney films on video-cassette in a highly cautious and selective manner in the early 1980s. The cautiousness of his approach can be attributed to a long-held view from Walt's days that the company's main assets were its films, particularly the classics, and that they should be protected from overexposure. Walt had realized their potential when he re-released *Snow White* in 1944 and was able to change what would have been a very lean year into a moderately successful one. Eisner and Wells agreed that it would be unwise to plunder the film library but decided that a less prudent approach than

Walker's would not be detrimental. In the middle of 1985, beginning with *Pinnochio*, the company began to release some of the classics on video. *Pinnochio* produced a profit of $9 million within a year. The successive release of the videos brought in massive and much-needed injections of cash. In order to limit possible future damage to re-releases of the film in cinemas, the videos of the Disney classics were usually only available for a certain length of time.

The problems associated with the cable TV channel were handled by increasing the budget available in order to improve programming and marketing. By cutting the wholesale rate to cable operators, the Disney Channel became less expensive. Even lower rates were offered to hotel chains and as a result a number of major groups were taking the channel. By the end of 1987, the channel was growing at an annual rate of 20 per cent and had subscriptions from nearly four million households. But the company's television-related activities did not focus exclusively on its cable channel. First, Eisner felt that the previous regime had been wrong to pull Disney's regular weekly television programme on network television so that it did not compete with the cable channel. He felt that it was a mistake to remove Disney's presence in this way, with its attendant advertising potential. From February 1986, Disney was again a presence on television on Sunday evenings. Second, Eisner and Katzenberg were concerned to develop new television series. The team had an early hit with *The Golden Girls*, while children's series were developed in 'limited animation', such as *Disney's Adventures of the Gummi Bears* and *Disney's Wuzzles*. However, the early success of such series did not continue and many new programmes developed by the company have had a very short life. Even *The Magical World of Disney*, a new series first shown in October 1988, only lasted two years.

Theme park attendance was declining at the time Eisner and Wells took over. This problem was tackled from a number of angles. One was to advertise the parks. Walker had never advertised them because he felt that they received free advertising through the Disney specials on television. But Eisner decided to advertise and promote them much more aggressively. A second tactic was developments which would be more attractive to teenagers. They announced a collaboration with George Lucas to develop a Star Tours ride based on *Star Wars*, a short 3-D film featuring Michael Jackson, and Videopolis, an open-air dance arena in Disneyland featuring rock bands and recorded music. At Walt Disney World, Pleasure Island was later developed to provide an area of late-night discos and bars for young adults. Other attractions were being developed, such as a pavilion at EPCOT dedicated to health-and body-related issues. Wells signed up Metropolitan Life to put up over $70 million for its construction. The image of EPCOT was also improved by placing Disney characters throughout the park and by increasing the number of ethnic restaurants which had proved very popular. Eisner and Wells also decided that they could carefully increase entry prices to the parks in order to boost revenue. The previous regime had been reluctant to increase prices, but following market research Eisner and Wells found that small but regular increases could be sustained without a reduction in patronage. The effect of this strategy has been continual increases in the cost of admission, to the degree that the author of the *Unofficial Guide to Walt Disney World* writes that the *Guide* contains no information about admission prices because they 'seem to change as often as the prime rate' (Sehlinger, 1994: 90). Eisner also believed that the previous management had been far too slow to build hotels at Walt Disney World and he committed the company to a vast increase in the number of hotels at the resort.

Pleasure Island opened in 1989 in the same year as three other new parts of the vacation resort in Florida: Typhoon Lagoon, a water theme park; Discovery Island, a small island with exotic animals and plants; and the Disney–MGM Studios theme park. The latter was embroiled in a race with MCA to complete its construction before the latter's new Universal Studios tour was built in Orlando. Disney won the race. Eisner and Wells believed that the Disney–MGM park would benefit the company, not just in terms of revenue deriving directly from it, but also because it would help to fill the hotels. The new park also demonstrates the ferocious negotiating skills for which Disney executives have become almost legendary, in that they managed to secure unlimited use of the MGM name and logo from MGM/UA at the park for next to nothing.

Meanwhile, the tremendous success of Tokyo Disneyland prompted Eisner and Wells to take up an idea that had been mooted by Walker and Miller – a European theme park. In fact, they and their staff began to explore the possibility soon after their arrival. However, they wanted a very different arrangement from the Tokyo park. The caution which had been a hallmark of the Tatum–Walker years had affected the financing and owner-ship arrangements for Tokyo Disneyland. Disney did not own the park but in return for its small investment and the use of its name, the company received 10 per cent of admissions, 5 per cent of food and merchandise sales, and 10 per cent of corporate sponsor-ship deals. While the arrangement made a sizeable contribution to Disney profits, the bulk of the money went elsewhere. In the case of the European operation, to be built in France, they ended up with a 49 per cent interest. The Disney representatives bar-gained very hard with the French authorities to get preferential interest rates and a low rate of VAT on goods sold in the park compared with elsewhere in France. Also the land would be sold to Disney at 1971 prices, roads to the park would be improved, and the TGV express rail network would be extended. The deal was very attractive to the investment community, and when the shares were offered for sale in October 1989 the flotation was a success.

In the area of merchandise and licensing, the new management team made a number of important moves, including bringing back comics. But the most important innovation in this area was the idea of the Disney Store. After a pilot operation in 1986 near Burbank, Disney Stores have multiplied. Previously, Disney re-ceived royalties for licensing the use of Disney characters, but a large percentage of the profits went to retailers. With the Disney Stores the company could have a greater share of the profits that accrued. They could also be used to advertise the parks, hotels, and new films. The company has also developed new merchan-dise lines, including computer software, publishing, records and mail-order catalogues. They even moved into the fast-food restaurant business, in the form of Mickey's Kitchen, though this venture turned out not to be a success (Masters, 1994).

All of these developments have taken place against a back-ground of much tighter financial controls and a more strategic approach to financial matters than in earlier years. In 1985, Eisner and Wells had brought in a new chief finance officer, Gary Wilson from Marriotts. Wilson's influence resulted in a much tighter rein being kept on projects. Also, new and imaginative approaches to financing major new areas of capital investment, which reduced the exposure of the company to risk, were developed. Wilson left Disney in 1989.

The effect of Eisner and Wells on Walt Disney Productions

(which became the Walt Disney Company in 1986) was dramatic. Compared to 1983, the last full year of the old guard, the 1985 figures, which relate to Eisner and Wells's first full year in charge, show an increase in net income from $93.2 million to $173.5 million; revenue from films nearly doubled from $165.5 million to $320 million. By 1987, net income had risen to $703.3 million and revenue from films had grown to $875.6. In 1990, net income had grown to $824 million (nearly nine times the 1983 figure), with revenue from films at $2,250.3 million (nearly fourteen times the 1983 figure). However, 1991 was a poor year with net income down to $636.6 million, leading to speculation in some quarters that the Eisner–Wells turnaround had run its course. The following year, the upward path was resumed and net income increased by 28 per cent to $816.7 million against the background of a very gloomy picture for the US economy in 1992. However, a massive problem was awaiting Disney: its European operation was losing vast amounts of money and in 1994 the Walt Disney Company had to come to its aid by agreeing a refinancing package with the banks which had huge outstanding loans on the project. Other problems on the theme park front confronted the company. Around 1992–93, it became evident that attendance at the US parks was no longer increasing, and in some cases was declining. Also, at the end of 1993 Disney announced plans for a new theme park based on American history and sited at Manassas in Virginia where two notorious battles of the American Civil War were fought. The plans provoked strident opposition from an alliance of historians, politicians, environmentalists and others. The various groups objected to an anticipated trivialization of American history and to its location on sacred ground. The company took a public-relations drubbing and in September 1994 announced that it would not proceed with the project.

There was also a recognition that, starting around summer 1990, the film division had lost its way. The main symptom of a growing malaise was *Dick Tracy*, which, contrary to Katzenberg's normal policy, had been expensive to produce and was not subjected to the normally close control over costs and production. The result was an expensive failure which did not generate the merchandise interest that had been anticipated. The division's problems led to Katzenberg sending out a much-publicized memo to his staff, in which he signalled very directly the need to get back to their normal way of producing movies:

Having tried and succeeded, we should now look long and hard at our blockbuster business . . . and get out of it. . . . The number of hours [Dick Tracy] required, the amount of anxiety it generated and the amount of dollars that needed to be expended were disproportionate to the amount of success achieved . . . DT was a great experience . . . but as much as DT was about successful filmmaking, it was also about losing control of our own destiny, and that's a high price to pay for a movie.

(Kasindorf, 1991: 40)

Katzenberg also indicated his intention to make less-expensive films in future and to give more freedom to creative staff. In large part, this greater freedom has been necessitated by the huge increase in the number of Disney films: in 1994 60 films were planned, 37 more than the 1992 output (Grover, 1994). But Hollywood Pictures had not enjoyed a major box-office success. Grover (1994) reports that since 1989, only 11 of its 26 films have achieved a gross of over $20 million.

As with Walt himself, many commentators have drawn attention to a dark side to the Eisner–Wells reign (the term 'dark side' is used explicitly by Flower, 1991). Indeed, the lower levels of profits in 1991 seemed to bring forth a stream of adverse comment about the company's practices and its key figures, notably Eisner and Katzenberg, which contrasted starkly with the near-ritual acclaim that they were receiving in the 1980s. Disney's success and some of its practices (see pp. 43–5) meant that as one Hollywood commentator, Michael Medved, observed: 'Everyone wants Disney to have a big black eye' (in Freedland, 1994). The problems with Dick Tracy, the tailing off in the 1990s of the studio's stream of box-office successes and Katzenberg's highly publicized memo seemed to bring a frisson of *schadenfreude* to many Hollywood watchers. The revelations about the dark side of the new Disney seem to revolve around a number of recurring themes. First, there are many testaments to the company's meanness. In an interview, actor Bill Murray said that the company's reputation for 'being very difficult to work with and tough with a buck and stuff like that' was true (Boyer, 1991: 66). Grover quotes the agent for both Richard Dreyfuss and Nick Nolte, who worked on *Down and Out in Beverly Hills*: 'There was no way to overestimate their stinginess' (1991: 90). However, from some quarters, Disney has earned praise for its policy of not paying a fortune for box-office superstars and for emphasizing instead the importance of the quality of the story (for example, Medved, 1993). Second, there are frequent references to the obsessive control of story and production. A screen-writer is quoted as saying:

> Most studios just sort of listen to you and get the gist of what you want to do. At Disney, they want to know every single detail; they want to take as much spontaneity out of the process as possible. They write down every word you say. It's like giving a deposition – it's like you're testifying. And they are obsessed with details that don't matter. You'd pitch *Lawrence of Arabia* and they would want to know what shoes he would be wearing.
>
> (In Kasindorf, 1991: 36)

According to another writer: 'They give you more notes on screenplays than any other studio in town' (in Rose, 1990: 110). Third, the company's representatives are often cited as ferociously fierce negotiators. In contracts, writers, producers and others are often signed up for multi-picture agreements, so that if an initial film is a success, they are tied to Disney at a lower rate than they could command in the market. Rose quotes the case of a writer, Leslie Dixon, who had a success with *Outrageous Fortune* for Disney and found afterwards that she was tied contractually to write another script for them. She did so, but was so incensed that she changed the message on her answering machine, so that it finished with 'and if this is anybody from Disney, *fuck off forever!*' (in Rose, 1990: 110). More generally, the company is renowned for lacking a sense of give-and-take in negotiations. Flower (1991) reports that when Jim Henson's company was in negotiation to sell the Muppets to Disney, the Henson representatives were appalled by the way their opponents fought for one issue after another. Rose (1990) quotes Tom Selleck as describing Disney negotiators as 'brutal'. Fourth, the company's legal department is notoriously litigious, which occasionally results in public relations blunders, such as filing a suit against the Academy of Motion Picture Arts and Sciences for dressing an actress up as Snow White at the 1989 Academy Awards presentation. In fact, stories of Disney filing suits over copyright infringements are legion; another illustration is a suit that was threatened against three day-care centres in Hallendale, Florida, for painting Disney characters on its outer walls. The company's legal department are also relentless adversaries when someone attempts to sue them. Disney executives recognize that the public relations damage sometimes outweighs the legal issues, and when this happens the lawyers are restrained (Cox, 1989). Fifth, the company is known to exercise very tight control of its employees, who refer to their workplace as 'Mauschwitz' or 'Mouschwitz' (Freedland, 1994; Turner, 1991).

There is no doubt that the modern Disney is a ravenous and highly combative corporation, but the revelations about the company's dark side sometimes smack of hypocrisy and have often been fuelled by disgruntled former employees. Much of Disney's seamy side can legitimately be viewed as the operation of a modern capitalist corporation which for some people has been almost too successful for its own good and which is the target of critics who relish the contrast of the hard business realities and the fantasy world with which the company is associated. Even the issue of the defence of copyright stories neglects the damage that could be done to the company if it failed to defend its rights, since it could be deemed thereby to have surrendered its title to them, while it could also be damaging if its characters were associated with activities or products of which it disapproved. There is also a lack of appreciation that some of the 'dark side' features are continuations or extensions of traditions that existed prior to the Eisner–Wells era. In the Miller–Walker years, for example, the company had a reputation for litigiousness (Adler, 1983). Davis (1980) noted the company's alleged stinginess toward creative individuals and the typically tight control of the creative process, while a firm hold over stories was very much a feature of the studio's operation in Walt's day (Barrier, 1974). Davis quoted a former Disney film-maker as saying: 'The place is run more like West Point than a creative community' (Davis, 1980: 150). The policy of not paying huge amounts for box-office stars and instead searching out new talent or stars whose fortunes had changed was also evident prior to the Eisner–Wells era, when there was a frequently quoted adage that 'Disney gets you on the way up or on the way down'.

THE ROUTINIZATION OF CHARISMA AT DISNEY

Reference was made in Chapter 1 to Weber's (1968 [1925]) writings on charismatic leadership and how these provided an interesting way of examining Walt Disney as a leader. However, one of the issues with which Weber was especially concerned was how charismatic leadership can be transformed into a relatively stable force. Weber recognized that charismatic leadership was inherently transitory and that it needed to be placed on a stable footing for it to persist beyond the specific circumstances that give rise to the charismatic leader's ascendancy or beyond the leader's lifetime. Weber employed the term 'routinization of charisma' to describe the process by which charismatic leadership becomes an enduring force, arguing that a failure to routinize a leader's charisma will almost inevitably result in the dissipation of that charisma. In fact, the issue of the routinization of charisma occupied Weber's attentions more than the nature and genesis of charismatic leadership as such because he recognized that without routinization charisma is bound to be ephemeral. There are two main aspects to the routinization of charisma in Weber's writings (Bryman, 1992, 1993). One is that charismatic leaders have to create a structure which incorporates and enshrines their charisma. This will establish continuity for the visions of charismatic leaders and provide a sense of security for their followers. Thus, the *development of structure* is one aspect of the process whereby permanence can be given to charismatic leadership. Second, there is the issue of the *succession* to the charismatic leader. In other words, what will happen when the charismatic leader dies or leaves the organization or movement? Weber delineated a number of different ways whereby succession might take place: the charismatic leader designates a successor; charisma becomes associated with a bloodline; the successor is 'revealed'; or charisma becomes associated with an 'office' or position. Weber recognized that charisma is changed by the process of routinization, since it becomes something that can be transferred and as such no longer attaches to a special person by dint of his or her extraordinary qualities.

Weber's notion of charismatic leadership was developed out of the religious context where charisma means 'gift of grace'. He applied it to a variety of religious leaders and then broadened it further to encompass political figures as well. In recent years, a number of writers have sought to explore the notion within business organizations (for example, Bass, 1985; Biggart, 1989; Bryman, 1992, 1993; Conger, 1989, 1993; Gaines, 1993). It was suggested in Chapter 1 that Walt Disney fits fairly well the image of a charismatic

leader in the business sphere, but how successfully was his charisma routinized? Of course, in the first of the two senses of the
idea of routinization, Walt did routinize his charisma in that he
created an organization and a culture that embodied his visions.
In fact, it is hard to envision a charismatic leader in the business
context for whom at least the creation of an organization does not
apply. As to the second aspect of routinization, it is clear that Walt
did not specifically nominate a successor. When founders of organizations, such as Steve Jobs of Apple Computer, leave (or die)
there is a profound sense of loss among those left behind (Rose,
1989), and it is apparent that Walt's passing engendered a similar
sense of despair. While Roy was an obvious successor, it has to be
remembered that he was over eight years older than his brother
and that he had been considering retirement at the time of Walt's
death. He was able to continue as part of the Disney troika and it
seems that, for the five years of their reign, this triumvirate successfully routinized Walt's charisma, in large part due to the
continued presence of a Disney in the leadership. The troika also
had the advantage of a stream of activities that Walt had set in
motion so that they were to a significant extent executing his
visions.

Roy's death in 1971 ushered in a period in which there was no
longer a Disney at the helm. It is also clear that neither Tatum nor
Walker enjoyed charisma of office, in that they were not able to
bathe in the glow of positions which were viewed as emblematic
of Walt's charisma. To make matters worse, as Potts and Behr
(1987), have observed, Walt's successors were trapped by a 'strong
culture'. In the early 1980s, a number of management writers
pointed to the advantages to organizations of having a strong
culture and the importance of having leaders who foster such a
culture (for example, Deal and Kennedy, 1982; Peters and
Waterman, 1982), although later evidence suggests the need for a
much more cautious assessment of the advantages of strong
culture s (for example, Kotter and Heskett, 1992). In the case of
Disney, it is easy to see why greater caution might be necessary.
The company had developed a strong culture which was an
extension of Walt's vision for the company – a preoccupation
with quality, perfectionism, and a commitment to providing
family entertainment. To this was harnessed a belief in customer
satisfaction which would be particularly relevant to the operation
of the theme parks, while the Disney University became the vehicle

for inculcating these core values. However, the Disney executives of the Tatum–Walker years were ensnared by this strong culture, as signified by the 'what would Walt have done?' refrain of that period. It prevented them from responding to changes in the public's tastes, for whom Disney's particular form of family entertainment in films had become increasingly unattractive. This failure to recognize such changes affected the theme parks too. However, a key element of Walt's vision – a preparedness to try new things – was less easy to inject into his company's culture, not least because his predilections in this area often conflicted with his brother's greater conservatism. Even the name EPCOT was retained, according to Walker, 'because it was inspired by Walt', although it departed very significantly from the entity that Walt had in mind (in Ross, 1982: 64). Moreover, the *name* of Walt Disney in films had increasingly come to be seen as meaning bland, asinine humour which appealed less and less to families and their teenaged members in particular. Even when new departures were tried, like *The Black Hole* and *TRON*, the name of Disney was not enough to carry them and they often did not go far enough. Moreover, the theme parks were in danger of going in a similar direction.

Accordingly, the 1972–84 period corresponds to a period in which there was a failure to routinize Walt Disney's charisma. If we take the two elements of routinization – establishing a structure and culture and addressing the succession problem – we find that the first was partly in place, but the second was not. The structure of the corporation remained intact (although the takeover attempt could have changed this forever), while the strong culture was largely an amplification of Walt's vision. However, from the point of view of the issue of succession, Walt's charisma had evaporated, since none of those who came after him was seen as a legitimate successor to him.

The Eisner–Wells period is an example of the kind of business turnaround that achieved considerable attention in the 1980s as the public seemed to have an insatiable appetite for stories of the dramatic reversals of ailing companies (for example, Carlzon, 1987; Iacocca, 1984; Jacobson and Hillkirk, 1986). In these stories, chief executives are depicted (or depict themselves) as changing the fortunes of companies by injecting them with new visions, changing the cultures of those organizations to make them more sensitive to the external environment, transforming organizational

54

structures, and so on. These emphases betoken a trend in the late 1980s and the 1990s which extolled visionary, transformational leaders who lead by using their vision for the organization to induce members of the organization to contemplate new ways of doing things and new possibilities (for example, Peters and Waterman, 1982; Tichy and Devanna, 1986; Westley and Mintzberg, 1989). Michael Eisner is often depicted in these terms (for example by Snyder *et al.*, 1994), but it is difficult to see exactly what his vision is. At a number of points, Flower (1991) refers to Eisner's vision or to him as a visionary. When making his present-ation to Sid Bass, just after moving to Disney, Flower writes: 'Eisner presented his five-year vision for Disney, describing for the meeting the value of video and cable, the new opportunities available in syndicated television, and more than anything else the extraordinary opportunities in a revitalized Disney studio' (1991: 145). He also writes that in 1985 Eisner 'was laying the basics for a grand vision of Disney as an international conglomerate' (1991: 164–5). Grover also refers to Eisner's vision on a number of occasions. For example, at a party in January 1990, Eisner outlined a host of plans for the theme parks which Grover describes as 'an impressive display of vision and fiscal strength' (1991: 270). But the truly visionary elements in these descriptions are not im-mediately obvious. There is little of the far-flung dreams which are supposed to be the mark of a visionary; instead, the vision inheres in making the company successful, a highly laudable aim, but it is questionable whether it warrants being called visionary.

Gomery (1994) takes this point somewhat further, arguing that in fact, Eisner and Wells have from the beginning employed two 'common textbook strategies' (1994: 81). The first strategy is 'if a company is languishing sell some of its assets', which was re-vealed in the highly successful exploitation of the film library by careful releases on video. The second strategy is 'do more of what you already make money with', which lies at the heart of the massive expansion of the theme park business. This may be a reasonably accurate perspective on the initial years of the Eisner–Wells era, but it fails to take account of a number of events, such as the reversal of the parlous state of the film division and the resuscitation of Disney animation. It also fails to reflect fully the huge expansion in profits accruing from merchandise and licensing that is a feature of their reign due to a widening of the range of products and the Disney Stores or the recognition by

Eisner and Wells of the potential importance of imaginative financing deals for expensive projects and other areas. However, whether all these things warrant the attribution 'vision' rather than more mundane and possibly more accurate terms such as 'business strategy' is arguable. Also, precisely because the Eisner–Wells approach was to 'expand in all directions at once', as Flower puts it (see p. 42), it is not easy to detect the visionary elements that can more readily be discerned in Walt Disney, who was described in the previous chapter as a 'serial visionary'.

Peters and Austin have described a vision as 'the concise statement/picture of where the company and its people are heading' (1985: 284); Nadler and Tushman refer to it as a 'picture of the future, or of a desired future state' (1990: 82); and in a similar vein Snyder *et al.* describe it as 'a picture of what the future should and could look like' (1994: 18). Vision is therefore much more to do with images which are projected into the future, while the listing of areas of an organization that can be improved or exploited or of new departures do not readily convey an image of where a company is supposed to be heading. Indeed, the point could be made that some of the company's successes had been set in motion during the previous regime, such as the creation of Touchstone Pictures, the building of the EPCOT Center, getting into cable television, exploring the possibilities of theme parks abroad, and changing the public's perception of Disney pictures. Potts and Behr quote Wells as listing contributions of his predecessors at Disney, to which he added: 'They did all those things. We're just here to build on them' (1987: 157). The truly visionary elements in the Eisner–Wells era relate to their recognition of the need to change an aspect of the company's culture which had built up in the 1972–84 period, namely the 'what would Walt have done?' mentality. Such thinking was changed to focus more on what kinds of film or theme park experience would attract people. Wells is quoted as saying:

We've never sat around and looked at each other and said, What would Walt have done? What we have rather done is say, What will work? What will be successful? What will please? What will draw people? What will attract people?

(Potts and Behr, 1987: 156)

And again:

56

We say, What will attract and interest and draw people to the parks? What will be entertaining to people? And [we] always ask the [next] question as well: Is it in good taste, because that's the one legacy we really do have – is it in good taste – and is it consistent with what Disney stood for?

(Potts and Behr, 1987: 157)

One of Walt Disney's greatest personal traits was an ability to understand what people wanted and would like. He would have almost certainly recognized that people would want changes to the films, theme park attractions or whatever, so that using a 'what would Walt have done?' test was irrelevant because he responded to changes in public taste (though he often created that taste as well). Eisner and Wells needed to shift the Disney culture away from its obeisance to a largely irrelevant rule of thumb towards a concentration on the kind of attitude ('What will work?') with which Walt might have been very comfortable. At the same time, many other Disney axioms would remain, such as the emphasis on family entertainment, on quality, and the like.

This management of the Disney culture by Eisner and Wells is not inherently visionary, but it is a reflection of Eisner's vision in particular of an organization in which the Disney approach was restored, albeit embellished by practices required by the modern business environment. Moreover, Eisner used himself to symbolize and signal this return, and it is at this juncture that the notion of the routinization of charisma becomes relevant again. Eisner's approach was to associate himself with the aura of Walt Disney by presenting himself as a true heir to Walt's way of doing things. He moved into Walt's old office when he became chief executive. This move, coupled with his decision to host the Sunday-night television show prompted Boyer (1991) to describe part of Eisner's strategy as 'becoming Walt'. Boyer quotes one of Eisner's associates: 'Michael's whole life at Disney is becoming Walt' (1991: 68). Such a view is probably too extreme because it would be very risky and transparent to attempt to turn himself into a Walt Disney. A more likely scenario is that he has made a conscious attempt to mould himself into the kind of smiling, zany, child-like persona with which Walt was associated. This too was a construction (see Chapter 1), but it was a memorable one and it is with these qualities, redolent as they are of Walt Disney, that Eisner has sought to associate himself. Central to this persona is the view of a man having fun. Just over a year after he took over at Disney, he was quoted in the *New York Times Magazine* as saying that running the company was like being left in a toy-shop: 'I don't know which toy to take home because they're all fabulous and they all work and I'm so excited I can't sleep at night' (Harmetz, 1985: 13). This quotation has been recycled in a number of publications and the image of Eisner as childlike and as a big kid having lots of fun takes its cue from comments such as this. He is regularly portrayed as a fount of zany ideas. In a *Newsweek* article, he was reported as suggesting placing an aircraft carrier at the Disney–MGM Studios theme park. His aide enquires: 'Sixty miles from the nearest ocean?' Eisner replies: 'Yeah, it'll be fun to look at, don't you think' (Leerhsen, 1989: 14). He is regularly described in magazine articles as childlike and boyish. His reports to shareholders are full of quirky homilies and remarks, as well as of tales about his family. He is regularly photographed in magazines with a wide grin and often with Mickey or Mickey's shadow, in contrast to the rather unsmiling 'boardroom' photographs that were common in the 1972–84 years. The persona serves him and the company well, in that it is easy for his opponents to underrate him, when he is in fact known to be a highly creative and powerful negotiator. Equally, as with Walt, the zany, childlike persona allows him to associate himself with the dream-like fantasy world and to deflect from himself a complete association with the world of business.

None the less, the visionary component of the Disney turnaround should not be overstated. The notion of a 'dark side' to the Eisner–Wells years is not simply a matter of drawing attention to some discreditable aspects of a visionary leadership team. Instead, the 'dark side' can be viewed as a basic component of their leadership which has been pursued in tandem with the more visionary flourish to which many management commentators have drawn attention. When that 'dark side' is scrutinized, it is apparent that it is highly redolent of traditional management practices. The 'dark side' turns out to involve close financial controls, tight management supervision, a combative approach in negotiations, ruthlessness over contracts, and driving management. When these points are coupled with Gomery's (1994) observations about the traditional approach of the Eisner–Wells team at least in the early years (injection of cash by selling off assets and doing more of what is already profitable), the 'dark side' can be viewed as more of a core ingredient than is often acknowledged. The frequent recourse by management writers to Eisner as a visionary leader is in large part a *template* that was imposed on the business heroes of the 1980s and 1990s, which often failed to take into account the traditional aspects of their management approach and which used the language of the day (*à la* Peters and Waterman and others) to exaggerate the more striking and dashing aspects of leaders and their turnaround strategies.

CONCLUSION

The Eisner–Wells era represents the kind of dramatic turnaround which was the focus of much interest in the 1980s and early 1990s. After a period in which the company's fortunes were languishing, in large part due to uninspiring management, Disney nearly succumbed to a takeover which almost certainly would have resulted in its being broken up. Eisner and Wells engineered a new and highly successful Disney, most notably in the film division. However, it is important not to underestimate the contribution of the era associated with Tatum, Walker, Miller and Watson, in that they laid foundations and began experiments upon which Eisner and Wells were able to build.

The reign of the Disney troika could capitalize on projects and initiatives which had been set in motion by Walt, and with Roy's prominent involvement could associate itself with Walt's charisma. In the 1972–84 period, there was a failure to routinize Walt's charisma both within the company and externally. Eisner has to a large extent tried to associate himself with the kind of persona that Walt and others created. This has been an important move in that the company comes to be associated with a quirky, innovative public figure, and as a result is not seen as solely concerned with the bottom line. To a certain extent, the childlike, zany image sits uneasily with the controlling, litigious, grasping corporation that it is known as in many quarters, but it is also a useful tactic which helps to mask these less admirable charactersistics from public view as well as establishing Eisner's charismatic credentials as Walt's heir.

In spite of evidence of travails in certain areas, in 1993 the Walt Disney Company was the sixth most admired corporation in the USA (Welsh, 1994); but at the point that this book went to press, it seemed as though Disney was about to enter a new post-Walt

phase. Wells's death in April 1994 did not result in the appointment of a successor. Instead, Eisner took over much of Wells's
work but in July 1994 needed quadruple heart bypass surgery.
Also, in August 1994 Katzenberg announced his departure, presumably because he had not been nominated Wells's successor.
At around the same time, it was believed that many senior Disney
executives were leaving and that many more were likely to go. On
the face of it, the company seems to be continuing to enjoy the
success inaugurated by Eisner and Wells, with the huge success
of *The Lion King*, its Broadway show *Beauty and the Beast*, and its
first major TV success for a number of years, *Home Improvement*.
Thus, in the first nine months of the fiscal year ending 30 June
1994, revenues were up 16 per cent and operating income up 12
per cent (Alexander, 1994). However, the continuing problems
with the Hollywood Pictures division, Hollywood Records and
Euro Disneyland, flat US theme-park attendances, the con-
troversy over the Virginia theme park (and Disney's ignominious
withdrawal of the project), and the loss of Katzenberg's energy
and creativity and of Wells's deal-making ability, cast a pall over
its immediate prospects. Towards the end of 1994, then, Disney
was beginning to look like a turnaround that had run out of
steam. This, coupled with a sick chairman and a succession problem,
made the prospects for a new post-Walt phase appear a distinct
possibility, albeit one in which Eisner would remain a highly
significant ingredient (Masters, 1994; Meyer, 1994; Mooney, 1994).

Part II

THE DISNEY THEME PARKS

3

BACKGROUND TO THE
DISNEY THEME PARKS

This chapter outlines some basic features of the Disney theme parks in order to provide a backcloth for the examination in the later chapters of various commentators' views about them. Inevitably these descriptions are brief and mainly cover the attractions and rides that have been especially singled out for attention by commentators. Readers wanting greater detail should consult standard guides. The vast bulk of the examination that follows concentrates on Disneyland and Disney World, rather than on Tokyo Disneyland and Euro Disneyland. The main reason for this is simply that it is the US parks which have typically been the focus of attention for the various commentators covered here. In fact, there is a basic structure to the parks which has been replicated in the Japanese and French models and they all share many common rides and attractions, but it is the US parks which have typically been the object of attention. Unfortunately, there are no pictures here of the parks' buildings or landscape due to the fact that the Walt Disney Company has copyrighted many of the buildings and structures, so that even a tourist guide like *The Unofficial Guide to Walt Disney World* (Sehlinger, 1994) contains no photographs. In his discussion of the Disney parks, Sorkin turns these restrictions into parody by printing a photograph of the sky above Disney World to which the following inscription is added:

> This is the sky above Disney World, which here substitutes for an image of the place itself. Disney World is the first copyrighted urban environment in history, a Forbidden City for postmodernity. Renowned for its litigiousness, the Walt Disney Company will permit no photograph of its property

without prior approval of its use. Is there a better illustration of the contraction of the space of freedom represented by places like Disney World than the innocent sky?

(Sorkin, 1992: 207)

All the Disney theme parks are united by a common approach which distinguishes them from conventional amusement parks. The share prospectus for Euro Disneyland provides a good account of their thinking and this forms a useful backcloth to the discussion that follows:

> Rather than presenting a random collection of roller coasters, merry-go-rounds and Ferris wheels in a carnival atmosphere, these parks are divided into distinct areas called 'lands' in which a selected theme (such as exotic adventures, childhood fairy tales or the frontier life of the nineteenth century American West) is presented through architecture, landscaping, costuming, music, live entertainment, attractions, merchandise and food and beverage. Within a particular land, intrusions and distractions from the theme are minimized so that the visitor becomes immersed in its atmosphere. . . . Restaurants and retail stores at Disney theme parks are designed to entertain guests and support the theme.

DISNEYLAND

Disneyland is situated outside Anaheim, a town to the south of Los Angeles. It is built on a 160-acre orange grove which Walt bought following a feasibility study by the Stanford Research Institute which had been hired to find a suitable site. It is said that Walt's original notion was for a small playground across the road from the studio, but as the vision grew this idea was eliminated. Schickel (1986) notes that Walt sent some of his staff to examine ideas which could be seen at existing amusement parks and to find manufacturers. Apparently, these informants felt that his idea of having a park without a roller coaster or a Ferris wheel or barkers was absurd. Nor were they impressed with his notions of not having outdoor hot dog stands or the sale of beer (he disliked the smells they created). But the exclusion of these symbols of the amusement fair may have been a deliberate strategy of product differentiation, whereby he could establish the distinctiveness of his enterprise and its market niche. Roller coasters were added in later years as visitors made it clear that they wanted more exciting fare, but the heavy theming of these rides disassociates them from traditional roller coaster rides. Disneyland opened on 17 July 1955 at a cost of $17 million. One problem with describing a park which has been in existence for 40 years is that it has changed greatly over the intervening period. Many of these changes are summarized in Bright (1987). When it opened there were 26 attractions, though 12 more were added before the end of 1955. Nowadays, there are over 50 attractions. Walt once said that the park would never be finished, and both he and his successors have been true to that commitment.

Basic to the theming of the parks are the 'lands' and some other areas which have distinctive narratives. The four basic lands are Adventureland, Tomorrowland, Fantasyland, and Frontierland. A fifth land was added in 1993, Mickey's Toontown. The other main regions are: Critter Country; New Orleans Square; and Main Street, USA. There is also an area called Rivers of America. The entire Magic Kingdom, other than Toontown, is circled by the Disneyland Railroad. Once past the ticket booths, visitors move to the Town Square, then down Main Street, round a Central Plaza with the Sleeping Beauty Castle inviting them forwards, and then they fan out to one of the lands.

The Main Street buildings give a false perspective, with the ground floor being to seven-eighths scale and the first floor to five-eighths scale, which was designed by Disney Imagineers (who dream up, design and build the attractions) to pull the visitor towards the castle. There are few attractions on Main Street, since most of the buildings are in fact shops. Two attractions of special interest are Great Moments with Mr Lincoln, in which an Audio-Animatronic Abraham Lincoln discourses on a number of themes, the Walt Disney Story, which presents his life and various artefacts, and the Main Street Cinema, which continuously plays six black-and-white silent cartoon classics, including *Steamboat Willie*.

Adventureland is meant to evoke exotic settings from areas as diverse as the South Seas and the Caribbean. Probably the best known attraction in this section is Jungle Cruise, an eight-minute guided cruise through dangerous waters and close to menacing shores where model animals and natives lie in wait. It is often enlivened by a humorous *spiel* from the guide. There is also a

Swiss Family Treehouse, based on *The Swiss Family Robinson*, and Enchanted Tiki Room, in which Audio-Animatronic birds sing.

New Orleans Square's attractions are Pirates of the Caribbean and Haunted Mansion. In the former, there are various sets in which Audio-Animatronic pirates and animals act out various acts of plunder, raiding, and singing. In Haunted House, visitors walk or are transported on a Doom Buggy through spooky settings, in which ghosts and other inhabitants of the other side try to frighten them out of their wits.

The architecture and landscaping of Frontierland, along with the dress of its hosts and hostesses (Disney language for 'employees'), conveys the impression of the era of America's pioneers. Its best-known attraction is Big Thunder Mountain Railroad, which is essentially a themed roller coaster in which intrepid visitors are transported at considerable speed through mines and a mining town setting. Other attractions include Mark Twain Steamboat, which takes visitors for a ride in a paddle wheeler, and Tom Sawyer Island, a themed adventure area.

Critter County was originally known as Bear County and is meant to suggest a wilderness populated with various creatures. The main attraction is Splash Mountain, a themed flume ride based on sequences in *Song of the South*, some of the animated characters from which appear along the way. Among other attractions, there is also Country Bear Playhouse, in which Audio-Animatronic bears perform a hoe-down.

Fantasyland has a large number of attractions. It includes Peter Pan's Flight in which visitors are given the impression of soaring over London and other settings, and various other rides based on classic Disney films like *Third Man on the Mountain*, *Alice in Wonderland*, *Dumbo*, *Snow White and the Seven Dwarfs*, and *Pinnochio*. Also in Fantasyland is It's a Small World, one of the attractions built for the New York World's Fair. It comprises a boat trip in which the visitor encounters miniaturized scenes and buildings from different parts of the world, as well as native Audio-Animatronic figures.

Tomorrowland is meant to convey an exciting future, but there is very little here that would prompt the visitor to feel reflective about the world of tomorrow in spite of its being dedicated to 'a world of wondrous ideas signifying man's achievements'. The bulk of the futuristics are based on space and space travel. A major attraction is Star Tours, which was designed by George

Lucas and is based on his *Star Wars* trilogy. It uses flight simulator technology to link programmed movement of visitors' seats to a film to give the illusion of movement. Space Mountain is a roller coaster ride wrapped up in a space travel theme. Captain EO is a 3-D musical in which Michael Jackson plays the part of a fairly inept space captain. Tomorrowland Autopia offers the opportunity to drive model sports cars. Submarine Voyage provides what its title implies. Tomorrowland also houses World Premiere Circlevision, a wraparound 360° cinema which shows either *American Journeys*, a tour of well-known sites which explores America's heritage, or *Wonders of China*, which does much the same for China.

Mickey's Toontown provides attractions which are orientated to a young audience. It is itself divided into zones: Downtown Toontown, Toontown Square, and Mickey's Neighbourhood. There are around 50 shops in Disneyland and a large number of restaurants. Entertainments are regularly available for visitors, including fireworks displays, parades, and bands and shows in a number of different locations.

WALT DISNEY WORLD

Walt Disney World (which will be referred to in this book, following common practice, as 'Disney World') is built on 27,400 acres of predominantly reclaimed swamp land in central Florida just outside Orlando. As can be seen from a casual comparison with Disneyland, it is vastly bigger than the California park. It is not a theme park in itself, in that it is a vacation resort at which the visitor is expected to spend a large amount of time; the idea has been to turn into a total holiday destination, rather than a place to visit as part of a visit to the region. In order to attain this goal, the company has successively added attractions and theme parks to its land, as well as several hotels, which in particular have grown in number during the Eisner–Wells era.

Whereas the visitor to Disneyland would probably purchase a one-or two-day pass, in Florida a four- or five-day multi-park ticket is the norm. Disney World comprises three main theme parks, two water theme parks, and two minor theme parks. This book will be mainly concerned with the three main theme parks: the original Magic Kingdom which Roy opened in October 1971; EPCOT Center which opened in October 1982; and Disney–MGM Studios, which opened in May 1989. The two water theme parks are the older River Country and Typhoon Lagoon, which opened in 1989. Both of the parks are heavily themed. A further water theme park, Blizzard Beach, is scheduled to open in 1995. The two minor theme parks are Pleasure Island, an area for night-time entertainment, and Discovery Island, which is a very open zoo with a special emphasis on birds, and which offers some shows. A third minor theme park, Disney's Boardwalk, is scheduled to open in 1996. According to Sehlinger, it will be 'an amusement park in the style of Atlantic City and Coney Island. Game arcades, rides, music, food, and bright lights will render a Disney-clean version of America's traditional amusement park' (1994: 17).

Disney's transportation system, which includes a futuristic monorail system, ferries visitors between the theme parks. A 5-Day Super Duper pass gives access to all the parks and allows transportation between them. Thus, a family not staying at one of the Disney hotels, can leave their car at the EPCOT Center to book an evening meal at one of the restaurants there, travel on to Disney–MGM Studios on Disney transportation, visit that park, return to EPCOT for the meal, evening fireworks and their car. According to Sehlinger (1994), attendance at Disney World varies from around 13,000 per day in early December to around 70,000 at Christmas. In the busy summer months, attendance is around 55,000. Sehlinger's guide indicates that on one day alone, 92,000 people have visited the Magic Kingdom, though this is far from normal. Disney World and Disneyland share many attractions, though similarly named attractions often differ in content.

The Magic Kingdom

This park is conceptually very similar to Disneyland. In addition to Adventureland, Frontierland, Fantasyland, Tomorrowland, and Main Street, USA, there is an area called Liberty Square and Mickey's Starland, which was originally called Mickey's Birthday-land. This last land was opened in October 1988 to celebrate Mickey's sixtieth year in show business.

Main Street, USA is mainly about shopping, but it also comprises a cinema. The Walt Disney Story used to be shown on Main Street, but was withdrawn in 1993.

Adventureland has a Jungle Cruise, a Pirates of the Caribbean (which was a New Orleans Square in Disneyland), a Swiss Family Treehouse, and the Enchanted Tiki Birds.

Frontierland's attractions include Tom Sawyer Island, Splash Mountain and Big Thunder Mountain Railroad, as well as a number of other features that rarely attract the attention of commentators.

Liberty Square's theme relates to colonial America during the era of the American Revolution. It has a Haunted Mansion and is a docking point for the Liberty Square Riverboat, a steamboat similar to Disneyland's *Mark Twain*. The Square also plays host to the Hall of Presidents in which Audio-Animatronic figures relate America's history. Part of it is based on Great Moments with Mr Lincoln.

Fantasyland has Peter Pan's Flight and various other attractions deriving from classic Disney films. There is also It's a Small World and Magic Journeys, a Kodak-sponsored 3-D fantasy film which originally appeared in the EPCOT Center.

Tomorrowland has a Space Mountain and World Premier Circlevision: *American Journeys*. Mission to Mars is a space travel simulation and Dreamflight, sponsored by Delta Airlines, presents a ride which provides a humorous history of flight. Carousel of Progress was originally designed for General Electric for the 1964 World's Fair. It is a show based on Audio-Animatronics which relates how our lives have improved through electricity and electrical goods. It was originally based at Disneyland, but moved to Disney World in 1975. It has recently been updated and the modern family is given a more contemporary appearance. At the time of writing, Tomorrowland is undergoing a substantial face-lift which will give it new attractions and a more futuristic appearance.

Mickey's Starland is orientated to small children and includes miniature buildings, shows, and the opportunity to meet Mickey.

In addition, there are around 50 shops and a large number of mainly fast-food eating places. There is a fairly continuous round of shows and entertainment.

EPCOT Center

EPCOT Center is in many ways two theme parks comprising two distinct parts: Future World and World Showcase. The World Showcase pavilions are arrayed around a lagoon; in order to get to them from Future World, which most visitors pass through first, the visitor has to cross one of two large bridges. The Future World pavilions encircle a central area comprising Spaceship

Earth and Communicore East and Communicore West. EPCOT is in the midst of major changes. In 1994, it was relabled 'EPCOT '94', the Communicores were substantially changed and renamed 'Innoventions', and changes to the contents of the Future World pavilions were announced.

Future World

Spaceship Earth, sponsored by AT&T, is close to the Entrance Plaza and is the well-known geosphere, which looks like a huge golf-ball. It houses two main features. One is a ride through the past, present and future with a pronounced emphasis on information and communication. It moves through tableaux representing, for example, cave dwellers' paintings, Ancient Egypt, the Roman Empire, the Italian Renaissance and so on, and finally zooms us into the future. The second main attraction is Earth Station, an information centre where visitors can reserve the all-important tables at World Showcase's popular ethnic restaurants.

Communicore East and West contained lots of hands-on exhibits which demonstrated the uses and attractions of modern technology. Attractions in the Communicores were housed in large crescent-shaped buildings and had a more obviously educational purpose than many other exhibits. For example, American Express Travelport allowed the visitor to find out about various holiday destinations using a touch-sensitive screen. At Energy Exchange, sponsored by Exxon, the visitor could find out about different energy sources by pushing buttons or touch-sensitive screens to produce calibrations or information. Expo Robotics introduced people to the science of robotics. But in June 1994, Communicore East and West were redubbed Innoventions East and West. The bulk of the content of the two buildings was changed in the process. Innoventions West mainly contains exhibits which depict the application of electronics, computers, virtual reality, and information technology. The accent tends to be on home entertainment systems, with Sega alone taking up 10 per cent of the whole of the Innoventions floor space with its games machines that visitors can play on (Jackson, 1994). CD-ROM technology is presented by IBM, which also demonstrates the power of its lap-top computers. Other companies like AT&T present products along similar lines. The building also houses part of Disney Imagineering Labs, in which the audience is introduced to the process of creating new attractions and the role of computer-based animation and virtual reality in both the design of attractions and modern animated cartoons. In Innoventions East, various predominantly electrical consumer products are paraded in a variety of settings, such as fanciful rooms. The products are typically from the very recent past or the present, or they provide hints about future developments.

The remainder of Future World is made up of seven pavilions representing different aspects of our world or ourselves. Each of them houses rides and/or exhibits.

The Living Seas, sponsored by United Technologies, has an underwater ride beneath a massive aquarium; but the ride is probably not the main attraction here; instead, the opportunity to gaze at a huge undersea world through thick windows represents the main feature. A number of films can be viewed and the visitor is introduced to fish-breeding techniques.

The Land pavilion, which is sponsored by Nestlé, has three main attractions. First, Listen to the Land is a boat ride which introduces the visitor to past, present and future methods of agriculture. It presents a very upbeat depiction of the application of technology to farming. This ride was renamed Living with the Land in 1994. Second, at Kitchen Kabaret we are told about nutrition by Audio-Animatronic figures in the shape of food or kitchen appliances. In 1994, this attraction was displaced by Food Rocks which does the same kind of thing but uses rock music as the musical medium. Third, in the film *Symbiosis* we are told about the need to respect the environment. It portrays some ecological disasters, but also shows how ingenuity has overcome them, such as the resuscitation of the Thames and Oregon's Willamette River.

Journey into Imagination, sponsored by Kodak, has a ride which features Figment, a small purple dragon, and Dreamfinder, who searches out new ideas. It celebrates the use of the senses in different areas of activity, such as the arts, literature and science. Image Works has hands-on exhibits which allow visitors to play around with sound, colour and light. It also contains the Dreamfinder's School of Drama in which children can play parts in short plays. Finally, this pavilion housed Captain EO, which is found in Disneyland's Tomorrowland, but in 1994 this attraction was withdrawn and a new one scheduled to take its place later in the year.

The main attraction of the World of Motion pavilion, sponsored by General Motors, is an Audio-Animatronics-based ride which tells the history of transport. The tone is humorous rather than educational and it revels in the apparent absurdities of early methods of conveyance, such as ostriches. There is also TransCenter, which has exhibits including General Motors cars and some short films.

Horizons, sponsored by General Electric, comprises a single attraction, a ride which portrays changing conceptions of the future. It takes us into our current notions of the future which depict modes of human habitation in space, the desert and undersea. The attraction shows how various electric innovations will play a part in the future.

Wonders of Life, sponsored by Metropolitan Life Insurance Company, has four main attractions. First, Body Wars is a simulation ride in which the rider chases through the human body after a splinter. Second, Cranium Command is based on a boy and how his brain, in the form of an Audio-Animatronic controller, regulates his functions. Third, *The Making of Me* is a light-hearted film about human conception and birth. Finally, there is an area populated with hands-on machines which give people information about their health, life-styles, and so on.

Finally, the Exxon-sponsored Universe of Energy pavilion has a single attraction: a theatre presentation and ride which presents forms of energy, followed by a film about fossil-fuels, then the age of dinosaurs, and finally a long film about energy in the future.

Between 1994 and 1997 (and probably beyond) substantial redesign of Future World pavilions is planned, particularly with respect to the major attraction in Spaceship Earth, Universe of Energy and World of Motion (Jackson, 1994).

World Showcase

There are eleven country pavilions in World Showcase. Unlike the Magic Kingdom which retains the integrity of the narrative enveloping each themed land by restricting the visitor's view of other lands, in World Showcase many of the countries are visible from a vantage point. Each country is made up of buildings which either stylistically or representationally symbolize it. There is often a marked degree of landscaping consistent with the impression of the nation. The buildings and landscaping serve as iconic signifiers of each of the countries. Each country also has shops selling typical products associated with it and a restaurant (in some cases more than one). There are often shows in each pavilion's grounds.

Mexico's main attraction is a boat ride, The River of Time, which transports visitors through ancient Mexican cultures. In addition to shops, there is a Mexican market selling pottery, baskets, hats, and similar ethnic merchandise.

Norway also contains a boat ride, Maelstrom, in which the visitor encounters scenes of the country's Viking past and its mythology. It touches base with the present in the form of a North Sea oil rig. As with the Mexican ride, considerable use is made of Audio-Animatronic figures. When the ride has finished, visitors are decanted into a theatre in which they watch a short film about Norway.

The main attractions in China, Canada and France are films. China has a 360° Circle-Vision film about the country and its people, *Wonders of China*. Similarly, Canada's main attraction is a Circle-Vision film, *O Canada!* France has a 200° film, *Impressions de France.*

Germany, Italy and the United Kingdom have no attractions at all other than the typical fare of buildings, landscape, shops and restaurants. Japan has a small gallery, but no other specific attractions. In Morocco, the only other attractions are a bazaar, which sells leather goods, pottery, and similar items, and a museum of Moorish art.

The United States pavilion is referred to by the name of its main attraction, the American Adventure, an account of American history based predominantly on Audio-Animatronic figures. The narration is done by Mark Twain and Ben Franklin. Like many such presentations in the Disney parks, there is an emphasis on the authenticity of the detail. As the official guide to Disney World puts it:

> Throughout the show, the attention to historical detail is meticulous. Every one of the rear-projected illustrations was executed in the painting style of the era being described. The Chief Joseph and Susan B. Anthony figures are speaking their originals' very words. The exact dimensions of the cannonballs in another scene were carefully investigated – then reproduced. In the Philadelphia Centennial Exposition scene, Pittsburgh's name is spelled without the *h* that subsequent years have added.
>
> (Birnbaum, 1989: 144)

Towards the end of the show, there is the Golden Dream sequence, a collage of images or film of key figures in US history, including Walt Disney.

The Disney–MGM Studios

This third theme park, which opened in 1989, is essentially about the motion picture and television industries. Its aim is to envelop visitors in the nostalgia, the excitement and the glamour of these industries. There are three main constituents. First, there is Hollywood Boulevard, an area in which park services, shops and restaurants are found within an ambience that aims to recreate Hollywood's golden age. It functions as the equivalent of Main Street, USA in the Magic Kingdoms in that it is the point of entry and immediate orientation for the visitor. A similar setting, Sunset Boulevard opened in 1994.

Second, there are studio tours which give visitors the chance to view Hollywood's tricks of the trade. One is the Animation Tour in which the visitor is introduced to the art of animation and can see artists at work. Visitors gaze through large windows on animators in much the same way that they gaze on the fish and sea mammals in the Living Seas. The tour ends with a film about animation and its accomplishments. The other main tour is the Backstage Studio Tour, in which visitors are introduced to film production while either seated on a long tram or walking. The idea is to give a behind-the-scenes impression of the world of movies and television. While on the tram, visitors find out about props, gaze on landscapes fabricated for films, and risk their lives as fire and flood befall Catastrophe Canyon. The walking part of the tour is mainly about the creation of special effects.

The third component of the park is made up of various rides and attractions. One of the best-known rides is the Great Movie Ride in which visitors move from a replica of Hollywood's Chinese Theater to vehicles which transport them through highly recognizable sets of famous Hollywood films in which Audio-Animatronic figures mouth the words of John Wayne, Gene Kelly, Humphrey Bogart and others. Other attractions include: the same Star Tours that was referred to in the context of Disneyland; the Monster Sound Show, in which a few members of the audience try to synchronize sound to a spooky film starring Chevy Chase; the Indiana Jones Epic Stunt Spectacular, which

74

shows how stunts in the film were created and allows some participation for a few of the 2,000 or so people in the theatre; a 3-D film based on Jim Henson's Muppets; and Superstar Television, in which a few audience members are able to participate in a television production. There are some shows and plays based self-referentially on Disney films, such as *Beauty and the Beast*, *The Little Mermaid*, and *Honey, I Shrunk the Kids*. A new ride, The Twilight Zone Tower of Terror, opened in 1994.

TOKYO DISNEYLAND AND EURO DISNEYLAND

The two foreign Disney theme parks have been constructed, albeit with minor modifications, like the Magic Kingdoms in Anaheim and Orlando. That is to say, they comprise the same four basic lands, a castle, a Main Street funnel, and landscaping as the two American parks. Many of the rides in the American parks have been replicated.

Tokyo Disneyland, which opened in April 1983, is not owned by Disney but, as mentioned in Chapter 2, its staff were and are heavily involved in devising attractions and the integrity of the theming. The park has been a huge success, with currently around 14 million visitors per year, and has spawned a large number of alternative theme parks in Japan. Seventy-five per cent of visitors have been before (Simons, 1990). Tokyo Disneyland is located on a 114-acre site of reclaimed land about a 90-minute journey from Tokyo. It is unashamedly American in orientation at the request of the Japanese. Simons quotes an executive from the park's owners, Oriental Land Company: 'When we built Tokyo Disneyland, we made the decision to keep the American flavor as much as possible' (Simons, 1990: 43). When Sayle visited the park, he was moved to remark: 'Apart from the customers, there is nothing Japanese in sight' (1983: 42). There are some differences from the American parks: there are more covered-in areas because of the less benign weather than in Florida and southern California; there is no Nautilus submarine (as in 20,000 Leagues Under the Sea at Disney World) because of Japanese concerns about nuclear weapons; Hall of Presidents is replaced by an animated history of Japan, sponsored by Matsushita, makers of Panasonic electrical goods; the World Bazaar has replaced Main Street, USA as the main shopping area; and there is a Japanese restaurant for older visitors. According to a *Business Week* writer:

'American as it may be, [Tokyo] Disneyland appeals to such deep-seated Japanese passions as cleanliness, order, outstanding service, and technological wizardry' (Neff, 1990: 39). So successful and admired is the Disney approach to training and management that, as Neff (1990) and Fusaho (1988) report, Japanese companies are flocking to the park to find out how it is all done. Yoshimoto suggests that the Disney attributes of cleanliness, quality, and so on are so central to the Japanese mind-set that Disneyland 'is arguably the most Japanese institution in the United States' (1994: 197). For this writer, the synchrony between the Disney approach and Japanese preferences, coupled with the small differences from the US parks, which he suggests are by no means trivial, means that it makes no sense to view Tokyo Disneyland as a sign of American cultural imperialism.

No such favourable response was to greet Euro Disneyland, which covers 138 acres (the whole site is 1,500 acres) and is located about 20 miles east of Paris. It is 49 per cent owned by Disney (or was when it opened) who felt that their predecessors had made a mistake in not having a greater financial stake in the Tokyo park. The company also receives a management fee, as well as 10 per cent of gross revenues from admissions and fees from participants and 5 per cent of gross revenues from merchandise and food and from hotels. Six themed hotels were available for visitors, giving a total of 5,200 rooms. The park opened on 12 April 1992. Its structure is very much the same as the American parks. Unlike Tokyo Disneyland, Euro Disneyland does have a Main Street, USA, but its Tomorrowland is called Discoveryland. Most of the attractions are versions of those found at the US parks. As with Tokyo Disneyland, there are subtle concessions to the local culture and conditions. There are more covered areas than in the US, because of the less reliable climate of northern Europe, while small Gallic touches were introduced. However, these concessions to French taste were not sufficient to quell dismay about Mickey's arrival. It was branded by some as a 'cultural Chernobyl' and was greeted with near-universal derision by French intellectuals. The French unions railed against the 'fascism' of the company's recruitment policy, with its stress on a certain 'look' (Jenkins, 1992). Bill Bryson expressed the requirements as follows:

No one on the Disney payroll is allowed to smoke, wear

flashy jewellery, chew gum, tint their hair an unnatural shade, possess a visible tattoo, be fat or fail to subdue their sweat glands. Men must wear their hair short and may not have a beard or moustache. The Mormons ask less than this.

(1993: 18)

Even before the park's opening, articles began to appear in newspapers questioning its viability. Articles typically focused on the receptivity of Europeans to such an icon of American culture, the problem of the weather, and whether Europeans could be made to conform to the Disney way of doing things. Even around a week after the park's opening, there were signs that all was not well, as can be seen from some newspaper headlines: 'British bookings slashed as fantasy park opens' (*The Sunday Times*, 12 April 1992); 'Hi-tech Mickey – over-priced, over the top and over here' (*Guardian*, 13 April 1992). Two months later, newspapers and magazines were reporting lower-than-expected attendance, complaints about the cost of food and merchandise and high labour turnover: 'Trouble in paradise' (*Investors Chronicle*, 12 June 1992); 'Queuing for flawed fantasy' (*The Financial Times*, 13 June 1992); 'Slow ride at Disney' (*The Sunday Times*, 21 June 1992). By July it was reported that prices were being reviewed as a response to disappointing attendance and that the cost of hotels and food was being reduced. On 24 July, the *Guardian* suggested that a net loss was likely and accompanied the article with the kind of cartoon that would be a feature of the treatment of the park in the media: it showed seven dwarfs facing Snow White who says 'I'm going to have to let you go'. In fact, as many of the articles over the summer of 1992 showed, attendance at the park during that period was very good, almost too good on one day when 92,000 descended on it. On the other hand, attendances were *generally* lower than expected and more importantly there were concerns about numbers in the cold, wet autumn and winter months. Also, there was growing evidence that the park was going to make a substantial loss because of poor merchandise sales and hotel occupancy. Within four months of opening, Euro Disneyland announced that it would close one of its hotels because of poor bookings. In November, a net loss of £23 million for the year to 30 September was announced, along with a warning that it was not expected to make profits in the first full year of operation. Fleet Street was again in its element with the following headlines from

The Sunday Times on 6 December: 'Rain stops play from Goofy and the boys' and ' Hi ho, hi ho, it's off the cliff we go'.

News continued to deteriorate in the new year and in January 1993 it was announced that Euro Disneyland's chairman, Robert Fitzpatrick, was quitting and would be replaced by its then president, Philippe Bourgignon. Over the winter, there were rumours of attendances as low as 3,000 on some days, but as spring approached there was some optimism. However, by April 1993, it was apparent that losses were increasing and there were the first indications of a move by the European operation to discuss refinancing with its American parent. In July 1993 it was announced that Euro Disneyland had lost £60 million in the quarter from April to June inclusive. On 15 August, *The Sunday Times* ran a story whose headline 'Euro Disney future in doubt' was to portend a theme which ran through many articles in newspapers and magazines, though Disney itself rejected the suggestion. During this period Fleet Street had a field day with its headlines, as did *The Sunday Times* on 22 August: 'Euro Disney: Dopey and a little Grumpy', 'Euro-Dismal' and 'Magic rubs off the Disney Kingdom'. During these months of analysis about the park's failure and speculation about its future, the following themes were recycled time and time again: poor weather meant that off-season attendances were too low; admission prices were pitched too high; hotel, food and merchandise prices were also too high; the proximity of Paris and of cheap hotels coupled with good road and rail links meant that the profitable resort hotels were underused; the predominantly French staff would not throw themselves into their roles as smiling hosts; poor value for Europeans compared with the cost of a trip to Disney World; and cultural resistance. In other words, it was in the wrong place and it was too expensive, so that when a Disney executive on secondment to the park was asked whether the park might have done better somewhere else, he replied 'Yeah, Milwaukee' (Langley, 1993: 9).

In October 1993, further reductions in hotel and restaurant prices were announced, fears of a rights issue of shares were surfacing, news of a reduction of the size of the workforce emerged, and British Airways announced that it was going to cease selling package holidays to the resort. The following month brought news of increased losses (nearly £500 million for the year to September 1993) and mounting speculation about closure.

Financial analysts were increasingly being quoted as wondering whether the whole Euro Disneyland project was fundamentally flawed, since although it had not failed catastrophically in meeting its attendance targets (around 9.5 million against a projected 11 million for the first year) it was still haemorrhaging money. It was becoming increasingly apparent that an injection of money and a preparedness for the banks and Disney to reschedule its debts and even to write some of them off were a *sine qua non* of its survival. Coincidentally, Disney seemed to keep itself very distant from the park's troubles and was quoted as taking a hard line on the park's problems, such as when Eisner was reported at the end of 1993 as saying that he would do nothing that would endanger the parent company's health. By February 1994, it was apparent that losses were deepening. However, in March 1994 Disney and the banks agreed a deal in which the former agreed to forgo £220 million of revenue and royalties for five years and the banks waived a large proportion of interest due to them. Disney also agreed to put up extra credit and to buy certain assets from Euro Disneyland. A rights issue of shares would finance the restructuring, with Disney taking up 49 per cent and the banks underwriting the remainder. But on 1 June there was an announcement that Prince al-Waleed bin Talal bin Adulaziz, a member of the Saudi royal family, would buy up to 24 per cent of Euro Disneyland shares from its bankers and would invest $100 million in a convention centre at the park. The deal was seen as providing the park with a lifeline and security. However, in August 1994, doubts about the park's viability resurfaced due to suggestions that there had been a decrease in patronage during the year and to a growing belief that its attendance targets were unrealistic. Figures released in November 1994 showed a sharp reduction in losses, but this was due to cost-cutting rather than to an increase in the number of visitors or their per capita expenditure, both of which were in fact down on the previous year.

One of the chief problems for Disney and its European operation in all of this was not just the park's survival, but the maintenance of fantasy. During this period, Euro Disneyland almost became a byword for a flop, but just as importantly the preoccupation with numbers of visitors, financing, prices, and so on diminished the sense of fantasy that the company is always at pains to create. The adverse publicity made people more aware of the park's nature, that is as a business, than Disney would have wanted. As we have seen, Walt and more recently Eisner sought to elevate the sense of fun and fantasy and to camouflage the more obviously commercial side of their enterprise. The financial problems were damaging, not just because they threatened the park's future but because the publicity focused too much attention on the park as a business organization to the detriment of the sense of fantasy the company is at pains to create. Such considerations may have been behind the decision toward the end of 1994 to rebrand Euro Disneyland as 'Disneyland Paris' in advertising and publicity

4

A FAMILY PILGRIMAGE

In this chapter, I begin an examination of the writings of various authors on the Disney theme parks. The aim is to explore the kinds of issues that these authors see as deriving from the parks – what they have made of the parks. Inevitably, my own observations will intrude, but the main aim will be to concentrate on what others have seen as significant and interesting. The writers represent a very diverse group. We find those who are unabashed enthusiasts and those who are inveterate detractors. The latter tend to decry the world of Disney as kitsch, shallow culture, as when Apple writes of the post-Salk vaccine era of Disneyland leading to 'a paralysis of taste' (1983: 166). For the novelist Julian Halevy, in Disneyland as in other Disney products everything has been 'reduced to a sickening blend of cheap formulas packaged to sell' and he felt 'sadness for the empty lives which accept such tawdry substitutes' (1958: 511). The enthusiasts have often waxed lyrical about the imaginativeness and innovativeness of the parks, with architects frequently being at the forefront of such enthusiasm. But this has by no means been the only dimension on which commentators have differed. They have often varied in terms of the intellectual traditions with which they have been associated. In the commentaries on the parks we find a wide diversity indeed, including semiotics (Eco, 1986; Gottdiener, 1982; Mechling and Mechling, 1981), structuralism (Marin, 1984), postmodernism (Baudrillard, 1983; Fjellman, 1992; Stephanson, 1987), deconstructionism (Dennett, 1989), and analyses with fairly clear Marxist overtones (e.g. Bukatman, 1991; Wallace, 1985). Many other writers have exhibited no obvious theoretical commitments, preferring to reflect in a general way on the significance of the Disney parks. Thus, for King (1981) the parks represent 'traditional values in futuristic form', while for Moore (1980) and Kottak (1982) the visitor is a pilgrim. Still other writers have related the Disney parks to wider projects in which they are interested. Real depicts Disneyland as one of a number of forms of 'mass-mediated culture' in which various media 'transmit in a mass manner from a single source to many anonymous receivers' (1977: viii). Zukin (1991) depicts Disney World as an illustration of the operation of 'landscapes of power' in which the physical environment is underpinned by economic power. For Findlay (1992), Disneyland connects with his interest in 'magic lands', the innovations that he sees as having a profound impact on concepts of urban living after 1940. There is a further group of writings which seem to comprise fundamentally of observations about the parks but which have no obvious single theme or position. By far the most comprehensive and best treatment of the parks is Fjellman (1992), which is specifically about Disney World. It weighs in at nearly 500 pages and represents the most significant analysis available. It draws on ideas associated with postmodernism and consumerism, which are coupled with detailed, travel-book descriptions of rides and attractions.

As this very general summary implies, writers have approached the parks from a variety of angles and have generated from them a number of different implications. In spite of this apparent diversity, these writers have not differed greatly in terms of the kinds of theme to be presented in Part II. In other words, although quite a wide range of themes have been extracted in the analysis to be presented here, writers have often contributed to each theme independently of their theoretical positions or of their individual projects when examining the parks. This commonality is interesting in itself since it means that writers working within frameworks as diverse as Marxism and semiotics can generate conclusions which are consistent, if not almost identical. Perhaps the power of 'theming' exerts greater influence over writers than they or we as readers are aware.

It should also be borne in mind that although terms like 'the Disney parks' have been employed in the preceding paragraphs, as a number of writers have observed, there are differences between them that affect writers' observations and inferences. Eco (1986) suggests that Disneyland is more coherent than Disney World, while Fjellman (1992) depicts Disney World's Magic Kingdom as 'intimate' whereas EPCOT is 'massive and impersonal'.

Blake (1972) suggests that Disneyland's smaller scale creates a greater sense of excitement. Francaviglia (1981) argues that Disney World's Main Street, USA is different from Disneyland's, in that the former is wider and has more striking buildings. He also characterizes the Disney World version as more exotic and bizarre than at Disneyland, whose buildings he feels are more consistent. At Disney World the buildings themselves are the object of attention; at Disneyland, Main Street itself is meant to be the focus of attention as a coherent entity. Francaviglia argues that these contrasts reflect the different kinds of vacation associated with Florida and Southern California. For the most part, however, the parks are sufficiently similar to warrant generalization across them, although the relative absence of social commentary on Tokyo Disneyland and Euro Disney (other than the sometimes near hysterical anxiety about cultural contagion in the case of the latter) means that the Florida and California parks will dominate the discussion. The fact that many attractions exist in more than one park makes generalization across the parks more feasible, although, as we have seen with Main Street, there may still be differences lurking behind the superficial similarities. Moreover, as Fjellman's contrast suggests, the differences within Disney World may be just as if not more striking than is implied by a comparison of Disney World and Disneyland. Indeed, EPCOT and its messages seem to have greatly increased the amount of interest in the Disney parks, perhaps because it more self-evidently has a cluster of messages than those aspects of the parks which have a greater component of fantasy.

The various commentators by and large have viewed the parks as constituting texts to be interpreted and understood. As texts, they have been seen as ripe with meaning and significance. But the parks are not inert texts. Walt always said that the parks would never be finished, and he and his successors have been true to this belief. Not only have new attractions been continually added (while others have been dropped), but also many have been changed and redesigned. Thus, as shown in the previous chapter, at the time of writing, the EPCOT Center is in the throes of numerous alterations to its Future World attractions, but the commentators to be discussed have based their observations on earlier versions of those same attractions. Consequently, just as the Disney theme park attractions are continually undergoing change, interpretations of the theme parks need to shift.

In an imaginative, but curiously inconclusive article, Nye (1981) has explicated eight different ways of examining amusment parks. These are:

1 as fabricated, controlled environments, which are designed to be different from everyday life;
2 as fantasy lands in which visitors can enjoy ephemeral contact with exotic and sometimes erotic worlds;
3 as spectacles which provide visitors with all-encompassing visual and aural experiences;
4 as liberation from the obligation to engage in mundane behaviour;
5 as an entertainment experience specifically designed for families;
6 as a direct consequence of improvements in transport;
7 as a place where visitors can take risks while knowing that they are unlikely to be harmed;
8 as a context within which the major forms of human play can be enacted.

There was no need for Nye to arbitrate between the virtues of these eight possibilities, since they are not really inconsistent. It will become apparent that the eight approaches can be discerned in different degrees in the writings of the various Disney commentators. However, the writers on the Disney parks have typically sought to go beyond the sorts of focus implied by this list, in that by treating the parks as a text (or as texts) they have probed possible meanings of the text which have to be divined and interpreted. It is precisely the themes which various commentators have detected that is the focus of the following discussion.

A number of writers have pointed to the importance of clear narratives in the Disney parks. This is another way of referring to the 'theming' of the parks and it is this feature which sets them apart from traditional amusement parks. In theme parks, the visitor is encompassed by narratives in the form of stories or of linked attractions which relate to particular motifs. These narratives function not just by virture of the names which they are given (such as Frontierland or Norway), but also by combinations of architecture, sounds, shops, restaurants, costumes, arts and crafts, and occasionally smells which enhance the feeling of being wrapped up in a time and place. These qualities apply equally to the regions of the parks (such as Adventureland) and to the attractions themselves (such as Pirates of the Caribbean). Disney goes to great lengths to protect the integrity of these narratives so that when in a land within the Magic Kingdom the visitor generally cannot see other lands. This integrity is protected at all costs: a Euro Disneyland spokesman was quoted in the *Independent* as saying to prospective employees: 'You are employed to work in one land. When you are a cowboy working in Frontierland, you cannot walk through Fantasyland on your way to lunch' (in Arlidge, 1992: 3). Waldrep (1993) observes that in the Magic Kingdom the function of narrative is to help the visitor move from one world to another (Adventureland to Frontierland). The visitor then has the opportunity to participate in the narratives that Disney have provided. In EPCOT, the use of buildings to encompass themes in Future World and of nation-states in World Showcase renders the narrative elements more transparent. In treating the Disney parks as texts, one of the main tasks will be that of decoding these narratives.

However, before beginning the analysis of the themes noted by various commentators, it is worth noting that a number of them have drawn attention to the way in which essentially cinematic techniques are employed to enhance the narrative elements and the visitor's experience of them. Finch (1973: 393) has pointed out that a key difference between Disneyland and earlier amusement parks is that it was devised in the manner of a film set. He suggests that both film sets and a theme park require similar presentational skills. In particular, since film-makers are taught to conceptualize films in terms of a series of events, this kind of narrative skill was very relevant to conceptualizing the park and its constituent parts. It facilitated the creation of narrative flow within which guests were to be submerged. It is probably not surprising, therefore, that many writers should depict the theme park experience as having cinematic overtones. Real, for example, writes: 'The visitor passes through a Disney experience just as a viewer is carried through scenes of a film by a camera' (1977: 47), while King (1981) tells us that the different lands give the impression of being in a film. Yoshimoto (1994) argues that the creation of narratives within self-contained spaces controls the experience of guests and that as such the theme park is an extension of the cinema. But it is also a form of cinema in which guests become part of the action. They participate in that action, albeit in a controlled and sometimes passive way.

The cinematic roots of the parks is futher evident in the fact that many of the rides are like being at the cinema in that guests are made to sit and gaze while surrounded by darkness. The difference is that these seats are in vehicles that move (in Disney parlance 'people movers'), but this adds to the sense of being part of the action. For Kuenz (1993), this is a distinctly cinematic experience for the guest and for Bukatman (1991) the parks provide a 'hypercinematic experience'. King takes a similar perspective when she argues that these rides function much like a movie camera:

> Each car is wired for stereophonic sound and turns electronically so that the occupant sees only what the designer has intended him to see throughout the programmed 'show' – exactly in the way the movie camera sees. The cars behind are invisible and those ahead obscure, so that these rides have an intimate, private feeling closely connected to film viewing.
>
> (King, 1981: 120)

The Disney theme park experience is heavily contingent on the artful creation of narratives which are heavily reliant on a cinematic approach to their presentation. In other words, the link between the new kind of amusement park that the Disney parks represent and a film studio is by no means accidental. However, with the building of the Disney–MGM Studios we are faced with the irony of a theme park in which the same cinematic skills have gone into the creation of narratives *about the cinema*. It is as though the visitor comes full circle. In the case of this theme park, the visitor is given insights into some of the artifices of the cinema ('houses' which are just façades, fabricated water marks, how animation is really done). Moreover, visitors (or at least a selected few) can literally become part of the action by being recorded or filmed, while others enjoy a vicarious participation in the action as they move around the various 'sets'. The Disney parks have often been seen as emblematic of this kind of elision of the boundaries between reality and fantasy but the self-referential nature of the Disney–MGM park seems to take this feature a further stage. However, the specific issue of the disjunctures between reality and fantasy, which is a particular focus of writers influenced by postmodernism, will be addressed in Chapter 8. The aim of the present discussion is to suggest that the skills and know-how that go into movie production have been central to precisely what makes a theme park distinctive – its use of narrative to envelop the guest. The aim of this book is to discern what various commentators have made of these narratives.

THE FAMILY AS THEME AND CONTEXT

It is well known that Walt Disney and the company after Walt fashioned films for a predominantly family audience. Walt frequently repudiated the suggestion that his films were designed for children, arguing instead that they were for everyone. He once said: 'I don't make pictures for children, at least not just for children.'[1] On another occasion, he said: 'The one thing for me . . . the important thing . . . is the family, and keeping the family together with things. That's been the backbone of our whole business, catering to families' (in Zehnder, 1975: 278). Indeed, the theme of family was extremely strong in many of the studio's most popular films, such as *Bambi* and *Dumbo*, which enhanced his credentials as someone who provided family entertainment. The very idea of Disneyland was founded on the premiss of an amusement park which could be enjoyed by adults and children alike, in other words by families. It is not surprising that the family should feature in Disney attractions. Kuenz (1993) notes that attractions are full of happy couples and families. Fjellman (1992) sees EPCOT's Horizons ride as a particular case in point. Guests are taken on a ride that examines how the future was conceived in the past and are then transported into the future where they visit FuturePort and encounter a family and its home. The dress and environment are manifestly futuristic, but the family context is highly familiar. We see the future through the experiences of a mother and father who gradually age and have children with whom they keep in touch in highly futuristic fashion (for example, with the aid of holographic images). Of course, their daughter is by now married and has a family of her own. The family is the focus for the changes in our material circumstances through the ages that is depicted in the Carousel of Progress. Similarly, while waiting for the Michael Jackson science fiction rock fantasy, *Captain EO* (also in Future World), the assembled crowd is treated to a treacly Kodak-sponsored series of photographs which depict the cycle of couple, babies, growing up, courtship, marriage, and back to babies. The implicit message of such presentations is clear: the conventional nuclear family is secure and will endure the vicissitudes that the future will bring to bear on it. Moreover, in many attractions, adults only appear as parents, so that so far as the Disney parks are concerned adulthood inheres in parenthood (Kuenz, 1993).

As Kuenz (1993) and Rojek (1993a) have observed, the resulting series of images provides a very conventional cast to the family and its future. This is the heterosexual nuclear family in action. A ripost to such observations is that a future of homosexual or single-parent families would hardly provide the kind of escapist entertainment with which Disney is associated. Nor would it provide acceptable entertainment for often quite young children. These are not unreasonable responses, although it could be countered that the idealized images of the family that such presentations impart do not provide children with the preparation that they need to handle divorce, separation, or the death of a parent. Moreover, a large percentage of children will have endured one of these events. The really important point about the conventional nuclear family that continually resurfaces in the parks' attractions, as a number of writers have observed, is that this family context is the location within which consumption takes place. It is the family that consumes the electrical gadgets in Horizons and Carousel of Progress, both formerly sponsored by General Electric, and which buys the cameras and film in the ante-room to *Captain EO*. The specific issue of consumption and consumerism will be returned to below, but the issue is worth registering here, because the association of the family unit with consumption provides a powerful image. It connects the purchase of the sponsors' products with the family which is the context within which many people go to the Disney parks. Moreover, it is also the context within which products at the theme park will be consumed – in the merchandise shops, restaurants, and so on. Thus, the connection of the family image with consumption is a powerful one which reinforces the consumerist goals of the parks.

It is often believed that the Disney parks are designed for children, but a number of writers have questioned this contention. For one thing, the ratio of adults to children at the parks is 4:1 (Findlay, 1992; Lawrence, 1986). Findlay (1992) has suggested that advertisements for Disneyland have often been designed specifically to appeal to adults. It could even be argued that

Walt's avowed aim of constructing the parks so that the outside world, with its implication of work and humdrum existence, could be banished from view was more likely to appeal to adults than to children. Adults would need to be convinced because they would be the ones driving the cars, spending the money, and taking the time off from work. Moreover, the parks' nostalgia, which is often remarked on, is much more likely to appeal to adults than to children, since arguably the latter have little to be nostalgic about. The recognition of the parks' appeal to adults recalls Walt's frequent dismissal of the views of those who suggested that his films were designed for children. It also recalls a scathing critique by Sayers (1965) of the effect of Disney renditions in his films and books of classical children's literature when she remarked that Walt did not address his films to children, but to adults. Sayers noted that the books and films employed symbols from the world of adults, such as heroes looking like Cary Grant and girls looking like Hollywood starlets. However, the appeal of the parks to adults has been crucial to their success. In the midst of the despair about Euro Disneyland in 1994, it was reported that the park's executives had discovered that it had a significant appeal to the older generation (aged 55 and over) who came without children (Elliott, 1994: 5). The company planned to mine this market through promotions to travel firms specializing in holidays for this older generation. The appeal of the park for such visitors is viewed by the company as explicitly nostalgic. Elliott quotes Euro Disneyland's senior vice-president: 'Obviously, they were not rushing to the white-knuckled rides but they were walking around happily taking in the atmosphere and clearly reliving their youth' (1994: 5).

The parks differ in their degree of appeal to adults. Waldrep (1993) notes that in Disney World, the Magic Kingdom is more obviously child-centred. The 'lands' with their concentration on adventure, fantasy, and for Americans at least, the near-mythical period of the frontier conjure the kinds of image that have a specific appeal to children. As Waldrep puts it, children can discover the new anew while adults enjoy the memory of that discovery as children (seeing *Peter Pan*, *Swiss Family Robinson*, *Cinderella* and other Disney films which have spawned attractions) as well as nostalgic recollections of the kind of place symbolized by Main Street and of encountering images of US presidents while at school. The child-centred nature of Disney

World's Magic Kingdom has been magnified by the addition of Mickey's Starland, an area of child-like scale and with specifically child-like interests. By contrast, EPCOT is a park in which the child, especially the young child, occupies a more peripheral position. Future World perhaps has more of interest to children (Captain EO, sea mammals, intimations of space travel, cars, hands-on exhibits), but it is cloaked in emphases about corporations and the future which seem more likely to register in adults than the young. In World Showcase, however, the child is almost displaced, since with the exception of such attractions as the small number of rides (in Mexico and Norway) and the American Adventure, much of it involves gazing at models of buildings or landscapes. While some of these may be familiar to children, such as the Eiffel Tower, others are less likely to be so, for example, St Mark's Square in Venice. The British pub, the German beer-hall, and some of the waitress-service restaurants also seem more geared to the wishes of adults than of their offspring.

Waldrep (1993) argues that in the Disney–MGM Studios park, the displacement of the child is taken even further. While there is plenty that will appeal to children, especially rides such as Star Tours and shows like the Indiana Jones Epic Stunt Spectacular, many other aspects seem designed for adults. The Animation Tour, the demystification involved in learning how films are made, the creation of nostalgia through film sets and seeing familiar props, and Audio-Animatronic figures representing much-loved actors of the past (the Great Movie Ride) are more likely to appeal to adults for whom these recollections will have far greater resonance. In contrast to the EPCOT and Disney–MGM parks, the Magic Kingdom seems childlike, even child*ish*. In some of the minor Disney World parks, such as Discovery Island and Typhoon Lagoon, there is a greater orientation to the world of children, but within a framework in which adults can have lots of fun too.

Thus, the theme parks have been constructed in such a way that they have a very direct appeal to families and to the adults within those families. Perhaps one of the reasons why many Americans revisit the parks, often many times, is that parents know that they too will have an enjoyable experience, since a great many of the attractions are designed for them, if not exclusively, then at least in part. The involvement of adults in the Disney experience and more specifically targeting that experience to adults as well as children, has been crucial to the success of the parks. The most obvious aspect is that adults are more likely to want to go to the parks when there is something in it for them. But it was also important for Walt that adults were engaged in the experience of the parks. He noted when he took his daughters to the old amusement parks that adults frequently looked bored while their children played. He did not want a park where adults sat around looking uninterested since they would not want to visit again, but also by engaging their interest he would be more likely to get across to them some of the themes that he wanted Disneyland to symbolize and to announce. Also, engaged parents would be more likely to consume – to buy merchandise, drinks, and food which are in many ways the key to the profitability of the parks. By being caught up in the total experience they would be less inclined to exhibit their normal caution about spending money on non-essential purchases. To a large extent it has been Walt's successors who have appreciated fully the importance of consumption to the parks' success and have greatly expanded their ranges to the extent that there is now a part of Disney World which is explicitly for consumption (Village Marketplace). It is also Walt's successors who have added parks and attractions which have a more obviously adult appeal. They have probably recognized even more than Walt the importance of appealing to parents.

Safety

One of the main appeals of the Disney parks that many writers have noticed is that they are safe environments. Writers have noted how the outside world makes a stark contrast with the parks (which was of course Walt's intention), in that the parks represent a haven of safety in a world which is riddled with fear and the threat (whether real or imagined) of danger. In the Disney parks, families can walk around free from concerns about the worries associated with large urban areas in the United States. As these worries have intensified, Walt's original plan to create a Utopian fantasy world has become more rather than less fitting. King detects a parallel with McDonald's in these respects:

> For both, providing a clean and attractive haven for families as a barrier against the corruption of the outside world gives them the defensive quality of temples dedicated to preserving

a sense of safety and certainty – even dignity – in a darkening urban world.

(1983: 118)

The safety of the Disney parks provides a highly attractive lure for middle-class families, many of whom come from areas like Los Angeles and Miami with their attendant images of danger and menace. Moreover, when in the parks, families are relieved from the need to engage in security precautions of the kind often undergone on the outside. The absence of traffic in the parks also obviates any concern about being run over by vehicles or having a traffic accident. The sense of safety may heighten the experience of some of the thrills-and-spills rides. Of course, although the parks give the impression of a haven of safety, when people return to their cars in the massive parking areas, they are also returning to the world of danger from which they have been cocooned. Disney World is sometimes promoted as a total holiday destination so that families will be encouraged to stay in the Disney hotels and thereby remain in the protection of the parks. This lure undoubtedly received a boost in 1992 and 1993 when there were a number of well-publicized attacks on tourists in Florida.

Appealing to the middle class

However, the appeal of the Disney parks to families and to adults has to be qualified by a recognition that it is *middle-class* families and adults who are typically found in the parks, and that in the main these are *white* middle-class families and adults. As long ago as the 1930s, Walt recognized the importance of appealing to a middle-class audience. Writing about the Mickey Mouse comics, Andrae has noted how Mickey himelf underwent a process of embourgeoisement to appeal more directly to the middle class:

> But Mickey had already begun to evolve into a less energetic character in the late thirties. By the next decade his youthful exuberance, symbolized by his shoe-button eyes, short red pants and oversize shoes, had given way to an even more humanized and contemporary mouse sporting polo shirts and slacks – stolidly middle class and clearly 'adult'.

(1988: 24)

Separately, Smoodin (1993) has suggested that in the 1930s Walt was attempting to capture a more middle-class audience for his products. In the 1930s, a series of hardbound books – Mickey Mouse Movie Stories – was started. The books derived from the cartoon films and contained copious illustrations from them. Smoodin also points to the fact that in the 1930s, Walt placed a nursery rhyme each month in *Good Housekeeping*, accompanied by sketches. He suggests that by placing the Mickey series in hard-back, Walt was attempting to gain literary credibility among a middle-class clientele, while *Good Housekeeping* was closely associated with middle-class homemaking. Smoodin writes: 'In each instance, while not excluding a lower-class audience, Disney was working within a network of bourgeois concerns and consumer habits' (1993: 17). One of the aims of *Fantasia* may well have been an attempt to gain cultural capital with the affluent middle class.

Right from the outset, Walt intended to instil this close association with middle-class values and interests in the parks. He aimed very specifically to differentiate Disneyland from the more working-class overtones and clientele of the older amusement parks like those at Coney Island, although ironically in the early years of the twentieth century these parks had also sought to create a distinctly bourgeois atmosphere to attract more affluent customers (Kasson, 1978; Weinstein, 1992). In so doing, King (1981: 119) suggests that, in conjunction with the use of theming, Walt created a new type of park which was clearly differentiated from the traditional amusement park. King writes: 'The [Disney] parks are middle-class and family-oriented as opposed to the lower-class "carney" atmosphere of traditional amusement parks.' There are guards at the gates of the Disney parks who are reputed to keep out the more 'lumpen' elements of the lower class. Gottdiener (1982) suggests that the high price of admission screens out the poor, but his observation is ironic, because the cost of admission has increased greatly since he wrote. Certainly, the costs of a full Disney World holiday are most likely to be within the reach of middle-class families. In the *Washington Post*, Bob Garfield, a writer for *Advertising Age*, detailed the costs of his five-day Disney World holiday for his family of four. A distinctly unimpressed visitor, he writes:

[We] purchased entry into the Magic Kingdom, Epcot Center,

Disney-MGM Studios and Typhoon Lagoon water park, where we luxuriated in 113 hours and 47 minutes [the fact that he was counting is a bad sign] of eating, sleeping in our 'affordable Disney' accommodations, riding on buses and standing in line, punctuated by a cumulative 6 hours and 47 minutes of fun, fun, fun. That amounts to $261 c.p.f.h. (cost per fun hour), and it is by no means the most horrifying statistic I can cite.

(Garfield, 1991: B5)

As these statistics imply, writers like Gottdiener are right to suggest that the cost of a visit to the Disney theme park screens out many sections of the community.

That the parks are the province of the white, middle class is very apparent and it is not really necessary to subject the assertion to detailed testing, but such hard evidence is available. Van Ansdale France, the founder of the University of Disneyland, refers to a market research survey undertaken around 1958 to determine the nature of Disneyland's primary audience. France reports: 'The results showed that we had an ELITE AUDIENCE, people from the middle and upper income areas' (1991: 52; capitals in original). Findlay reports that surveys around that time showed that 'visitors were disproportionately well educated, well paid, and well positioned compared to American society as a whole'. Writing about Disney World, Wallace (1985) informs us that the median income of visitors was $35,700 and that 75 per cent are managers or professionals. He also writes that 3 per cent are black and 2 per cent are Hispanics. Nor is the middle classness solely a feature of the guests. John Van Maanen, a sociologist who worked at Disneyland as a ride operator, has described ride operators as a 'distinctly middle-class group' (1991: 61). Sayle (1983) attributes much of the success of Tokyo Disneyland to the huge increase in the Japanese middle class after the Second World War.

The Disney theme parks, then, are closely connected with the middle class. Targeting the parks at the middle class served to act as a strategy of product differentiation (to establish their difference from the conventional amusement park) and to attract the most affluent sections of the population. The latter would be most likely to own cars on which Disneyland was heavily dependent and they would be more likely to afford the price of admission and to spend heavily once in the park. They would also be less likely to engage in the kind of boisterous behaviour which would destroy the ambience of the parks as regions for family entertainment. As will be seen, many of the features of the Disney theme parks which will be explored below were designed to dovetail with the world-view of the middle class. This occurred in two ways. First, many of the parks' features were designed to appeal to a middle-class audience (their cleanliness, safety, concern for the visitor). Second, many of the motifs to be explored below affirmed the middle-class world view. The parks provided an image of a Utopia that is not only congruent with middle-class values; the Utopia *is* middle-class America.

THE FAMILY PILGRIMAGE

A number of writers have described going to the Disney parks as a pilgrimage for visitors. When construing the Disney parks in this way, we find at least two different ways of using the term. One is to use it in a very general way of a feeling of compulsion to visit a sacred region. For example, King writes:

> The parks serve as Meccas, sacred centers, to which every American must make his double pilgrimage, first as a child (for whom the Disneyland experience is a focal point), later as an adult with his own children. The power of the Disneyland imperative in this role is demonstrated in the litany of answer and question in our society, beginning with the question 'Have you been to Disneyland yet?' A 'yes' answer leads to recounting of the experience. But if the answer is 'no,' an explanation seems called for . . . Disneyland has presented all generations of Disney-raised children – and adults – with a larger pilgrimage as an extension of the minipilgrimage made as family groups attend Disney films at local theaters . . .
>
> (King, 1983: 117)

This impression of a trip to Disneyland or Disney World as a visit to a near-religious shrine which one feels compelled to visit is a notion expressed by a number of writers. It is almost as though a visit to a Disney theme park is a benchmark by which parents judge themselves (and perhaps are judged by their children) as parents. Bob Garfield, unsurprisingly in light of his previously mentioned calculations, refers to Disney World as 'a monumentally unrewarding pilgrimage, characterized by anthropomorphic vermin infesting my wallet' and as 'the middle-class hajj, the compulsory visit to the sunbaked holy city' (1991: B5). The quasi-religious status of the Disney parks is underscored by MacCannell's (1992) observation that a visit to one of the parks is often the 'last wish' of terminally-ill children (see also Kottak, 1982: 64).

The second use of the term 'pilgrimage' in connection with the Disney parks is consistent with the more general use of the term, but adopts a somewhat more technical frame of reference by examining the constituents of a pilgrimage and how these apply to a visit to Disneyland or Disney World. These analyses have typically taken the work of Victor Turner as their point of departure (for example, Turner and Turner, 1978). Turner depicted a pilgrimage as a sequence in which the pilgrim leaves a familiar place and goes to a remote area and comes back to the familiar again. When at the remote area, Turner writes of the pilgrim being in 'liminoid' state. The pilgrim is not simply in an unfamiliar setting but is also outside normal and conventional obligations and constraints. He/she is freed from routine duties and responsibilities. Unconstrained by conventions associated with his/her social status, the pilgrim bonds with other similarly unfettered pilgrims in a state of *communitas* or communion. This transient community represents an alternative social order which Turner described as anti-structural, characterized by playfulness and sponteneity and by the inversion of normal rules. While this representation of pilgrimage has been criticised from a number of quarters (see Reader, 1993a, for a summary), Turner's remarks about their relevance to understanding tourists in these terms has been found insightful (for example, Shields, 1991).

It is hardly surprising that some commentators should have taken up this framework. Moore (1980) notes how the Disney World pilgrim has to travel through land owned by the Disney company to a huge car park where they leave their cars (which are themselves symbols of identity) and then board the monorail or ferryboat to the Magic Kingdom (the only part of Disney World open at the time Moore made his observations). This is the equivalent of the ludic journey of the pilgrim. After disembarking visitors

> enter a giant limen, a replica of a baroque capital, whose central avenue is the symbol of the dominant culture form of

nineteenth century America, Main Street. Passage through
each attraction takes the form of mini-phases of separation,
transition, and reincorporation as the passenger journeys
past electronically manipulated symbols evoking well known
myths.

(Moore, 1980: 214)

Moore, then, depicts the Magic Kingdom as a giant area of liminality to which the pilgrim travels and returns from, but within
the Kingdom itself there are many mini-pilgrimages involving
the same processes of separation, transition (and presumably
liminality) and reintegration. He argues that the sacred nature of
Disney World is underpinned by a number of other features.
First, there are various cultic objects (Hall of Presidents and the
recreation of Walt's office, which was removed in 1993). Second,
there are symbols such as the castle and Mickey's ubiquitous
image. Third, there are features of anti-structure which are characteristic of liminal zones, such as people dressed as animals.

Kottak (1982) has attempted a very similar analysis, but sees
the main function of the Magic Kingdom within the pilgrimage
metaphor as one of 'representing, recalling, and reaffirming' both
Walt Disney's creativity and the values of American society.
Fjellman writes about a visit to Disney World as a playful
pilgrimage in which the pilgrim's 'passage through the gates and
barriers leads over the threshold into liminal space' (1992: 221).
Moreover, as a liminal state, Disney World exhibits the classical
characteristic of anti-structure, which is in fact what people are
drawn to: 'Animals are portrayed by people. People are portrayed by robots. Ghosts dance. Children make family decisions'
(ibid.: 222). The sense of community is also revealed in a number
of ways: 'Children and adults mingle, the latter often acting more
childlike than the former. People talk to and eat with strangers,
offer advice, and commiserate about the heat and lines' (ibid.:
222).

The metaphor of the Disney park visitor as a pilgrim is a
suggestive one, but it has its limitations. Moore's (1980) notion of
a series of mini-pilgrimages within one of the parks is uncon-
vincing, because almost any aspect of life could be construed in
these terms (such as going to work). Second, while there is a
superficial similarity between the notion of liminality and the
experience of Disney World, the correspondence is not entirely

convincing. As Cohen (1988) has observed, the experience of liminality for Turner's pilgrims is one of spontaneity and abandon. This kind of experience has been described by Shields (1991) as being characteristic of Brighton beach in much of the nineteenth century and of Niagara Falls during much the same period. These two sites became contexts for licence and exuberance, which, while organized to a degree, were characterized by a carnivalesque mood. It is not at all clear that these characteristics travel well when the Disney parks are examined as pilgrimage centres, since the visitor/pilgrim is to a very significant extent controlled by the structure of the theme park experience and by the ever-present security staff. The centrality of control at the Disney parks provides a further theme to be examined in the next chapter. Third, as Hunt and Frankenberg have observed, although the Disney visitor arrives 'like a pilgrim to participate in the clean and wholesome fun of Disney' (1990: 107), unlike the conventional pilgrim, he or she does not return home with a new sense of reality. This is not because the Disney parks represent fun and nothing else, so that there is no new sense of reality being promoted, but because the parks present an essentially conservative image of the world which confirms and reaffirms the conventional and the normal. This theme too will be examined in further detail, but a glimpse of this commitment to the status quo has already been caught: it has been noted that the parks present a highly traditional image of the family and of courtship, which is simply projected into the future as if further to ratify that conventionality. What is more likely is that American pilgrims to a Disney park will return with a renewed sense of their roots. Reader notes that for many pilgrims their quest is about 'holding on to the past, to what appears to have been lost to the present, and of reconstituting the past in an idealized and romanticized way' (1993b: 231). The creation of this sense of the past will be addressed below.

5

CONTROL AND PREDICTABILITY

A major theme of the Disney parks, which melts into many of their facets, is *control*. This element is in evidence in a variety of ways and of levels. It operates at the fairly mundane level of how the visitor is handled while in the parks to the way in which the parks relate to their immediate environment. In the following discussion, six levels at which the theme of control operates are presented.

CONTROL

Control of the theme park experience

The movement of visitors at the theme parks is highly controlled and as a result their experience of those parks is controlled. Francaviglia (1981) notes how in Disneyland and in the Magic Kingdom the castle acts as a visual magnet to which people are drawn. People first encounter Main Street (via its main square) and are then funnelled to the next open space – the plaza. From there, the visitor has a number of choices, in the form of the different 'lands' that can be visited, but the number of routes that can be taken is substantially circumscribed. Less overtly, movement is simultaneously maintained and constrained by what Walt referred to as 'wienies', visible lures which draw people on to the next attraction in one of a number of predetermined sequences. In this way, the visitor's movement is both overtly and covertly controlled by the park's physical layout and by its inbuilt narratives. The opportunity to cross 'lands' is highly restricted so that the integrity of their themes can be maintained. To a certain extent, modern guidebooks like *The Unofficial Guide to Walt Disney*

World (Sehlinger, 1994) attempt to undermine this control, by proposing alternative sequences based on experience of traffic flows, the popularity of attractions at various times and the amount of time available to the visitor. In so doing, they risk disrupting the narrative flows which the parks' designers try so hard to create and may even create new flows of their own, but they provide strategies of independence (at least to a degree) from the physical and narrative control. Fjellman (1992) notes that in EPCOT's Future World movement is controlled by limiting what can be seen at the pavilion exits. In this way, visitors are covertly steered in a certain direction because of the use of landscaping to block alternative perspectives. Indeed, at EPCOT visitors seem more controlled than in the Magic Kingdom because most of the time they have only two directions to take if they are unfamiliar with the park's layout. In the area of queuing, the Disney designers have often won great praise for the parks' humane control of visitors. The queues seem to bend back on each other and give the impression of constant movement. They also give the impression of being much shorter than is in fact the case, which has the advantage of reconciling people much more to the fact of queuing.[1] In fact, standing in lines is almost the quintessential Disney theme park experience, as can be discerned in the quotation on page 94 from Garfield's (1991) humorous account of his Disney World holiday. Willis even suggests that in the Backstage Studio Tour in Disney–MGM Studios, the distinction between a ride and its queue has been eroded, 'condemning the visitor to a two-and-a-half-hour-long pedagogical queue that preaches the process of movie production' (1993: 124).

A further element of control is in the attractions themselves. Rather than allowing people to move around freely to look at Disney images of the future or wonder at the Audio-Animatronic movie stars and the holographic ghosts, the visitor rides in a car. This means that each person will only spend a few moments gazing at the scenes and objects that the Imagineers have created. As a result, Disney can control the amount of time that each person expends on the attraction so that large numbers of people can be allowed access to it. The fact that these are rides also means that visitors experience such attractions in the same way. Each person will see the same as everyone else so that the experience of many theme park attractions is controlled and thereby standardized. The EPCOT Center seems to have a particularly large incidence of such rides in which, in the words of one writer, one finds 'environmental robotic dioramas that audiences are transported through' (Nelson, 1986: 135). Attractions which function as shows (such as the American Adventure and the Hall of Presidents) also exhibit a combination of control and standardization of experience.

The high level of control has brought the accusation from some commentators that Disney theme park visitors become passive and lack spontaneity (Eco, 1986) and that as a result they do not engage with the parks in a creative manner (Johnson, 1981). In the previous chapter, it was remarked that some writers have suggested that the parks are like film sets in which the visitor is part of the action. However, the visitor is not a full participant in that he or she is little more than a passive onlooker. It is rarely the case that visitors are in a position such that they must or can respond to a stimulus of some kind. One feels an almost childlike glee when at the end of the Horizons ride, the passengers in a car can choose which of three dioramas about the future (sea, desert and space) they would prefer to see. The choice is based on a 'majority wins' principle. Kuenz (1993) notes that even when there is an audience participation show, people are not really integrated into it. In the Monster Sound Show in Disney–MGM Studios, for example, a few people have the chance to add sounds to a spoof horror film starring Chevy Chase, but the participation is limited, by and large, to the select few. In fact, the chosen few perform their task poorly (and hence humorously for the audience) which limits their ability to participate, as well as signalling the need for professional expertise of the kind offered by Disney. Similarly, Kuenz notes that at the Adventureland Theater members of the audience are plucked out, dressed up and then essentially ignored, as the big dance number starts up to which they can only contribute feebly. Thus, the visitor is forced into a predominantly passive role. In both cases, apparent participation disguises the fact that a standardized product is being presented to the visitor.

Control over the imagination

In her attack on Walt Disney's renditions of classical children's literature with respect to *Pinnochio*, Sayers accused him of labelling everything and leaving nothing to the child's imagination. She went

on: 'Disney takes a great masterpiece and telescopes it. He re-
duces it to ridiculous lengths, and in order to do that he has to
make everything very obvious. . . . There is nothing to make a
child think or feel or imagine' (1965: 604). Similar comments have
been made in relation to the theme parks. Waldrep (1993) remarks
that the parks bombard visitors with Disney ideals (which are
explored in further detail below) and in the process the possibility
of exercising the imagination is curtailed. Findlay (1992) argues
that this has been a deliberate strategy since visitors could be
induced to behave and think in ways that Walt knew best. He
quotes from an interview with John Hench (who at the time was
Vice-President in charge of Design at Disney World):

> John Hench explained that Walt Disney knew how to make
> people 'feel better about themselves' because he could make
> them 'believe about themselves the way he felt about them'.
> If Disneyland could communicate effectively, its guests would
> *respond correctly*.
>
> (Findlay, 1992: 79, emphasis in original).

Real (1977) goes so far as to refer to the way in which Disneyland
controls the imagination as 'brainwashing'. One of the chief
strategies for controlling the imagination is the selecting out of
undesirable elements from the purview of visitors. Thus in its
portrayal of the past, which will be the focus of an extended
discussion in Chapter 6, Wallace quotes a Disney Imagineer:
'What we create is a "Disney realism", sort of Utopian in nature,
where we carefully program out all the negative, unwanted elements and program in all the positive elements' (1985: 35). As a
result, they are able to produce, in the words of another
Imagineer, 'what the real Main Street should have been like'
(ibid.: 36). For Zukin, such quotations are indicative of 'totalitar-
ian image-making' (1991: 222). Writers differ about the implications
of the anodyne images created by Imagineers, and Main Street is
a case in point. Francaviglia (1981: 146) quotes Rowe and
Koetter's (1978) criticism of Disney World's Main Street that its
'elimination of unpleasantness, of time and of blemish' leaves 'the
imagination unprovoked and the capacity for speculation un-
stimulated' (quoted in Francaviglia, 1981: 146). King (1981) views
Main Street as an idealized setting which conveys a sense of the
familiar and of happy memories but without the disappointment
that is often experienced on returning to places that one remembers

from one's youth. The desire to suppress the less-attractive aspects of reality was one of Walt's main intentions when conceptualizing Disneyland, but in so doing he left himself open to the charge of creating a sanitized world which left the imagination unaroused. Moreover, the essentially passive stance that visitors are induced to submit to contributes to the capacity of the parks to control their imagination by reducing their capacity for reflection on the messages with which they are surrounded. Even the cinematic underpinnings of Disneyland, referred to in the previous chapter, had much to do with control over the imagination. Thomas (1976) argued that Walt wanted to establish continuity in the park, as in a film, so that as visitors moved between scenes the complementary surroundings would not result in a jolt and would make the whole experience more memorable.

As a result of these processes, it is often suggested that children lose the capacity for play and spontaneity. Hunt and Frankenberg (1990) note that, unlike amusement parks in the United States, in the Disney parks there are few climbing frames and playground-type activities. These authors argue that the number of such attractions is limited because they cannot be controlled since children will use them in their own way and at their own pace. The tendency for so many attractions to involve a programmed series of events in which children are passive spectators limits their ability to engage in their normal more impulsive behaviour. When children encounter the less-programmed areas of the parks, they seem to relish their empowerment. In the Wonders of Life pavilion in EPCOT, there are a number of 'hands-on' exhibits for testing senses, conducting computer-based analyses of health and life-style, and using exercise equipment. In their normal playful style, children relish the opportunity to tear around from exhibit to exhibit and to try out each one in a climate of playful exuberance. Likewise, Fjellman (1992) argues that many people enjoy the Image Works in the Journey into Imagination pavilion, where there is a host of electronic and other devices which allow experimentation with colour, music and sound. He comments that children often become very involved in these activities and have to be dragged off by parents who do not feel that such pursuits are what the Disney experience is all about. The new Innoventions attraction in EPCOT also acts as a magnet for children who relish the computer games and other hands-on information-technology-based exhibits. Many adults stand around waiting to whisk their children off at the earliest opportunity. Schultz also bemoans the absence of play and spontaneity:

> We lose the power of play to repeat a story or game never the same way twice. We lose their socializing as well as their inventive power, the resolving of conflicts and points of view, and the accommodating of differences and complexity. We lose the willingness to imagine and act on our own, individually and in groups.
>
> (1988: 300)

Willis (1993) writes that she did not notice the absence of imaginative, spontaneous play until she saw some children who, unlike the hundreds of others dutifully waiting in line, began dancing on the steps of the Mexico pavilion in EPCOT's World Showcase, while all those around them kept to the pre-programmed itineraries that had been created for them.

These writers' comments about the relative absence of playful spontaneity are interesting because they are emblematic of the pervasiveness of control at the Disney parks. The comments also reveal an element of criticism, a dislike of the suppression of individuality and of the programmed, rationalized elements of modern life. A not unreasonable retort to the accusation that the Disney parks control visitors' imagination and that they programme their activities is that, from Walt's original concept onwards, Disney has aimed to create a land of fantasy and magic for large numbers of people and that it is inevitable that in the process the more positive aspects of life will be brought to the fore and even exaggerated. Moreover, the large crowds have to be organized. The real issue, however, is that many writers have railed not simply against Disney's proclivity for controlling the imagination, but the channelling of the imagination in particular directions that result in a distortion of such areas as the presentation of the past and of technological progress. These issues will be examined in later chapters. The present discussion also reveals a problem that was hinted at in the previous chapter with the metaphor of the pilgrimage: the highly programmed nature of the Disney theme park experience sits uneasily with the notion of liminality which is characterized by playful exuberance (Shields, 1991; Turner and Turner, 1978). While pilgrimages are undoubtedly organized, the emphasis on conformity with the Disney schedule to which many writers have drawn attention suggests that the notion of a trip to a Disney theme park as a pilgrimage is limited.

Control as a motif

The theme of control turns up as an often none too heavily disguised sub-text in some of the attractions themselves. Findlay (1992) has noted that the designers of Disneyland conceptualized nature as something which had to be controlled and saw it as part of their role to get this image across to visitors. Nature was envisioned as a source of 'accidents' which, while not totally capable of being managed, could at least be brought to heel. Wilson (1992: 180) remarks: 'Nature is relentlessly evoked in Disney World, yet it is always a nature that has been reworked and transformed; subsumed by the doctrine of progress.' Both Wilson (1992) and Fjellman (1992) single out the Kraft-sponsored (now Nestlé-sponsored) boat ride, Listen to the Land (now Living with the Land), in EPCOT. *The Unofficial Guide to Walt Disney World* describes this attraction as follows:

> A boat ride which takes visitors through a simulated giant seed germination, past various inhospitable environments man has faced as a farmer, and through a futuristic, innovative greenhouse where real crops are being grown using the latest agricultural technologies. Inspiring and educational with excellent effects and a good narrative.
>
> (Sehlinger, 1994: 321)

The seemingly innocent remark about 'inhospitable environments' is a clue here to the way in which Disney tends to think about the land and nature – as something that needs to be cajoled to behave itself. However, it is not the simple farm that is presented as the way forward, but technology-based farming associated with large corporations like Kraft. Wilson quotes the narration:

> Each year the family farm is being replaced by business as farming becomes a science. With better seeds, better pesticides and better techniques, we're moving into a new era.
>
> (1992: 185–6)

We are also told: 'Nature by itself is not always productive' (ibid.: 186). In this attraction, the sub-text of control of the land and nature is casually and apparently irrevocably linked to technological progress and to the importance of large corporations which look after 'our' interests. Arguably, these themes have little to do with listening to the land, but with exploiting and controlling it. As Fjellman puts it: 'The land is to be manipulated, tricked and beaten into submission, told what to be, and certainly not listened to' (1992: 270). It is not just the land and nature with which we are all familiar that will be subjected to control. The Horizons ride suggests that space and other planets are going to be subjected to the same processes too. Even the Living Seas pavilion is concerned to get across ideas about aquaculture. The narration has many references to our being on a voyage of discovery in which we (or more particularly United Technologies) are finding out new things about the seas, but allusions to the seas' 'resources' are also slipped in. The message of potential exploitation and hence control of the seas is clear.

In the Land pavilion, a film entitled *Symbiosis* is also shown. This film draws attention to a number of problems that have occurred when people have tried to control the land, but the upbeat message gives the impression that we have all learned from these experiences. It shows some examples of ways in which problems have been reversed (such as the River Thames), but such illustrations merely underline the message that we can all get it right in the future and that we can correct problems that have occurred. The ability to master the land through technology under the control of large corporations remains undiminished as an optimistic refrain. In this way, the theme of control of the land and nature overlaps considerably with two further themes to be examined below – technological progress and corporatism.

The control motif surfaces in other regions of the parks. In Frontierland in Disneyland and the Magic Kingdom, one finds essentially a paean to the taming of the American frontier. Marin (1984) observes that here we find narratives of how the West was won, a theme which illustrates the appropriation of land and resources. Similarly, in its representation of conquest over the Indians, it is also a narrative about control over peoples. Marin suggests that the rides in Disneyland's Frontierland 'involve penetration into and victory over the lands of the first inhabitants, the Indians' (1984: 250). As Real (1977) notes, white people are implicitly depicted in the familiar cinema western role of bringing civilization to the new world, but the elements of appropriation and control of land are concealed by conveying an image of *discovering* it. Thus, a pictorial souvenir of Disney World reports that Frontierland captures the spirit of the Old West 'a time when prospectors panned for gold and courageous settlers homesteaded the wilderness'. Adventureland also implies similar notions of conquest and control, for example of the African jungle, within a framework of imperialism and the triumph of whites, both of which are ultimately about control.

The control motif is powerful, not least because it is relatively easy to cloak with euphemisms and neutral terms, of science, of progress, and of overcoming wilderness, and by eulogizing the intuition or courage of those who manage to (or seek to) overcome adverse conditions. On the other hand, the message is sufficiently transparent for a number of different commentators to have drawn attention to it. But perhaps its main force comes with the realization that it ties in so well with many other themes about Disney park narratives which have been touched on here and which will be examined in greater detail below. The theme of control acts as a connecting point which links other major Disney preoccupations, such as faith in progress and in corporations.

Control over the behaviour of employees

When Walt opened Disneyland, guards and many other staff who had been hired lacked experience of handling people and the kind of service he wanted to provide. The staff who sold merchandise and food were employed by lessees. Randy Bright (1987), a Disney Imagineer prior to his early death, reports that the operators of the attractions were the only staff who did not cause problems. The security guards seem to have been a particular difficulty since they were often surly and aggressive towards visitors. Because of complaints about food, Walt fired the restaurateurs and took over the food concessions himself. As a result of these early problems, Walt realized that he would have to train his own staff to behave in the Disney way. The Disneyland University was created to introduce new and existing staff to the Disney approach to handling people (France, 1991). Part and parcel of this approach meant being introduced to a new language which conveyed an alternative way of thinking about theme park visitors. The language seems to convey the impression for employees and visitors alike that the former are at play rather than at work. As a result, visitors are not reminded of the world of work and can continue to feel that they are at leisure and participating in fantasy. Some of the more common terms and their everyday equivalents are presented in Table 5.1. Most of these terms have their origin in a cinematic metaphor. Through the training received at a Disney university, employees learned about such Disney principles as the importance of quality of service and pleasing the visitor. People who go to a Disney park often comment on the friendliness of the Disney employees and the cleanliness of the environment and these qualities are seen as important to the creation of a mentality which places an emphasis on the customer and on quality of service.

At the Disneyland University, Van Maanen reports that new employees are given an introduction to key Disney values, such as 'the customer is king' (Van Maanen and Kunda, 1989). The aim is to draw new staff into a strong corporate culture: 'Inspirational films, hearty pep talks, family imagery, and exemplars of corporate performance are all representative of the strong symbolic stuff of these training rituals' (Van Maanen and Kunda, 1989: 64). Blocklyn (1988) describes the training at Disney World as involving an introduction for new employees to the history, achievements and philosophy of the park, followed by an introduction to Disney

Table 5.1 Some examples of Disney language

Everyday term	Disney term
customer / visitor	guest
employee / staff	host / hostess or cast member
public areas	onstage
restricted areas	backstage
ride	attraction / adventure
hiring for a job	casting
job interviews	auditions
crowd	audience
accident	incident
uniform	costume
queue / line	pre-entertainment area
designer	Imagineer
talking robot	Audio-Animatronic figure

policies and procedures. He indicates that part of the introduction aims to induce a feeling of being part of a family and of creating a spirit of teamwork. Instruction manuals and handbooks provide information about correct appearance, how to answer questions and various other bits of in-role information. Considerable use is made of quotations from Walt. Findlay (1992) argues that the quotations and lessons drawn from Walt's life and deeds act as a kind of scripture which is meant to motivate employees and to give them an understanding of Disney thinking. They are also instrumental in giving a sense of his lingering presence and have 'served both to glorify Walt Disney and to solidify his organiz-ation, even after his death' (Findlay, 1992: 76). In fact, there is evidence that the Walt Disney approach is so ingrained in this training period that many park employees become sensitive to what they see as unacceptable departures from his precepts (Smith and Eisenberg, 1987). When talking to park visitors, employees have to use a script and not introduce variations on what they have learned. Their appearance is heavily monitored. Women are asked to have a clean-cut look with limited makeup and jewellery. A hostess at the Preview Center was quoted in 1971 as saying: 'We girls don't tease our hair or wear makeup – mascara and a little bit of powder are okay, but that's it. Out at Disneyland, we had one girl who went without a bra, but you couldn't tell anyway' (in Zehnder, 1975: 183). Zehnder reports that on Disney World's opening day, a monorail pilot was grounded because her black underwear showed through her lime-green jumpsuit. Men are told not to have long hair, sideburns, or moustaches and beards, leading to the well-known quip that Walt would probably not have been hired for a front-line job at a Disney theme park because he sported a moustache. Bryson's (1993) account of re-quirements for Disney employees at Euro Disneyland were cited on page 77.

These characteristics of training for work at the theme parks are highly redolent of the features of a strong corporate culture of the kind revered by writers like Peters and Waterman (1982) and Deal and Kennedy (1982). Strong corporate cultures include pre-cisely the kinds of attributes that have been noted: celebration of organizational heroes (not only Walt but illustrations of exemplary behaviour); clearly articulated values and beliefs; distinctive language; precepts about physical appearance; and myths and legends about the organization and its heroes. Thus, the Disney company represents an interesting case of an organization which exhibits a strong culture at both the managerial (see Chapter 2) and operational levels. Shearer quoted Dick Nunis, Vice-President in charge of theme parks: 'When we hire a girl [as a hostess], we point out that we're not hiring her for a job, but casting her for a role in our show. And we give her a costume and a *philosophy* to go with it' (1972: 4, emphasis added). The company recognizes that not everyone will fit the culture. Writing about the placement of culinary students from a Rhode Island college, Gindin quotes a Disney representative: 'Disney requires employees to abide by a clean-cut look. They are told to get a haircut, to shave, to take off jewelry, make-up, and nail polish. Chefs tend to be rather independent; they don't like to be told what to do. But the Disney look is very important, so the students conform' (1984: 242). In order to enhance the likelihood of securing people who will fit the roles and ethos that Disney envisions, applicants are heavily screened and a certain 'type' tends to be appointed. Van Maanen and Kunda describe the kind of person typically recruited for the role of ride operator: 'Single, white males and females, in their early twenties, of healthy appearance, possibly radiating good testimony of a recent history of sports, without facial blemish, of above-average height (and below average weight), with conservative grooming standards' (1989: 59). They add that the company prefers college students for such front-line positions. In similar fashion, Johnson (1981: 159) describes what he calls 'above ground workers' in the following terms: 'young white, college-age, well-groomed and scrubbed'. To Harrington, Disney World's Magic Kingdom seemed to be run by people who were 'disproportionately blond and blue-eyed' (1979: 38). Haden-Guest (1973) quoted a director of employee relations at Disney World as saying that types of people were more important than specific skills when hiring for particular positions.

The strong corporate culture with which front-line workers are imbued at the theme parks arises out of a combination of intensive training practices coupled with the hiring of people who are perceived as most likely to be susceptible to those training practices. Interestingly, the Disney approach to training is so highly admired outside the company that it has developed a management seminar about its management approach and human relations strategy which it puts on for managers in other companies (Blocklyn, 1988; Eisman, 1993). In spite of the potential difficulty outsiders might expect many new recruits would experience in adapting to such a strong corporate culture, not to mention the repetitiveness of many jobs (such as ride operators) and meagre salaries (Johnson, 1981), turnover is low. Fjellman (1992) suggests that subsidized food and other employee-friendly practices keep turnover at Disney World below 20 per cent. Moreover, between 60 and 80 per cent of promotions to salaried positions are achieved internally (Blocklyn, 1988). Conformity with Disney rules and precepts is further enhanced by the use of supervisors who check on and frequently punish transgressions, such as experimentation with alternative scripts or an incorrect manner when dealing with visitors.

Interestingly, Martin (1992) regards Van Maanen's (1991; Van Maanen and Kunda, 1989) observations about and research on ride operators at Disneyland as indicative of a 'differentiation' perspective on culture rather than an 'integration' one. The latter places an emphasis on the coherence and unity within corporate cultures; a differentiation perspective stresses sub-cultural differences within the organization. The latter perspective would seem to imply that the Disney culture is not as strong at the operational level as has been implied here. Van Maanen's research *does* point to strategies of independence and defiance exercised by ride operators, but on balance his data point to a predominance of compliance with the culture and of cohesiveness, which are more indicative of an integration perspective. At one point Van Maanen and Kunda write: 'not all of Disneyland is covered by the culture. There are small pockets of resistance, and various degrees of autonomy are maintained by employees. But, none the less, the adherence and support for the "Disney way" is remarkable' (1989: 68). Thus, while there is evidence of independence and even rejection of the culture, the scales seem more firmly tipped in the direction of an integration approach providing a more accurate overall picture of ride operators. Even the esoteric Disney language tends to be absorbed easily. Smith and Eisenberg (1987) report that in their interviews with Disneyland employees, most saw their role as one of providing entertainment for visitors and no one used taboo terms like 'customer', 'amusement park', or 'uniforms' when talking about their work.

What is important about the strong culture among employees at the theme parks is that it is not simply an emergent product of interaction at the workplace; it is also, perhaps even primarily, a device for controlling their behaviour. Van Maanen and Kunda (1989) have noted that the work of ride operators exhibits the three levels of control of work explicated by Edwards (1979), though the following exposition differs slightly from theirs: hierarchical control (revealed in supervision of employees); technical control (mechanization of rides which restrict movement and variation); and bureaucratic control (use of manuals, rules, regulations and procedures to constrain behaviour). These three methods of control can be viewed in a linear sequence in the twentieth-century workplace with greater emphasis being placed on technical and later bureaucratic control as the century progressed. Van Maanen and Kunda distinguish a fourth level of control, 'culture control', which aims to influence the emotions and feelings about the company and about work. This level of control 'is intended to act on the values, loyalties, sentiments, and desires of employees' (1989: 90). This form of control, which is perhaps the main type in the Disney parks, also helps to reconcile employees to the other forms of control. There is little doubt that the growth of interest in organizational culture in the 1980s had much to do with the recognition of its potential as a control device (Barley *et al.*, 1988). This discussion suggests that the managers of the theme parks had realized this potential a long time ago and that they have created a highly efficient framework for controlling the behaviour of its front-line employees.

There may be cultural (in the sense of the nation state) constraints on the effectiveness of organizational culture as a control mechanism. There have been rumours that at Euro Disneyland, European workers (who have been mainly French, of course) have not taken readily to the Disney corporate culture and attempts to socialize them into it. It is believed that turnover has been high; in August 1993, Langley (1993) reported that it was estimated that as many as 50 per cent of the original 12,000 employees had left, and quoted the Disney University's manager as admitting that the French 'are not known for their hospitality'. In February 1992, Jenkins (1992) gave an indication of possible problems when it was reported that a government inspector had submitted a report declaring that the Disney pronouncements on dress were illegal. However, for those who did get hired, hope was at hand in the form of a French priest and member of a communist union who, at the behest of his bishop, secured a job at the park and became the employees' union representative (Lennon, 1993). However, in the long run, it may be that Disney's ability to build culture control will take root as well in France as it has done in the USA and in Japan. They have every reason to persist with it because, in conjunction with the other approaches to control that are employed, it represents an extremely effective means of controlling employee behaviour.

Control over the immediate environment

Of course, the Disney theme parks are themselves testaments to the ability of the Disney company to control land, creating fantasy worlds out of orange groves or swamp lands. It controls its own landscape by creating imaginary vistas in which impossible combinations of flora and fauna are transplanted. Findlay (1992) reports that even flowers and trees were frequently transplanted to give an impression of seasons changing. Walt and the company were so concerned to shut off the outside world that in 1963 they thwarted an attempt by Sheraton to build a 22-storey hotel within Disneyland's vicinity. Walt appealed to the Anaheim city council, arguing that it would undermine the ability of visitors to forget about the outside world. The city council prevailed on Sheraton to build the hotel only up to 16 storeys and also agreed to a new ordinance prohibiting the construction of tall buildings in the future. But Disney's control of the immediate environments of the theme parks goes much further than these very self-evident aspects in that it has shut off the outside world both at the intellectual level, through control of the imagination, and more literally and perceptually by creating surrounds for the parks which mean that one can neither see in nor out. Walt is often quoted for his remark: 'I don't want the public to see the world they live in while they're in the park.' This can be taken to mean both the elimination of the negative aspects of reality, as noted in the discussion of control of the imagination, or literally being unable to see the outside. In all likelihood he meant both meanings. Yet another way in which Disney World manages its own environment is through its banishment of utilities underground, so that power lines, transportation for employees, storage, pipes, and the like are consigned to a vast underground network of corridors. Access to the doors which allow entry to this underworld is concealed by such obstructions as foliage, artwork and walls.

113

However, the parks' immediate environment includes the surrounding land. Walt failed to exercise adequate control over Disneyland because he was unable to afford the additional land that would have allowed him to prevent encroachment on to Disneyland's environs. Instead, the area around the park became littered with motels, restaurants, and various other attractions. He felt that the area became unsightly and promised himself that if ever he built another park, he would buy sufficient land to control the surrounding area. Walt's irritation with the park's environs is often referred to in biographies and accounts of its development. Another anecdote is that while Disneyland was being built, a local private utility company proposed to Walt that they rather than a public utility company should supply electricity. By that time, Walt was a confirmed believer in the spirit of capitalist free enterprise and agreed. The company began its work but Walt was taken aback when he realized that the ugly wiring would be visible from within the park. He asked the company if they could place the wiring underground, to which they agreed – if he paid for it, which he did. Again, Walt realized that to achieve the kind of setting that he envisioned, it would be necessary to control the environing area and its supply of utilities himself. It is quite likely that it was not only such events and the aesthetic aspects of the area that grew up around Disneyland that exasperated him, but also that he was unable to share in the revenue from hotels in particular. Even the Disneyland hotel was not a Disney property but was built and run by the Wrather Corporation. Walt had been a close friend of Jack Wrather and had granted him a 99-year lease which allowed him to use the Disney name on any hotel he built in the area. Wrather built the hotel on a site adjacent to Disneyland and had an exclusive lease for the use of the monorail that linked the hotel to the park. The Walt Disney Company bought the hotel in 1988 and in the process restored its right to use the Disney name on hotels in the area. But the chief point is that Walt and the company were frustrated by Disneyland's immediate environment.

Therefore, when it came to buying land for Disney World in Florida, the acreage purchased was far greater than Disneyland. As a result, the company has been able to control its surrounding area and consequently the approach to Disney World is not encumbered by a mass of tawdry buildings. But it is likely that it was not simply the opportunity to control the aesthetic appearance of the approach to the park, but the opportunity to build hotels and thereby to control the competition that was an important factor in the decision to buy so much land (as well as the opportunity for far more expansion than is possible in land-locked Disneyland). Ironically, the construction of hotels was not as great as it might have been and it was not until the Eisner–Wells era that a huge expansion began of the number of rooms on the site. Even more ironically, many commentators believe that the same strategy of purchasing a large amount of land, controlling the immediate environment, and building ample hotel accommodation on the park grounds has been an element in the problems faced by Euro Disneyland, since hotel occupancy has often been low and has contributed to the park's failure to meet its financial targets in spite of attendances being not far short of the levels predicted. Thus, we can view the desire to control the immediate environment of the parks as partly to do with controlling the appearance of the approach and as a way of controlling the competition.

Control over its destiny

Walt's problems at Disneyland with power lines and encroaching high buildings seem to have convinced him and the company that at Disney World they needed far greater control over matters of governance which would impinge on it. Central to his strategy at Disney World was a mechanism that would give them such control, the innocuously named Reedy Creek Improvement District. This entity symbolizes the company's preoccupation with control as much as if not more than any of the other issues covered above. The Reedy Creek Improvement District gives the company more or less complete autonomy within its domain, so that it became an area of private government. The legislation on which it is based was passed in May 1967 after considerable debate. Walt had given the rationale for the special treatment that he and the company were requesting in a film presentation which was shown at a meeting in February 1967:

> We must have the flexibility in Disney World to keep pace with tomorrow's world. We must have the freedom to work in co-operation with American industry, and to make decisions based on standards of performance.

If we have this kind of freedom, I'm confident we can create a world showcase for American free enterprise that will bring new industry to the State of Florida from all over the country.

I believe we can build a community here that more people will talk about and come to look at than any other area in the world.

(Zehnder, 1975: 95)

The references to 'flexibility' and 'freedom' in this presentation can be read as euphemisms for 'control', because the company wanted nothing less than unfettered control of its domain.

In a news release which covered the February 1967 meeting, Donn Tatum was quoted as explaining the purposes of the relevant legislation:

[The] Act clarifies the District's authority to perform work of drainage, flood and pest control; amplified the District's authority to build and maintain roadways, utility and sewer systems, to provide and administer a public transportation system, police and fire protection, airport and parking facilities, and *to regulate and administer land use and planning within the District limits.*

(ibid.: 89, emphasis added)

The news release went on to say:

Tatum stated that one of the principal purposes of the District will be to permit the landowners to control the environment, planning and operations of the services and construction essential to the contemplated improvement and development of the property.

(ibid.: 89)

Interestingly, one of the main justifications given in the news release for this freedom was that it was necessary for the building of EPCOT, in order to serve 'the needs of those residing there' (Tatum, quoted in ibid.: 89). Tatum was referring here to Walt's original blueprint for EPCOT, not the theme park that opened in 1982.

One of the main advantages that the Act conferred on the company is implied by the emphasized portion of the foregoing extract, namely, it gave the company control over building, so that it did not have to seek building permits from the local county (Holleran, 1992). In addition, the company was not required to pay impact fees which are levied by the county on developers. According to Holleran, the impact fee for a 7,000-room hotel in 1990 would have been $18 million. This sovereignty was agreed to because of the tremendous growth in jobs and wealth that would be brought to the area, which was in any case growing and would have grown further even without the arrival of Disney World and was one of the reasons for its choice. Some voices in 1966 and 1967 were heard muttering concern about the power that the company was securing for itself, but the momentum of enthusiasm could not be stopped. In addition to getting the Reedy Creek legislation passed, the company was able to win substantial commitments from the local counties for massive road improvements. Traffic has proved the greatest problem for the local authorities, because the very success of Disney World brought a growing trail of cars in its wake. The cost to the two counties affected by this growth has been considerable. However, Disney World generates considerable revenue for Orange and Osceola counties from taxes. Holleran (1992) calculates that by 1990 Orange County alone had received $181 million in taxes from Disney.

The importance of Reedy Creek to Disney is illustrated by the fact that in 1988 it was persuaded to pay $1.3 million to Orange County to improve roads, in return for which the county promised not to sue Reedy Creek for the next seven years. Attitudes to Reedy Creek vary. Many commentators, such as Harrington (1979) have been astonished at its sovereignty. On the other hand, a libertarian writer applauded the fact that Disney was able to set up 'what amounts to a private government for the simple reason that such a legal device is necessary if one wants to get away with any "Imagineering" at all in our controlled society' and saw the park as magical because it 'was conceived, created and perpetuated in freedom' (Boehme, 1975: 86, 90). However, the main reason for the emphasis here on the Reedy Creek Improvement District is that it is so clearly symptomatic of the quest for control that pervades the parks.

PREDICTABILITY

The theme of predictability is closely linked to that of control, since one of the functions of controlling things is to render outcomes relating to them more predictable. Some writers have noticed that the high level of control exercised at the Disney parks is very attractive to many visitors. Zukin (1990) suggests that many parents relish the control exercised over them at the Disney parks because it enhances the predictability of the tourist experience. As Willis (1993) suggests, they do not need to be concerned about the things that concern them in everyday life (danger, worries about the children). The high level of control makes their normally unpredictable and troubled world predictable. Many of the rides are designed to engender a frisson of excitement in the sure knowledge that visitors will not come to any harm. Wilson (1992) and Waldrep (1993) point to the Jungle Cruise as a classic ride in which danger is dangled in front of the intrepid explorer but without the uncertainties that might be encountered with the real thing. Ride operators often spice up the suggestion of danger by suggesting that their charges bid farewell to people they know back at the dock since they may not see them again. But predictability is a much more important feature of many attractions than these observations imply.

As the previous discussion of control over the behaviour of employees indicates, one of the aims of training was to limit the amount of variability in visitors' experiences of many theme park attractions. Thus, a central goal seems to be that of making sure that each visitor will have much the same set of experiences as another. This goal is reinforced by the substantial control over visitors' movement within the parks. The fact that for many attractions visitors sit in moving cars further ensures that their experiences are consistent and hence predictable. There is a well-known anecdote, which has overtones of Scientific Management, in which Walt went on a Jungle Cruise at Disneyland and timed it at four-and-a-half minutes. He discovered that the ride should have been seven minutes, which prompted him to fulminate about the deficiency to Dick Nunis, who at the time managed Adventureland. Walt complained that the ride was so fast that he could not distinguish the hippopotami from the rhinoceroses! For three weeks Nunis retrained the boat operators until the rides were timed to perfection (Bright, 1987). While one issue in this anecdote has to do with Walt's concern that visitors were being short-changed, his other concern was almost certainly that visitors were not all being given the same ride. The strict appearance and dress codes for employees also seem designed to enhance the predictability of the visitor's experience. This consistency has been reinforced by discouraging ride operators and others from engaging in 'ad libs', or by at least having them approved first (Findlay, 1992), so that visitors would experience the same attraction. There seems to be slightly greater leeway in this regard in more recent years. Schultz (1988) suggests that employees are even encouraged to engage in a certain amount of ad-libbing. But there are clearly limits. A popular ad lib among tram guides taking visitors back to the car parks was to joke about EPCOT really standing for Every Person Comes Out Tired. Schultz indicates that the Disney authorities gave their assent to this banter, but only if they stated the official meaning of the acronym first.

But even rigorously trained employees cannot be made to behave with an absolute degree of consistency, and hence predictably, which was one of the reasons for Walt's interest in Audio-Animatronic figures which could be given a human form and human speech. For many of the attractions in which Audio-Animatronic humans appear, especially those which are essentially shows, such as Hall of Presidents and American Adventure, there is no reason why actors could not have been employed to speak from scripts. The advantage of Audio-Animatronic figures is that, breakdowns aside, their behaviour is absolutely consistent and they are extremely reliable – more so than human actors. Haden-Guest quotes Bill Justice, a Disney Imagineer, as explaining the superiority of Audio-Animatronic figures over actors in terms of the former's greater consistency: 'I've seen actors when they're better at times than they are at other times. But these figures perform the same way every time! They're reliable, and they don't belong to unions, and they don't go on strike, and they don't want more money' (1973: 243). Apple quotes Walt Disney in similar terms from a 1964 interview with the Canadian Broadcasting Corporation:

> We're not going to replace the human being – believe me on that. Just for show purposes. We operate [Disneyland] fifteen hours a day and these shows have to go on on the hour. . . . [Audio-Animatronic figures] don't have to stop for coffee breaks and all that kind of stuff.
>
> (In Apple, 1983: 167)

For the founder of the University of Disneyland 'one advantage of mechanical animation is that machines don't demand higher wages

119

and longer coffee breaks' (France, 1991: 48). Audio-Animatronic figures have the advantage of consistency and predictability, but according to both Justice and France, they offer the further advantage of political reliability because they do not strike or request wage increases. Similarly, the Audio-Animatronic animals are used for rides like Jungle Cruise for their predictability. Haden-Guest quotes John Hench as saying that live animals and fish are not used because 'they're just good at feeding times, and the rest of the people see them under a rock' (in Haden-Guest, 1973: 238).

The quest for predictability pervades other aspects of the parks in that it has affected the kinds of attraction that Disney find acceptable. As the last quotation implies, attractions involving live animals might be expected to be especially prone to the unexpected. When Disneyland first opened there was a stagecoach ride through part of Frontierland. On one occasion, a stagecoach led by four ponies, took off on a run, but without the driver. It ran into a coach which was loading passengers and knocked it over. On another occasion, steam from the train frightened the ponies and when a safety device malfunctioned the coach was released and turned over. According to Bright (1987), although the ponies and mules had been trained, they were regarded as too unpredictable, and after a number of mishaps the stagecoaches were closed in 1959. The mules in the Disneyland Pony Farm were especially unreliable. They often nibbled at visitors' souvenir hats, and when the operators responded by collecting hats before the rides, the mules sometimes exacted revenge by going for shoes. Even worse in Disney's controlled, predictable world, the mules often behaved according to their reputation and would suddenly stop and bray loudly. The mules were eventually withdrawn as well. Yet another early Disneyland attraction which fell foul of the unpredictability of live animals was the Mickey Mouse Club Circus. Bright reports a series of mishaps: the wheels of a pumpkin chariot brought down a post holding up the big top, which none the less did not fall down; a group of llamas escaped and had to be chased to round them up; and a black panther chewed off a tiger's paw. The show was withdrawn, not least because it was not a popular attraction.

It is not only attractions involving animals which have caused such problems. Bukatman (1991) says that an early Tomorrowland attraction in Disneyland, Autopia, had to be redesigned because children kept crashing cars. The cars were later put on tracks. Bukatman interprets the significance of this redesign as indicative of an inability of Disney to countenance evidence of technological breakdown, presumably because of its faith in technological progress, a theme that will be explored in greater detail below. It can also be interpreted as a response to an attraction which failed to be sufficiently predictable. Schultz (1988) reports that even visitors' interaction with costumed characters has become more programmed. He writes that this interaction is restricted to 'posed picture taking, autographing, patting children on the head, and close (almost mechanical) movements – perhaps because the tremendous enthusiasm and energy of the broad interplay with a variety of characters in the early days was perceived as leading to a more participatory, chancey theater' (Schultz, 1988: 310). Here again we can see the attempt to control the behaviour of employees in order to promote and enhance predictability, although there is evidently still room for a modicum of playfulness, since I remember being tapped on the shoulder by a mischievous Goofy because I was not paying him sufficient attention at a photo-opportunity session (I have to admit that he is one of my least favourite characters in the Disney pantheon).

Unfortunately, despite the immense care taken by the Disney management and employees to enhance predictability and to ensure the safety of visitors, accidents happen. The company's approach to such unpredictable incidents is to programme (and hence make predictable) the response to them. There are instruction manuals which detail how employees should respond to an accident (Adler, 1983). Following an accident the closest employee calls for first aid and for a supervisor. The manual tells the employees attending the victim to be friendly and helpful. Often visitors are in the throes of embarrassment, do not want to make a fuss, and are grateful to the employee attending them. They frequently blame themselves for the accident, citing their own carelessness. Such admissions are immediately written down, as are eye-witness accounts. Adler cites a lawyer, Dennis Hightower, who worked on personal injury suits against Disney World: 'While the person is still embarrassed about getting hurt, Disney employees get admissions. They're trained to get you to say things that are against your interests' (in Adler, 1983: 34). Toufexis (1985) quotes another Orlando lawyer: 'It's your dignity that really is on the line, and God knows what you'll say at the time: "I should have been looking where I was going. How stupid of me"' (in Toufexis, 1985: 40). Admissions of this kind occur frequently when the victim is disorientated or in pain and make it almost impossible for the victim to have any prospect of success if he or she subsequently decides to sue. Many victims are placated with free passes and airline tickets. Interestingly, even if victims do proceed with a suit, they are statistically unlikely to succeed since Disney World has won around 85 per cent of jury trials. Adler suggests that plaintiffs and their lawyers who do go to court encounter the combined problems of 'the biases of Orlando juries, their own distance from the city, and the opposing counsel's skill at exploiting the Disney image' (1983: 34). As one of the lawyers interviewed by Adler suggested 'it's like suing Snow White', while one of Toufexis's informants described such suits as 'like suing God in the Vatican' (1985: 40). However, the chief point of drawing attention to accidents at the theme parks is that they demonstrate how the company deals with such un-predictable incidents, namely, by controlling the responses of employees and by making the outcome more predictable. As a result, only about 50 personal injury suits per year were being filed in Orange County in the early 1980s.

THE McDISNEY THEME PARK?

Ritzer has written about a general social process which he refers to as 'McDonaldization', which he takes to mean 'the process by which the principles of the fast-food restaurant are coming to dominate more and more sectors of American society as well as the rest of the world' (1993:1). The idea and his treatment of it are heavily influenced by Weber's (1968 [1925]) pessimistic prog-nostications about rationalization, as Ritzer acknowledges. The point about Ritzer's notion of McDonaldization is not that McDonald's is imperialistically taking over the world, although he does describe the influence of its fast-food restaurant approach, but that it is indicative of wider trends in society. Thus, McDonald's is part cause and part symptom (with a decided emphasis on the latter) in Ritzer's characterization of McDonaldization. In describing the dimensions of the phenomenon, Ritzer delineates four factors:

1 efficiency – 'the choice of the optimum means to a given end';

2 calculability – an emphasis on quantifying things so that quantity comes to be an indicator of quality, but is in fact often to the detriment of quality;

3 predictability – people know what to expect and they get it so that they are served with identical fare on each occasion;

4 control – the quest for greater and greater control over employees and customers.

It is striking that two of these attributes – predictability and control – have been described as features of the Disney theme parks. Does this mean that they too are part of the process of McDonaldization?

In fact, some writers have drawn parallels between the Disney theme parks and McDonald's restaurants (for example, King, 1983; Nelson, 1986). There are even a number of superficial similarities between them: a strong focus on the family; they both have universities; they both depend on the motor car; both are concerned with order and cleanliness; both are concerned with the appearance of employees (who in both cases wear uniforms) and the employee–customer interface; most of the employees who serve are young; and both were started by self-made men 'with a flair for business creativity and innovation' (King, 1983: 106). McDonald's has created its own cartoon character (Ronald McDonald), while the Disney parks are heavily involved in fast-food restaurant service and the Walt Disney Company has started a chain of Mickey's Kitchen restaurants. There have also been promotional tie-ins between the products of the two companies. Ironically, according to Greene and Greene (1991), McDonald's founder, Ray Kroc, was in the same training unit as Walt before being shipped out to France at the end of the First World War.

Ritzer draws attention to a number of ways in which the Disney theme parks provide evidence of McDonaldization. He uses illustrations drawn from the Disney parks under the headings of both control and predictability. As regards the former, Ritzer draws attention to the tight control over the appearance and demeanour of Disney theme park employees. As evidence of predictability at Disney parks he draws attention to the orderliness, calling them 'a world of predictable, almost surreal orderliness' (1993: 92). He also points to the near-identical appearance of the theme park employees and the requirement for them to behave in the same way. Ritzer makes this last point in relation to another theme park, Busch Gardens in Virginia, but as the previous discussion suggests, they apply well to the Disney parks. What, then, of the other two attributes of McDonaldization? Under the heading of efficiency, Ritzer is particularly drawn to the efficient handling of people at Disney World as they are whisked from the car parks to the attractions and then through the attractions themselves:

> Once in the park, visitors find themselves on what is, in effect, a vast (albeit not self-propelled) conveyor belt which leads them from one ride or attraction to another. . . . Once the attractions themselves are reached, the visitors find themselves on one conveyance or another (cars, boats, submarines, planes, rocket ships, or moving walkways) that moves them through and out of the attractions as rapidly as possible. The speed with which one moves through each attraction enhances the experience and reduces the likelihood that one will question the "reality" of what one sees. . . . The entire system is set up to move large numbers of people through the entire park as efficiently as possible.
>
> (Ritzer, 1993: 51)

Ritzer also cites the efficiency of the disposal of trash (i.e. rubbish) as evidence of this dimension.

When discussing the fourth dimension of McDonaldization – calculability – Ritzer makes no mention of Disney or any other theme parks. In fact, the Disney parks do not sit at all well with this dimension. Ritzer shows that fast-food chains often emphasize the size of their products (Whopper, Quarter-pounder, Big Mac), which is treated as a tacit indicator of quality or value. The parks make only passing reference to the size of their sites or to the number of attractions that the prospective visitor will enjoy. Schultz has observed that Disney now eschews giving out details of the numbers of visitors who have attended each of the parks since they opened, 'apparently feeling that the Disney mythology becomes trivialized the more the figures move toward the infinity of McDonald's "Billions Served"' (1988: 275). A *Pictorial Souvenir of Walt Disney World* which was sold in the early 1990s does make reference to the number of visitors, referring to over 300 million visitors from over 100 countries since Disney World opened. It also refers to its acreage and to the fact that there are 101 ways in which the visitor can relax and play. But these references to numbers are not at all central to their marketing and advertising efforts. Instead, qualitative factors tend to predominate, with reference to the nature and the uniqueness of the experience of a Disney theme park. Ritzer writes that '[at] best, what customers expect from a fast-food restaurant is only modestly-good, but strong-tasting food' (1993: 64). Visitors going to a Disney theme park will know by experience if they have gone before, by word-of-mouth, or by reputation that they will be going to a holiday destination with high levels of customer service and of quality. Even among detractors of Disney theme parks, one often finds an admiration for the quality of the presentation, the attention to detail, and the like.

For the time being, then, the Disney theme parks only partially exhibit the characteristics of McDonaldization. As this chapter has shown, control and predictability loom large in the Disney world view. Ritzer's dimension of efficiency fits fairly well also. However, the Disney parks are less symptomatic in terms of the fourth dimension, calculability. This is in many respects the most important dimension from the perspective of the parks, since it strikes at the very heart of its commitment to quality of service and quality of the fabric of the parks themselves. It is not surprising, therefore, that in the twelfth annual *Fortune* Corporate Reputations Survey, in which the Walt Disney Company came sixth (out of 404 companies), the dimension on which it scored best was 'Quality of Products or Services', in which it came third and very nearly joint second (Welsh, 1994).

CONCLUSION

In this chapter, we have seen that control in a variety of spheres – of how the theme park should be experienced by visitors, of visitors' imaginations, of employees, of the parks' own environment and destiny, and as a motif in some attractions – is a recurring feature. Predictability is a conceptual relative, in that in many ways it is cause and outcome of control mechanisms. The fixation on control goes back to Walt's day as we have seen: control of people's movement and their experience of the park, of the behaviour of employees, and of the parks' boundaries with the outside world. The quest for control of the company's destiny can be seen as flowing from the day that Walt discovered that although he and his team had created Oswald the Lucky Rabbit, they did not have any control over the product of those efforts. Thereafter, he was insistent that he would control the rights to the company's films. His use of tight storylines has been described as a control device for the animators (Langer, 1992). He greatly disliked the participation of shareholders in the firm, since it signalled a loosening of control. He was quick to buy out ABC's stake in Disneyland. Starting their own distribution company gave the brothers much greater control of their films. He was greatly distressed by his inability to control Disneyland's environs and purchased more than enough land in Florida to ensure that he would have far greater control over his domain. This level of control was to be greatly buttressed by the Reedy Creek Improvement District. In an article on Walt, Davidson quoted a Disney executive in the following terms: 'Everything Walt does today is conditioned by his past problems. When he makes one of his tough deals, he negotiates like he's afraid some-one might take another *Oswald the Rabbit* away from him' (1964: 73). Walt's proclivity for control can also be discerned in his specification of his vision for EPCOT which was quoted on page 14. 'Control' over inhabitants and the environment permeates almost every sentence.

This preoccupation with control can be seen in the modern Disney, with some of the features described in Chapter 2, such as the tight control of scripts. And of course, the motif of control applies to the company's close control of information about itself and its key figures (Wiener, 1993). When Flower (1991) went to Orlando to join a journalists' junket for Mickey's sixtieth birthday, he was not even allowed access to press information, let alone interviews. It is small wonder that he described his experience as one of 'controlling paranoia' (p. 3). But the parks have not succumbed to the ravages of McDonaldization, and in not having succumbed to the demands for calculability, they still represent islands of quality.

6

BACK TO THE FUTURE
Representations of past and future

The past and the future, in particular of the United States, are abiding themes in the Disney parks. These preoccupations are quite conscious: Zehnder (1975) quotes from the company's 1968 annual report which proposed that Disney World would be like Disneyland in its celebration of the 'nostalgia of the past' and of 'the dreams for man's future'. However, as King (1981), Fjellman (1992), Kuenz (1993) and others have pointed out, the present is curiously absent or ambiguous in the parks. In part, this has to do with the wish of Walt and his successors to blot out the nasty realities of everyday life while people are in the parks; after all, those nasty realities are located in the present and are the ones that visitors worry about. When rides or attractions touch on the present, visitors' contact with it is fleeting and not particularly memorable. However, as we shall see, the suppression of the present has the effect of making visitors feel better about the world that they currently live in. By presenting rosy pictures of the past and the future, the problems of the present can be played down.

THE PAST

As many writers have observed, the Disney theme parks present a very positive view of the past. A vision is presented which mythologizes and steeps in nostalgia a past that never really existed. Main Street, USA, for example, symbolizes small-town America around the turn of the century, a dreamy place and time which conjures a good feeling about both the time and the place. How far it is based on Walt's Marceline is a matter of conjecture, but it is likely that he was influenced by his life there. But Main

Street, USA never really existed in the form in which it is presented in the parks. It was not the clean, commercially prosperous strip that is portrayed at the Disney parks. What we find in the parks is a reconstruction of the past which exaggerates positive elements and plays down or altogether omits negative ones. Two techniques which influence the depiction of the past are humour and omission.

The past is often presented as slightly zany, and humour is employed to convey the eccentricities of history. This is particularly evident in those rides and attractions in which visitors travel through time enclosed in moving cars ('people movers'). The household gadgets of the past are made to look quaint and so obviously inefficient that they were bound to be superseded. In the Carousel of Progress, mother marvels that her new washing machine takes only five hours to do a wash. In World of Motion, early experiments with methods of conveyance are depicted in a distinctly humorous context. In the Renaissance period, Mona Lisa is sitting for Leonardo, who is in fact ignoring her while playing around with a flying machine with an apprentice. The inefficiency of bicycles is demonstrated by the vulnerability of their riders to attacks from dogs and by someone else falling into the mud. In the near modern era, the first traffic jam is caused by a horse which has upended its cart and as a result its load (vegetables and boxes of live chickens) is strewn in all directions. A menacing, but obviously comical, police officer looks on, glowering while the farmer tries to get things moving again amidst the clamour of honking horns. In Dreamflight in Florida's Magic Kingdom, early experiments with flight are depicted through tableaux as bizarre or patently ridiculous. By conveying aspects of the past in largely humorous terms, it is possible to neutralize problems that have been encountered there. Problems become either not real problems at all or ones which, with our current know-how and expertise, can easily be overcome.

Omission is used extensively in the presentation of the past. In fact, one of the most popular games among writers on Disney history is to spot and often list what is *not* there. Omission allows the parks to present an upbeat, optimistic message for its visitors. To start us off, Wallace (1985) notes that the parks in their presentation of the past omit depressions, strikes, the squalor in which immigrants lived, lynchings, wars and mass protests. Fjellman (1992) adds to the list Indians, labour wars, and disenfranchisement of blacks. Real (1977) notes the omission of immigrants, cities, ethnic minorities, and factory and mine workers. Nelson (1986) notes the omission of acid rain and the arms race. Sayle writes of Tokyo Disneyland: 'Whatever happened to Japan's wars with China and Russia, the greater East Asia Company-Prosperity sphere, Nanking, Pearl Harbor, Hiroshima, Nagasaki, and all that militaristic jazz?' (1983: 45). Gottdiener writes that Disneyland 'offers a world free from the energy crisis and gas lines, free of pathological forms produced by an inequitable and class society such as slum ghettoes and crime' (1982: 153). Wilson (1992: 180) notes that the modern city is largely marginalized in the Disney theme parks and that as a result cultural diversity and productive labour disappear from view: 'Exchange, interdependence, the struggle for power – all the everyday functions of the city have been hidden, or banished.' The omissions highlighted by various writers could go on and on, but the gist of the omissions mentioned should be apparent from these few lists. Three elements stand out in these lists. One is that, by and large, the problems created by industry and corporations are given little if any attention. Second, issues of class and race (and gender too, which is less apparent from these lists) are side-stepped. In a sense, the attractions frequently pander to and reflect the interests of the predominantly white, middle-class American families who are the US parks' main clientele. Third, conflict is all but eliminated from the depiction of the past. It is these three elements that underpin and are reflected in the lists provided by the authors mentioned in these paragraphs.

Problems caused by corporations

The essentially pro-corporation stance of the Disney theme parks is a specific issue addressed in Chapter 7, but its role in relation to the presentation of the past will be touched on here. The problems caused by corporations are largely hidden from view. Thus, ecological horrors, the role of corporations in producing the instruments of war, dehumanizing work, and the like are largely omitted from accounts of the past. Harrington's remark about the plans for EPCOT – 'industry will speak, the public will listen, and the controversial will be filtered out' (1979: 42) – has proved remarkably prescient. However, the presentation of the past in EPCOT's Future World is somewhat more realistic than that of

Disneyland or Florida's Magic Kingdom. In Future World, problems are acknowledged. In World of Motion, the traffic jam is
rendered less objectionable by locating it in the fairly distant past
and depicting it as caused by the horse's upturned cart rather
than by vehicles as such. The use of humour also neutralizes the
incident. In the film *Symbiosis*, a number of ecological horrors are
graphically depicted – dust bowls, pollution, despoliation of forests
– but there is a highly optimistic tone, because we are then presented with corporate solutions to these mistakes of the past, as
the fish return to polluted rivers, and so on. It is the corporations
who are the source of hope. The message is that they have learned
their lessons from the mistakes of the past and have devised ways
to deal with them and we can be confident that the problems will
not recur. In attractions and rides such as this, we move rapidly
'through the troubled past into the Future' (Wallace, 1985: 45). In
the process, as Fjellman (1992) remarks in the context of the
presentation of the past at Disney World in general, difficulties
are turned into opportunities. This is underlined by the relatively
problem-free future with which the rides confront visitors. The
combined effect of this presentation of the past and the prog-
nostications for the future is to make the present and the role of
large corporations within it more palatable.

Class, race and gender in the past

A number of writers have suggested that the working class and
their labour are virtually absent from the presentation of history
in the parks. A similar omission has been discerned in relation to
Disney comics in which working-class individuals are largely
absent, as is their productive labour (Dorfman and Mattelart,
1975). When they do appear it is largely in the form of 'stupid,
incompetent criminals' (Barker, 1989: 282). As Dorfman and
Mattelart show, while a great deal of consumption goes on in the
Disney comics, there is little work. Wealth is frequently derived
from discovering treasure that is lying around. The concealment
of the working class means that class conflict and the very notion
of social class itself are eliminated from view and from the mind.
The absence of the working class from much of the visitor's
purview undoubtedly creates a similar effect; even the Pirates of
the Caribbean are searching for buried treasure rather than engaged in gainful labour. There has been a greater tendency for

manual labour to surface in EPCOT than there had been in earlier parks. Miners and oil rig workers are briefly portrayed in Universe of Energy, but overall the relative exclusion of the working class persists. However, in the apparently more modern American Adventure, there are few working-class individuals and little reference to class (Fjellman, 1992).

Issues of race are also skirted over. In the Jungle Cruise, racist stereotypes abound with its black porters and the white explorer. The latter is chased up a tree by a rhinoceros and is followed by the four black porters. In the Hall of Presidents, the plight of native Americans and of blacks after the middle of the last century is not mentioned; instead, we find references to freedom, the rights of individuals, and the dignity of 'man'. Some of these more obvious omissions and distortions are given a somewhat different cast in the American Adventure. In this attraction, blacks and native Americans are more prominent, with appearances from a robotic Chief Joseph and a robotic Frederick Douglass (a black abolitionist) dressed in a white suit and musing about the end of slavery while drifting down the Mississippi on a raft; we also hear the voice of Martin Luther King. But intimations of institutionalized racism within the contemporary United States are carefully avoided by locating matters of race firmly in the past and in forms that are more redolent of historical incidents and persons. Moreover, the issues surrounding racial conflict are not confronted. Audio-Animatronic of blacks and native Americans serve as symbols rather than as representatives of coherent standpoints or movements, since to elaborate on what these icons actually stood for would have meant allowing conflict to be much more central than is the case. Horton and Crew (1989) point out that the only blacks in the American Adventure attraction who are not well-known heroic figures appear in a depiction of southerners assembled on a front porch in the depression years of the 1930s. Here blacks are presented in heavily stereotypical forms: one strums a banjo and the other laughs in *Song of the South* style.

Gender issues surface in such a way as to reinforce conservative notions of social role and family. Perhaps one of the most prominent illustrations of this is the Carousel of Progress. Here the position of women is presented in terms of their gradual emancipation from the kitchen by virtue of the creation of labour-saving electrical goods. Bierman (1976) reports that when this attraction was moved from Disneyland to Disney World in 1975 it was updated. When it closed, a *Los Angeles Times* reporter described it in the following terms:

> The GE Carousel was a sexist hymn to all-electric progress in the 20th century. Through the years, dumb old Mom would fall off ladders replacing light bulbs and strident little Sis would be talking on the phone all day while working off the blubber with an electric exercise belt. Dad, of course, would be long-suffering.
>
> (In Bierman, 1976: 229)

When it was updated for Orlando, the more obvious sexist elements were eliminated. However, in its new guise 'mom' uses the free time, heaped on her by liberating electrical products, by working on the 'Clean Waters Committee'. 'Dad' is stuck in the kitchen attempting (and largely failing) to prepare a meal. Of course, depicting men as incompetent cooks, presumably because mom is usually in the kitchen, does not mitigate the stereotyping of women. However, the recently revised Carousel of Progress has got rid of some of the more obviously sexist scenes, though the notion of women's liberation through electrical products remains. Kuenz (1993) draws attention to other forms of sex stereotyping in the parks, though these are not always in connection with the past. She notes that the only female Audio-Animatronic figure that narrates an entire show is 'Bonnie Appetit' in Kitchen Kabaret where she appears in apron and fishnet tights educating the audience about food groups. Schultz (1988) has noted how the demeanour of male and female guides differ. He notes that women direct attractions in which a high degree of common response is needed and where 'a reverent, evenhanded, uniform efficiency' is required (1988: 305). With their appearance, demeanour and gestures they project a seriousness that turns them into custodians of cherished myths and traditions. Men, however, are often permitted a racier image. Schultz notes that the men often engage in sexual innuendo on the Jungle Cruise. Kuenz found that they often pretended to act as protectors to the young women in their charge. She also points out that many of the attractions adopt the perspective of men or are narrated by them. In Cranium Command we get to understand the functioning of the brain by entering that of a young boy, who predictably becomes infatuated with a new pretty girl at school.

The absence of conflict

Writing generally about Disney media, Schiller has written that what he calls 'the transcendent Disney message' is 'behold a world in which there is no social conflict' (1973: 99). Walsh (1992: 97) suggests that the Disney theme parks share with open-air museums this tendency to suppress conflict, while Wallace (1981) has also noted the suppression of struggle in history museums in the USA. At the Disney parks, the suppression of conflict occurs in a number of ways. The virtual elimination of social class (through the censoring of the working class) means that class conflict and its manifestations, such as strikes and even trade unions, are absent from view. In fact, as Wallace (1985) points out, labour history generally is absent from the American Adventure. Leaders of protest movements, such as Martin Luther King, do appear, but as we have seen, they do so as symbols of movements rather than in terms of their ideas or what they were reacting against. In this way, racial conflict similarly disappears from view. Along with the discontents of women and ecologists, those of blacks are 'presented as having been opportunities in disguise' which have actually made things better for everyone (Wallace, 1985: 52), a familiar tactic which was noted in connection with the discussion of ecological problems in the past. Moreover, in the American Adventure, the tendency to disregard conflict seems to increase the closer we get to the present. Wallace writes:

> The silences get louder the closer the show gets to the present. There are no 1960s ghetto uprisings, no campus protests, no feminist or ecology movements, no Watergate. Most notoriously, there is nothing about Vietnam. One of the designers explained that 'I searched for a long time for a photograph of an antiwar demonstration that would be optimistic, but I never found one.' (A picture of a helicopter was recently added – a distinctly minimalist response to complaints.)
>
> (Wallace, 1985: 52)

Kuenz notes a similar tendency in the Hall of Presidents, 'where the history of the presidency is told as a history of quelling domestic rebellion in the interest of solidifying authority' (1993: 76). In the slightly revamped American Adventure, the Vietnam War is symbolized by the white crosses at Arlington, so that it is the effect of the war, rather than warfare itself, that is represented.

In the Hall of Presidents too, conflicts close to the present day are largely ignored, giving the impression that conflicts were in the past.

The Disney theme parks provide a version of the past which is distorted by omissions and by a very upbeat message about the role of corporations in the past. It is easy not to notice the limitations of Disney history because the attention to detail in rides and characterizations of people and places is seductive. In fact, the authenticity of the surface appearance of the attractions usefully helps to conceal the inauthenticity of the message that underpins them. The sincere voices which narrate the story of what we are seeing, as we are transported from scene to scene, and the likeness of Audio-Animatronic figures to the people they are supposed to represent (at least physically) serve to render Disney history more palatable and its distortions less obvious. In the light of these doubts about the ways in which the past is depicted in the Disney theme parks, it is hardly surprising that there would be considerable anxiety about the company's plans for a new theme park on a 3,000 acre site in Virginia specifically about American history. While many locals welcomed the jobs that the project would bring, many historians expressed great concern about the distortions that might be wrought by Disney history (Long, 1994; Roberts, 1994).

THE FUTURE

In spite of what might be expected from Tomorrowland and from EPCOT's Future World, there is remarkably little about the future. What there is tends to be regarded by many commentators as bland and unimaginative. This view contrasts sharply with Walt's intention:

> Tomorrow can be a wonderful age. Our scientists today are opening the doors of the Atomic age to achievements which will benefit our children and generations to come. In Tomorrowland, we've arranged a preview of some of these wonderful developments the future holds in store. You will actually experience what many of today's foremost men of science and industry predict for tomorrow.[1]

Wilson (1992) suggests that Disney World shares with world's fairs a failure of the imagination. The future comes to be associated with the products of corporations, rather than with inventions and Utopian experiments. As a result, capitalism and corporations are left firmly in the driving seat of change as we slowly move into the future. Wallace expresses the point nicely when he writes: 'The progression goes like this: history was made by inventors and businessmen; the corporations are legatees of such a past . . .; this pedigree allows them to run Tomorrow. Citizens can sit back and consume' (1985: 47). The future that the corporations have in mind for us is an exciting one in which there will be no problems because they will have learned from the past. This future is full of machines and technological inventions that the corporations will have manufactured. Visitors have been prepared for this optimism because of the way in which the past has been presented to them – relentless improvement in their lot with the help of corporations which have recognized the problems of the past.

In fact, to many commentators, the future envisioned by the corporations is remarkably mundane and uninspiring. There are intimations of a sci-fi future of space travel and alternative modes of living, but little beyond that. Rugare (1991: 108) points out that the future presented in the Carousel of Progress is almost exactly the same as the future presented at the 1964 World's Fair 'except *that* future should have happened by now'. In the recently revamped Carousel, the future seems to comprise mainly of virtual-reality games machines, voice-controlled electric ovens, and computers. This future too, in its eagerness to be associated with products that touch base with those that are currently available or are impending, seems to lack the vision that is imputed to it. Spaceship Earth is typical of a brilliantly designed ride that runs out of ideas as we come to the future, which is depicted, as are a number of Disney futures, in space and presumably from where AT&T think that our future of communications will be launched. We are treated to an image of Tomorrow's Child playing amidst silicone chips and DNA strands and are then told: 'Now is the time of unprecedented choice and opportunity. So let us explore, question and understand. Learn from our past and meet the challenges of the future' (quoted in Fjellman, 1992: 90). Fjellman suggests that the disinclination of corporate sponsors to give away technological secrets may lie behind the low level of informational content and the mundanity of the futuristics at the parks. In fact, the future has been a continual problem for Disney planners because of the way the present rapidly catches up with

135

it. Findlay (1992) reports that between 1964 and 1967 some $20 million was spent demolishing and rebuilding Tomorrowland at Disneyland. In the process, space travel and atomic power were made less prominent. A radical redesign of Disney World's Tomorrowland is currently being undertaken. Nor have the new Innoventions exhibits given a more futuristic and visionary feel to Future World. Many, if not most, of the hands-on displays are readily recognizable items, such as Sega games machines, IBM computers and multimedia machines, and AT&T telephones and communication devices. There is little to suggest a realm of serious futuristics.[2]

The really interesting vision for the future that is found at Disney World will never be seen by visitors, namely, its underground service and utility passages. By consigning services to its basement and rendering them invisible and inaudible, the parks' engineers have won praise for their imagination and foresight (for example, Goldberger, 1972). One of the reasons that the future seems bland and unimaginative is that it is closely connected with the present. The future seems so familiar that one almost feels nostalgic about it. The future is expressed in terms and idioms of the present in order to connect them with the corporations' visions. The future has to be one in which the corporations have a clearly defined presence in order to link them with the present. The problems that they will be overcoming, the technology they will be generating and the visions that will be giving them momentum represent ways of boosting their image for today. Billig's (1994: 158) view that 'Disney's celebration of the past and future is always a celebration of the present' is another way of saying that the corporations' eulogizing of the past and present is a way of firmly locating their position in visitors' consciousness for the present day. Thus, in the quotation from the Spaceship Earth ride it is *now* that is the time of choice and opportunity. It is in the present that the past and future are firmly located. Thus, while writers like King (1981) are correct in their observation that the present is largely ignored in the Disney parks, it is only the present as a specific focus of attention that is absent; in fact, it permeates the presentation of both past and future to form a conceptual bridge between the two.

NOSTALGIA

Several commentators refer to the sense of nostalgia that pervades many aspects of the parks. That this feeling should be noted is hardly surprising since it was part of Walt's vision for the parks. Weinstein (1992: 149) refers to a memorandum written by Walt in 1948 about a then unnamed amusement park. This appears to be the earliest written reference to what was to become Disneyland. Weinstein describes Walt's concept of the park, as outlined in the three-page document, as 'an extremely sentimental and nostalgic place where children can experience the material culture of past generations and where adults can relive their or their parents' childhood'. In a 1953 document, Walt declared that Disneyland would be a place where the older generation could reminisce about the nostalgia of earlier years (Thomas, 1976: 257). The Disney Imagineers are often very explicit about the role of nostalgia in the impressions that they try to create. Fred Beckenstein, senior Vice-President of Euro Disneyland Imagineering was quoted in *The Sunday Times Magazine*:

> The whole idea is an escape from reality into a place where you can simply have fun. Life is full of problems, but it is our job to stop harsh reality intruding on the fantasy. Nostalgia, too, is a big part of the magic, but we're not into straight transliterations. Euro Disney has a turn-of-the-century feel to the principal streets and arcades – research proves that it is an era most nationalities feel comfortable with. But we're not trying to design what really existed in 1900, we're trying to design what people think they remember about what existed.
>
> (In Dickson, 1993: 34)

Main Street, USA has been most frequently described by commentators as the locus of feelings of nostalgia. It has been described for example as a

> a monument to an 'era of good feeling', a born-again belief in the squeaky clean virtues of front-porch USA, and nostalgia for a supposedly uncomplicated, decent, hard-working, crime-free, rise up and salute the flag way of life that is the stuff of middle America's dreams, an ersatz image of the past imposed within the here and now.
>
> (Mills, 1990: 73)

This nostalgic effect is hardly surprising in the light of Walt's belief that for 'those of us who remember those carefree times, Main Street will bring back happy memories'.[3] Dennett (1989) argues that the American Adventure is also imbued with a sense of nostalgia in its celebration of the myths of America's past rather than of its stark realities. For many writers, it is the drift towards nostalgia which is one of the most significant factors in the distortion of the past at the parks. Rojek (1993a) suggests that it is this nostalgia which is responsible for the tendency to disregard conflict, referred to above. Fjellman makes a similar point: 'There is no real history here, only historical items and nostalgia purloined in the interest of fun and commerce. There are no politics, no tragedy, no poverty' (1992: 251).

Giroux (1994) suggests that nostalgia is a device that is employed in a variety of Disney products to create a sense of innocence, a device through which both history and the present can be purged of unpleasant realities. The version of America that is thereby created comes to be associated with childhood naiveté, while in the process racism, conflict, poverty and unemployment can be legitimately ignored. It is also striking that in construing childhood as a period of innocence and naiveté, a particular vision of childhood is constructed, which is essentially rooted in a conventional, middle-class view of that period of a person's life. In fact, of course, the childhood that many children experience, by virtue of a variety of different factors (family breakdown, poverty, abuse, and so on), departs greatly from the socially constructed reality at the Disney parks. King (1981) argues that the sense of a return to childhood is the basic appeal of the parks (as well as other Disney products) and is the essence of their sense of nostalgia. In this she follows Starobinski's (1966) view of nostalgia as a longing for a return to one's childhood rather than to a place. It is striking that this view is highly congruent with suggestions encountered in Chapter 4 about the appeal of the parks to adults, since it is they who are most likely to experience the longing for childhood about which both King and Starobinski write. Lowenthal makes a similar point when he wrote that 'the adult world of yesteryear reflects the perspective of childhood' (1985: 8). King extends her analysis further by suggesting that there is an additional layer of nostalgia in the parks which is revealed in a longing for a return to the nation's childhood, as represented in turn-of-the-century settings like Main Street and the era of the conquest of the frontier.

Chase and Shaw (1989) argue that there are three preconditions of nostalgia: a sense of linear time; a sense that the present is deficient; and the presence of artefacts from the past. The first of these three preconditions is very clear at the Disney parks, since in spite of the frequent dislocation of artefacts from their historical contexts, there is a sense of historical progression from an exciting and misty past to an even more exciting and decidedly misty future. The sense of the present as deficient is ambiguous in the Disney parks. As we have seen, the essentially optimistic picture of the past and the future acts to reconcile us to the barely outlined present. On the other hand, the very fact that the negative features of reality are deliberately excluded from the visitor's purview by Imagineers suggests that something out there in the present is not quite right. Moreover, the fact that many visitors view the parks as a place of safety in the face of a world of danger and uncertainty further suggests that the nostalgia at the Disney parks is fuelled by a sense of the present as deficient, although as Lowenthal (1985) suggests, it is also frequently associated with fears about the future. Thus, the present, in its interstitial relationship with the future, represents for many people a time of uncertainty which results in the celebration of the certainties of the past (Lowenthal, 1989). The third precondition – the presence of artefacts from the past – is most definitely present in the parks, in the form of buildings, costumes, merchandise and atmospheres, and these undoubtedly act as signals for feelings of nostalgia. The nostalgia at the Disney parks is of course a *fabricated* nostalgia. Robertson (1990) similarly refers to a surge of 'synthetic nostalgia' in the modern (or more specifically in his case, the postmodern) world which he describes as 'wilful'. The nostalgia of the Disney parks is not fabricated simply to allow the ugly aspects of America's past to be placed out of view, but to allow the present to be cast in a more favourable light (and the future as well since, as suggested in the previous section, the unremarkable futures presented at the parks almost induce a sense of nostalgia about the future). Tester (1993) has remarked that nostalgia is not simply about repudiation but also about coming to terms with one's present position. Thus, while the fabricated nostalgia of the parks inevitably involves a looking backward in time and a sense of something lost, the clever way in which past, present and future are dissolved into one another helps to render the present more agreeable. However, the nostalgia created at the parks also links with the consumerism that underpins so much that goes on in them and which will be explored in greater detail in Chapter 7. As Robertson (1990) suggests, the growth of wilful, synthetic nostalgia in the late twentieth century is closely connected with consumption. Indeed, both Marin (1984) and Eco (1986) have argued that the fabricated nostalgia of Main Street merely conceals the commercial realities that lie behind it. The fabricated nostalgia at the parks, then, does not simply engender a distortion of the historical record; it also acts as a palliative for the present (and perhaps the future too) and a lure for the prospective consumer. As Lowenthal (1989) observes, it is this commercialization of nostalgia that is often the reason for the contempt heaped upon it by intellectuals.

UTOPIA

Wakefield (1990) has referred to Walt's formulation for Disneyland as a 'Utopian manifesto', and a number of writers have drawn attention to the Utopian elements in the parks' design and formulation of attractions. The use of the term 'Utopia' or the designation 'Utopian' in connection with the parks is sometimes confusing because it is used by writers to refer to a variety of levels and in relation to different objects. The parks themselves are sometimes described as Utopias. Goldberger quoted the noted architect Robert Venturi, the high priest of postmodernist architecture, as saying: 'Disney World is nearer to what people really want than anything architects have ever given them. It's a symbolic American Utopia' (1972: 41). Gottdiener describes Disneyland as 'a Utopian urban space' when compared to the environing Los Angeles (1982: 150). Fjellman (1992) remarks that the pedestrianism at the parks is a distinctly Utopian feature. But there are other Utopias at the Disney parks. Real (1977) describes the Disney account of the past as Utopian in its idealization of America's history by overlooking its less savoury aspects, so that the past is turned into a Utopia. Equally, the future is Utopian in the image of a world in which enlightened corporations have learned from the problems of the past and will create (indeed *are* creating) an idyllic future full of opportunities. As Nelson (1986) suggests, EPCOT's message is that things are under control or will be, so we can sit back and wait for the perfected future.

But precisely because the past, present and future shade into each other at the Disney parks, the Utopian past and the Utopian future come to symbolize a Utopian present. There is a sense in which America is being celebrated as a Utopia. By idealizing aspects of its past, present and future, the Disney parks celebrate America as a Utopian space. It is no wonder that many writers have seen in the parks the representation of the American Dream (for example, Wolf, 1979; Billig, 1994). The parks symbolize that Dream and as symbols, they convey the sense of Utopia attained (or nearly so) in the form of the contemporary USA, which is both signifier (of Utopia) and signified (by the parks). Such a view is consistent with Walt's vision which was given voice to by one of his closest associates, Bill Walsh, who in 1953 wrote the text for an early pamphlet on Disneyland:

> Disneyland will be based upon and dedicated to the ideals, the dreams and the hard facts that have created America. And it will be uniquely equipped to dramatize these dreams and facts and send them forth as a source of courage and inspiration to all the world. . . . It will be filled with the accomplishments, the joys and hopes of the world we live in. And it will remind us and show us how to make those wonders part of our own lives.
>
> (In Mosley, 1986: 221–2)

In this passage, America is not simply idealized but surrounded by Utopian imagery in such a way that the two merge. The *Encyclopaedia Britannica* describes the American Dream in the following terms: 'A democratic land of opportunity, in which social, political, economic and religious freedom prevail, one person is as good as another and individuals can achieve their dream if only they work hard enough' (quoted in Marling, 1993: 10). This is very much the image presented at the Disney parks through its portrayal of the past, in particular. It is not just the American Dream that is symbolized as having been attained but Utopia. The Disney parks reinforce the 'culture of comfort' (Galbraith, 1992) and thereby the legitimacy of the lot of the relatively affluent middle class who are their patrons. There are, then, a variety of ways in which the narrative of Utopia applies to the Disney parks – as descriptions of the parks, of America's past, of America's future, and of America itself.

CONCLUSION

In their presentation of both the past and the future, the Disney parks provide an anodyne picture. There are crucial silences about the past, while the future is bland and barely informs the visitor in spite of the pedagogical aims of the parks. However, in its presentation of the past, there is no doubt that the Disney Imagineers provide a form of instruction that is easily absorbed and which influences tens of millions of people for whom the Disney version of history becomes real history. As Horton and Crew (1989) suggest, they provide a view of history with which professional historians are unable to compete in terms of either the mode of presentation or the numbers of people touched by it.

The present appears largely by inference, as the point where the past and the future intersect. As a result, a broadly positive account of the present is provided, albeit by implication. The past is subject to heavy doses of nostalgia which not only results in a skewed account of the past, but also serves to link the warm feelings inspired by nostalgia to consumption. This nostalgia is particularly interesting because it seems to avoid the sense of melancholy with which it is often associated. Turner (1987) has shown that nostalgia is often indicated by a sense of loss – of a golden age, of moral certainty, of community, and of spontaneity. This pessimistic and melancholic sense of nostalgia is occluded within the Disney parks by conveying it in positive terms. In large part, this is accomplished by placing the narrative of nostalgia next to optimistic accounts of the future and of learning from mistakes in the recent past. In this way, the past and the future are depicted as Utopias, a realm in which the present and America itself also reside.

7

CONSUMING THE CORPORATION

For many writers, the Disney theme parks are panegyrics to capitalism. Some manifestations of this connection will be examined in the present chapter by drawing out a few themes, which are themselves highly interconnected. The three themes which form the framework for this chapter are: *corporatism* – the glorification of the corporation; *technological progress* – faith in the capacity of advanced technology to improve our lot, a theme that links with some of the issues raised in the previous chapter; and *consumerism* – the centrality of the consumer and consumer goods to images and practices within the parks. These three themes interweave considerably. Some of the ways in which overlaps arise will be explored, but it should be appreciated that these are not discrete motifs.

The parks are frequently referred to by writers as revealing the underlying principles of capitalism. Dennett describes the American Adventure as 'the self-serving politics of the growth and development of American capitalism which is being encouraged' (1989: 159). Drawing on a semiotic analysis, Gottdiener (1982) has gone slightly further than many writers in depicting Disneyland's 'lands' as signifiers of capitalism. The correspondences work roughly as follows:

- Frontierland – predatory capital;
- Adventureland – colonialism / imperialism;
- Tomorrowland – state capital;
- New Orleans Square – venture capital;
- Main Street – family capital.

As a result, Disneyland becomes 'the fantasy world of bourgeois ideology' (Gottdiener, 1982: 156). Quite aside from the arbitrary nature of some of these correspondences, Gottdiener recognizes that Disneyland cannot be interpreted solely as a reflection of forms of the capitalist system and argues that it is necessary to take into account Walt's intentions and background. In fact, of course, Walt was the archetypal self-made capitalist, so that even if one were to accept Gottdiener's mapping of Disneyland's lands, his experiences as a capitalist entrepreneur and his faith in the system that allowed him to accomplish what he did undoubtedly affected his confidence in that system.

This commitment to the values of capitalism is exhibited by the confidence in the ethic of individualism that is revealed in many attractions. Rojek, for example, suggests that the parks 'celebrate the inventive and creative powers of individuals' (1993a: 130). Dennett (1989) notes that the Golden Dream sequence at the end of the American Adventure symbolizes Americans as dreamers and doers (of whom one is Walt himself), while Fjellman writes of the attraction as a whole that its central image is of the American as a 'pragmatic, inventive entrepreneur, seeking freedom to go his or her own way, to make or sell her or his own inventions' (1992: 103). Thus, the celebration of capitalism at the theme parks is as much to do with the celebration of the values on which it rests, such as individualism and the freedom to dream and do. However, to anticipate very slightly some of the subsequent discussion, how well these tenets sit with Disney's glorification of the corporation is not entirely clear. It is not sufficient to depict corporations as legatees of individualism, since corporations do much to stifle competition. In the case of Disney World, for example, the company keeps competitors at bay by its control over the land. The rugged individualist may be celebrated but will have no luck on Disney land where even the buildings are copyrighted and therefore photographs of them cannot be published (Sehlinger, 1994; Sorkin, 1992).

In its affirmation of the capitalist system, the messages of the theme parks are heavily orientated to the support of the status quo, a characteristic that they share with other Disney media, according to Schiller (1973). Wallace suggests that EPCOT's Future World 'dulls historical sensibility and invites acquiescence to what is' (1985: 49), while Morison feels that the aim of EPCOT generally 'is to make people more comfortable with the world they live in' (1983: 77). In a similar vein, Sorkin suggests that both the circus and Disney entertainment are 'anti-carnivalesque' in that they are both 'celebrations of the existing order of things in the guise of escape from it' (1992: 208). Corporations, above all, have much to gain from the preservation of the status quo, and it is to their position and their images at the Disney parks to which we now turn.

CORPORATISM

The role of corporations in the Disney theme parks became more pronounced after Walt persuaded Pepsi-Cola, General Electric and Ford to sponsor attractions for the 1964 World's Fair, but it was greatly enhanced by the construction of sponsored rides and attractions at EPCOT's Future World pavilions. Interestingly, the only World Showcase exhibit which has a corporate sponsor is the American Adventure (American Express and Coca-Cola). Presumably, the various sponsors have felt that their association with Disney would provide high-profile publicity for the corporations themselves and their products. Wallace quotes a General Electric executive who cites as his company's reason for its continued involvement with Disney: 'the Disney organization is absolutely superb in interpreting our company dramatically, memorably and favorably to the public' (1985: 43). Moreover, exhibits like the Carousel of Progress fix in the minds of visitors the association of progress with consumption (of electrical appliances). Similarly, the World of Motion ride demonstrates the successive improvements in modes of conveyance leading up to the General Motors cars that people mill around just prior to exiting from the pavilion. Having been on a ride in which the visitor has been propelled through dioramas representing millennia of progress in locomotion, he or she is given ample time to dwell on the company's latest products.

The role of the corporation was implied by the analysis in Chapter 6 when the Disney account of the past and the future was examined. The corporation is depicted as gradually improving our position, as recognizing and overcoming the problems of the recent past, and as working on our behalf for the future. Fjellman (1992) notes the frequent use of 'we' in running commentaries. He views this as a device which links the middle-class visitor with the corporation. Their interests become fused in people's minds. Another device, not mentioned by Fjellman, is the use of 'they', as in 'Today, they're bringing good things to life that weren't even dreamed of a generation ago' (from the Carousel of Progress, quoted in Fjellman, 1992: 83.) 'They' was in fact General Electric who are working things out for 'us'. The implication is that we can sit back while the corporations are beavering away finding solutions on our behalf, inventing products that we will need, and developing technology to improve our lives. We can all be confident about tomorrow because 'they' will ensure that yesterday's problems will not be repeated if 'we' act wisely. As Fjellman points out, the message seems to be that of acquiescence to corporation-inspired solutions and initiatives. The message of Listen to the Land is that the corporation (previously Kraft, but now Nestlé) is finding technological solutions to agricultural problems on our behalf. Moreover, science and technology are primarily construed in these exhibits as the science and technology devised by and located in corporations. As Harrington observed about EPCOT before it opened, the meta-narrative of the pavilions is that planning for the future can be left to corporations which will 'maximize the common good' (1979: 86). Wasserman referred to such messages soon after the opening of EPCOT as 'costly industry propaganda' (1983: 34). For Wallace, EPCOT seems 'intent on inducing awe in the capabilities of corporations' (1985: 47).

The optimistic messages about the past and the future serve the sponsors well in associating them with a distinctly upbeat message about their products and their image. We see a 'dream ticket' which links the corporations to both the optimistic message created by Disney Imagineering and consumption.

TECHNOLOGICAL PROGRESS

A number of writers have noted that the portrayals of both the past and the future in the Disney theme parks are ineluctably linked by a narrative of progress – we've done marvellous things, we're still doing them, and things will get even better. Problems are increasingly alluded to, but they are placed within the perspective of continual progress and improvement, not least because the problems will be overcome. This theme of continual progress is especially apparent on those rides and attractions which take us through the centuries and even millennia from a dim and distant past to an exalted future, especially the Carousel of Progress, World in Motion, Horizons, and Spaceship Earth. As these four examples suggest, it is particularly *technological* progress that is exalted in the parks, a theme which seems to have become more prominent with the building of EPCOT and the growing involvement of large corporate sponsors. Bierman (1976) observes that there is frequent use of the word 'progress' in the opening statement of the Carousel of Progress. Fjellman quotes some of the opening words: 'On this and every turn we will be making progress. And progress is not just moving ahead. Progress is dreaming, working, building a better way of life' (1992: 81). The theme of progress can also be discerned in relation to attractions like the American Adventure, but the nature of the material with which this kind of exhibit deals is inevitably less futuristic. We are simply left with the impression that more great things are to come. When addressing *technological* progress, we are given a more direct insight into what is to come and are meant to be in awe of the plans that 'they' have in store for us. Morison sums up the message as 'don't worry' since 'machinery always does good (even the first traffic jam is blamed on a horse) and . . . it will soon do better' (1983: 76). Bukatman (1991) makes an interesting observation when he notes that it is not just the optimistic message in the portrayal of the future that is meant to reconcile us to the new technologies, but the way in which the rides in EPCOT's Future World and in Tomorrowland project the audience into the landscapes of the future and are thus incorporated by the futuristic technology 'they' have designed for us. Rugare (1991) notes that the vision of technological progress is specifically the motor for America's future. It is after all US corporations that are the sponsors of these attractions. He also notes that intimations of cultural diversity are the province of World Showcase, but not in the realm of technology. One of the effects of these connections is to associate technological progress very much with America and more specifically with American corporations.

There is a narrative in much of this of what might be called *disempowerment*. We are all supposed to sit back and let the corporations do the planning for the future on our behalf. We will benefit by the better world that the corporations will produce and we will benefit as consumers. We are given insights into the tremendous labour-saving devices that are being produced to make life even better than corporations have made it for us. That corporations want to portray us as consumers of their products is a separate matter which ties in with the issues confronted below, but the approach taken to the theme of technological progress is one in which our participation in such issues as which problems require technological solutions, the form of those technological solutions, and even control over the use of new technologies, is negligible. We will simply benefit from the things that are being devised on our behalf (Kuenz, 1993). Instead, it is through the proliferation and purchase of labour-saving devices that we will be empowered, according to the Carousel of Progress.

The theme of control surfaces again here, in that the image with which we are presented is that, in the name of technological progress, corporations should be left to get on with what they know best, which is, of course, one of Disney's intentions for its own destiny. In fact, individuals seem to disappear from view in the world of tomorrow. Whereas the past, as depicted in Hall of Presidents and the American Adventure, is all about dreamers and doers (like Walt himself who is one of the participants in the latter attraction's Golden Dream sequence), the emblems of individualism – people – do not figure in the world of tomorrow other than as consumers and beneficiaries of technological progress. In a sense, the marginalization of people in all this is surprising because in the 1975 annual report, Card Walker wrote about EPCOT being a forum in which individual scientists, as well as universities and representatives of the arts (as well as industry) would have the opportunity to demonstrate new technologies and ideas, but in practice it has been corporations that have firmly taken the place of individuals. In the rides which take us from the past to the future (Carousel of Progress, Horizons, etc.), corporations ('they') begin to be substituted for the inventors and entrepreneurs of yesteryear. In this way, a sign of technological progress is that whereas in the past individuals were the main movers in ushering in the modern world of which we have every right to be proud, in the future corporations will be the prime forces. Corporations are substituted for individuals as the heroes of the future. But the eulogizing of technological progress, as well as the glorification of the corporation as its agent, is a theme that is most likely to find acceptance in precisely the social strata which are drawn to the parks, the relatively affluent white middle class who frequently have a vested interest in such a message.

EPCOT and the world's fair tradition

A number of writers have drawn attention to the parallel between EPCOT and world's fairs, with many referring to it as a 'permanent world's fair' (for example, Morison, 1983; Wallace, 1985). In fact, the phrase was also used by Martin Sklar, Vice-President of Creative Development at WED Enterprises, in his Introduction to Beard's (1982) book on EPCOT. The bridge between the world's fair tradition and EPCOT is the New York World's Fair of 1964 for which Walt produced a number of exhibits with the aid of corporate sponsorship which were subsequently incorporated into Disneyland. It seems likely that the success of these exhibits coupled with a growing realization of the advantages of sponsors contributed to the creation of a park of similar attractions, which drew more generally on the world's fair approach. Thus, in an article that is very disparaging about EPCOT, Wasserman (1983) refers to it as an 'eternal world's fair'. Nelson (1986) argues that it is if anything closer to a world's fair, especially the 1893 and 1939 ones, than to a theme park. He writes:

> Separated by a huge moat, Future World and World Showcase express the foremost thematic concerns of world's fairs past: technological progress and cultural diversity. Future World borrows from the 1939 New York World's Fair with its huge geodesic dome, reminiscent of the Perisphere, and its corporate pavilions sponsored by GM, Kodak, and other companies who also participated in the 1939 fair. The World Showcase is an unabashed derivative of the Midway villages of the 1893 Columbian Exposition, with its attempt to condense world cultures into easily recognizable cuisines, behaviors, costumes, and architectural styles.
>
> (Nelson, 1986: 128)

As Nelson observes, by transforming technology into entertainment, world's fairs and EPCOT have been able to neutralize the worries that many people legitimately feel about their inability to understand it or to appreciate its consequences. In other words, it is a powerful tool in creating a benign image for technology and acquiescence to technological progress. The image of perfectibility through technology and other Utopian messages are also shared. Disney has contributed techniques developed in its parks – Audio-Animatronics, holography, rides, strong narratives – to spruce up the world's fair message of technological progress. There is also an overlay of national self-promotion in that other US fairs, as well as EPCOT, have been celebrations of American achievements and know-how.

While drawing attention to the continuities between world's fairs and EPCOT, writers have also suggested that there are differences as well. Rugare (1991) points out that at world's fairs the demonstration of a nation's material accomplishments was through the exhibition of vast numbers of manufactured artefacts. At EPCOT this sense of a munificence of products is largely lacking, which is at least in part a function of the lack of direct attention to the present. Nelson describes just one of the buildings at the 1893 fair as encapsulating

> towers of blazing electric lights, gigantic roaring furnaces, whirling dynamos, huge statues made of dried fruit, working model warships, railroads and cannons, glass containers filled with oddities living and dead, and at least a dozen examples of every conceivable and inconceivable type of manufactured and/or agricultural product.
>
> (1986: 110)

At EPCOT, by contrast, we are presented with images of products of the past and very sketchy, abstract images of what is to come. There are gadgets to play with at the Communicores (now Innoventions) and elsewhere but there is little to tell the visitor about achievements outside the realm of information technology on which many of the push-button and hands-on exhibits seem to be based.

Although parenthetical to this section's theme, writers have sometimes noted the similarity between the expression of cultural diversity at the 1893 exhibition in particular, where the foreign was made much more exotic and even erotic than at World Showcase. In addition, the variety of cultures on show was much greater:

> Tourists gawked at the extraordinary panorama of the world's peoples: Egyptian swordsmen and jugglers, Dahomean drummers, Sudanese sheikhs, Javanese carpenters, Hungarian gypsies, Eskimos, Chinese, Laplanders, Swedes, Syrians, Samoans, Sioux, and on and on. . . . Visitors were titillated by the prospect of the World Congress of Beauty

with '40 Ladies from 40 Nations', in reality an exhibition of native costumes. They pushed into the Streets of Cairo, the Algerian Village, and the Persian Palace of Eros to watch entranced as 'Little Egypt', and her colleagues and companions performed the 'danse du ventre,' popularly known as the hootchy-kootchy.

(Kasson, 1978: 24, 26)

Undoubtedly, Disney's emphasis on family entertainment and the political incorrectness of some of these attractions (beauty parades and gawking at people from other cultures) would render them inconceivable for a park like EPCOT, but the great variety of cultures on display and the exuberant climate within which they were displayed is quite striking from this description.

It is not clear whether the designers of EPCOT were consciously influenced by the world's fair tradition, but there is a good deal of evidence to suggest similarities between them. The chief point of this section has been to show how a number of writers have pointed to continuities with world's fairs and that in respect of the commitment to an ideology of technological progress and how best to present it, EPCOT shares many common features.

CONSUMERISM

Consumerism, in the sense of consumption of goods and services as a focal element in the individual's and the family's *raison d'être*, is a recurrent theme in the writings of many commentators. In large part, this theme arises out of a realization that consumption is increasingly replacing a person's occupation as the sphere from which people in modern society derive social meaning and personal identity. This notion has strong affinities with some of the central ideas in the stream of thought described as 'postmodernism', which will be more directly confronted in the next chapter. For many of these authors consumption is significant because of the sign value, rather than the use value, of many goods and services. Goods with sign value are symbolic goods which are purchased for their capacity to enhance people's ability to proceed with their (or their families' – the two are often indistinguishable) life-projects. People are increasingly pursuing life-styles (or are being encouraged to pursue them by advertisers) which define

151

them as individuals and which require symbolic goods for their realization. Through consumption individuality and distinctiveness are purchased, as is full participation as a modern individual. Through a host of artefacts including his/her home, decoration, car, clothes, and holidays, the individual is portrayed as forgeing a life-style which forms his/her own identity and how he/she is perceived by others. Featherstone (1991) rejects the suggestion that such concerns apply only to the world(s) of the young and the affluent – with the designer label suit as the emblem of its underlying mentality; instead, he suggests that through advertising and publicity we are all exhorted to spruce up our images and to become what we are capable of becoming, if only we buy the right things. Thus, for Bauman, one of the main exponents of these ideas from within the postmodernist approach 'Consumerism stands for production, distribution, desiring, obtaining and using, of *symbolic* goods' (1992: 223, emphasis added.)

Ewen (1988) characterizes modern consumption as concerned with *style*, which is supposed to shift our attention from a joyless emphasis on consumption for necessity. As he puts it:

Style, more and more, has become the official idiom of the marketplace. In advertising, packaging, product design, and corporate identity, the power of provocative surfaces speaks to the eye's mind, overshadowing matters of quality or substance. Style, moreover, is an intimate component of subjectivity, intertwined with people's aspirations and anxieties.

(Ewen, 1988: 22, emphasis removed)

Through advertising, packaging, and the construction of corporate images, companies help to define the good life for us, telling us what we want rather than what we need, and how we can accomplish the life-projects that they dangle in front of our eyes. Bauman (1992) argues that in the process seduction (through consumption) replaces control (at the workplace and beyond) as the chief means of social integration. People can then be left to engage in self-actualization through consumption rather than through work, pursuing symbolic goods. The quest for such goods is boundless since it is not constrained by the limitations of fulfilling basic needs, although Bauman recognizes that many are excluded from the opportunity to participate in this regime of consumption by poverty and low levels of income.

152

These views about consumption have not gone unchallenged. Warde (1994), for example, argues that Bauman concentrates too much on the individual and his/her project and that the importance of consumption as a source of identity is exaggerated. It has also been suggested that many of the writers within this tradition play down the importance of rational calculations of use value (Aldridge, 1994; Keat *et al.*, 1994). However, even though there have been some criticisms of the view of consumers as engaged in a search for personal identity through consumption, there is a general recognition, even among the critics, of a sea-change within the sphere of consumption. These ideas also draw attention to the importance for companies and for the consumer of adorning goods and services in signals of the consumer's engagement with something more that the manifest utility of the good or service in question (if indeed it has a manifest utility). Moreover, there is no suggestion that considerations of use value are completely replaced by considerations of sign value; it is manifestly the case that the former persists even among the affluent middle class. Rather, what is being drawn attention to is the growing deployment of sign value as a marketing tool and its growing acceptance among certain social strata. Indeed, if we were not to accept at least a minimalist version of the notion that goods and services are increasingly sold for what they signal in relation to people's self-concepts, it is difficult to visualize on what grounds certain goods or services are ever bought.

There are a number of different aspects of consumption at the Disney parks to which these ideas form a helpful backcloth. First, and perhaps most obviously, the parks are contexts for a great deal of consumption. In fact, they are set up to maximize consumption. The novelist E.L. Doctorow recognized this when he wrote: 'The ideal Disneyland patron may be said to be one who responds to a process of symbolic manipulation that offers him the culminating and quintessential sentiment at the moment of purchase' (1972: 295). The use of 'passports' as ways of entering the parks is an indicator of the significance of consumption at the parks. When Disneyland first opened, there was a small general entrance fee and visitors then had to purchase tickets for each attraction. Walt realized that on busy days people spent a great deal of time standing in line simply to purchase tickets for each ride. Some rides tended to be patronized too little, while other rides were the source of long queues. Some years after it was opened, the visitor was able to purchase a block of tickets for rides and attractions, which had been graded according to their popularity. Each block would have a certain number of tickets for each grade of ride. Even this approach was dropped when in 1982 the passes which are still used today were introduced and allowed unlimited access to the rides in any park. At Disney World, visitors typically purchase multi-park tickets which allow access to all the rides in all the parks (and the minor parks depending on the type of pass) over a set number of days. Findlay (1992) suggests that the continuous exchange of money in the early Disneyland years gave the impression of a visit being expensive. It may be that one of the concerns was that this 'psychologically bad situation', as one of the Disney Imagineers called it (Bright, 1987: 109), inhibited people's preparedness to spend money on merchandise. While the significance of the consumption of merchandise and food at the parks has grown greatly since 1955, it is likely that Walt and his associates were profoundly aware of its profitable nature, particularly in the light of its importance in the studio's early years (see Chapter 1).

A second register of consumerism at the Disney theme parks revolves around an observation that has been made in a number of guises previously, namely, that some of the corporate-sponsored attractions in the parks relate to the goods and services that they sell. In presenting to us pictures of past and future revolving around electrical goods (Carousel of Progress) and cars (World of Motion), the good life is construed in terms of our identities as consumers – we are what we buy. The new Innoventions buildings at Disney World can be viewed more appropriately as showcases for the electronics, information technology and computer products of companies such as IBM, Sega and AT&T. Kuenz (1993) suggests that a major reason for the frequent allusion to the family in the parks is that it is the chief locus of consumption. Stimulating this image acts as a prompt to remind the visitor of his/her identity as consumer of both the corporation's products and the Disney merchandise itself, though this is not to suggest that visitors are unreflective automata who rush to buy character dolls and tee-shirts as soon as they can, but that the image is a convenient, self-serving one.

The third context of consumerism relates to consumption at the parks themselves. Some commentators have written as though the parks are simply shopping milieux. Yoshimoto (1994) suggests that the point of providing guests with narratives to mould their experiences of the parks is to naturalize consumption, so that people consume without being aware of what they are doing. By making consumption part of the experience itself, its nature as consumption is not fully revealed. In Yoshimoto's view, the 'ingenuity of Disney magic lies in its attempt to integrate shopping as part of the attractions without destroying the autonomy of the latter' (1994: 187). It is not surprising, therefore, that more and more shopping malls are adopting a Disney approach to retailing, so that shopping takes place in themed environments. Increasingly, it is difficult to distinguish large malls with themed environments from theme parks. The most frequently cited illustration of this trend is the West Edmonton Mall in Alberta, Canada; to all intents and purposes it is a shopping mall which increasingly resembles a theme park (Crawford, 1992; Shields, 1989). In fact, West Edmonton Mall's publicity tries to give the impression that it provides a great deal more than a Disney theme park:

> Imagine visiting Disneyland, Malibu Beach, Bourbon Street, the San Diego Zoo, Rodeo Drive in Beverly Hills and Australia's Great Barrier Reef . . . in one weekend – and under one roof. . . . Billed as the world's greatest shopping complex of its kind, the Mall covers 110 acres and features 828 stores, 110 restaurants, 19 theaters . . . a five-acre water park and a glass dome that is over 19 storeys high. . . . Contemplate the Mall's indoor lake complete with four submarines from which you can view sharks, octopi, tropical marine life, and a replica of the Great Barrier Reef. . . . Fantasyland Hotel has given its rooms a number of themes.
> (Travel Alberta publicity material, quoted in Urry, 1990: 147)

However, even less extreme cases than this, such as the Metro Centre in Gateshead, sometimes exhibit this tendency to narrativize shopping by creating themed locations, such as a Mediterranean Village (Chaney, 1990). In large part, of course, the aim of theming the experience of shopping is to keep the shopper in that role for as long as possible and for shopping to become an attraction in its own right. Crawford (1992) argues that the advantage of theming is that mundane goods reap the benefit of 'adjacent attraction', whereby their display in exotic contexts renders them more glamorous and interesting. This is especially important in malls since they are typically populated by well-known retail chains selling very familiar goods, and each section of the mall duplicates other sections in terms of the spread of shops that are housed there. Crawford sees West Edmonton Mall and to a certain extent other large regional malls as drawing on Disneyland motifs: the use of a diversity of themes as contexts draws on the past, the future, different cultures, and literary texts which are temporally and spatially compressed in order to stimulate adjacent attraction and therefore to animate shopping.

Main Street in Disneyland and Disney World's Magic Kingdom and EPCOT's World Showcase are the regions of the Disney theme parks which have most frequently been referred to as essentially concerned with consumption. Wakefield (1990) argues that shopping and the fiction enshrined in the attractions are fused so that the visitor can achieve full participation in the experience of fantasy as a consumer. In this way, consumption is presented as an aspect of the fun and fantasy. To become a full participant, the visitor needs to consume. Similarly, Eco (1986: 43) writes: 'The Main Street façades are presented to us as toy houses, but their interior is always a disguised supermarket, where you buy obsessively, believing that you are still playing.' There are in fact few real attractions on Main Street other than the façades themselves, so that Eco's suggestion that the latter are simply 'fronts' for shops is not as extreme as it first appears. Main Street serves as a conduit to the rest of the park and creates a certain kind of atmosphere for the visitor, but the main business of Main Street is undoubtedly business. Moreover, in associating the goods sold in Main Street with the past, an explicit narrative is provided in which to contextualize and naturalize consumption.

More than anything else, the sign value of the goods purchased in Main Street and in many other locations in the Magic Kingdom and Disneyland is associated with the construction of childhood. As Giroux (1994) has pointed out, Disney as a company is associated almost umbilically with childhood. Writing about Disney output generally, he suggests that 'Disney's power and reach into popular culture combines an insouciant playfulness and the fantastic possibilities of making childhood dreams come true' (1994: 87). It is in their own childhoods that many parents will have developed their love for Disney characters, films, merchandise, and indeed theme parks. Advertising for the parks associates itself with childhood through the use of standard representations, such as Mickey, the castle, stars (the ones you wish upon), and so on, though often couched in ways that will appeal to adults, as noted in Chapter 4. It is the place where childhood dreams come true. Thus, 'childhood' provides one of the most pervasive narratives of the parks. The purchase by adults of much of the child-centred merchandise represents a sign of the child's engagement with and participation in childhood. To be a child means going to Disney films and theme parks and owning character dolls and similar merchandise. Purchasing such merchandise for children is therefore rendered normal in the sense of being part of the project of providing the wherewithal for childhood. The narrative of childhood is underscored by the inter-referential nature of Disney products with respect to childhood. They form a network of mutually reinforcing linkages in which films are at the centre, but television, the parks, merchandise, and publications are all involved in masterful interconnection. Yet another narrative implied by Main Street and by many of the attractions in Disney-MGM Studios is nostalgia. By providing fronts or attractions which adults associate with their pasts, purchasing commodities which rekindle enjoyable memories, often by virtue of the contexts in which they are purchased, is made to appear part of the experi- ence of the themed environments. Thus, the sign value of the goods purchased has much to do with fond memories and recollections, even though the memories and recollections have themselves been constructed for the visitor.

World Showcase has also been viewed as little more than a backcloth for consumption. Sertl goes so far as to suggest that the pavilions are 'little more than souvenir stands with restaurants' (1989: 142). Wasserman went even further when he wrote of the pavilions: 'The kindest thing to be said is that these villages are the most elaborately decorated entrances to restrooms ever devised' (1983: 39). In fact, remarkably little occurs in some of the pavilions, which are in some cases buildings and little else. Italy, Germany, and the United Kingdom contain buildings and shops and little more, other than occasional entertainment. Morocco has a small museum and a market place which, of course, sells real commodities – carpets, jewellery, belts, etc. In addition to their buildings, China, France and Canada have short films. Japan has a small art museum and elaborate gardens. Mexico and Norway are the only exhibits to have rides; the latter also has a short film.

Finally, there is the American Adventure, which comprises the American Adventure show and a theatre. Fjellman (1992) lists no fewer than 52 shops in the 11 country pavilions (Germany comes top with nine shops). In addition there are a number of very popular ethnic restaurants. Thus, architecture, restaurants and shopping are the only elements that are common to all 11 country pavilions. Each of the 11 pavilions provides its own narrative based on well-known symbols of architecture, sound and costume, but in most of them there is not a great deal to hold the visitor's attention for long, other than shopping. There is a lack of narrative continuity between the pavilions and this, coupled with the relative absence of theme park attractions, makes the emphasis on consumption in World Showcase highly transparent. None the less, the narratives provided by each country's pavilion justify 'the experience of eating its food, seeing its traditional dances, and buying its mass-produced souvenirs' (Rugare, 1991: 106). Nelson (1986) takes the view that the costume parades (information about the timing of which is given on entry to the park) are little more than ways of luring visitors to the food and souvenirs. Sorkin suggests that the 'knick-knacks' in the pavilions 'are stand-ins for the act of travel itself, ersatz souvenirs' (1992: 216).

The Disney parks have often been accused of commercialism by their critics (and sometimes by their enthusiasts too) and this charge seems to lie behind the quotations in the previous paragraph. Real (1977) found that this was a feature that some of the people who completed a questionnaire for him disliked in Main Street. King (1981) has objected to the charge of commercialism at the Disney parks. She argues that the charge is ironic for three reasons: consumption is not as central to the experience of a Disney theme park as it is at traditional amusement parks where there is a constant exchange of money for rides and attractions; commercialism is only one goal, whereas for many, if not most, amusement enterprises it is the sole aim; and most people think of the parks 'as a national shrine, monument, and living museum of American history and symbols' (King, 1981: 119). However, while not an *essential* ingredient, spending money at the parks is very much part of the Disney theme park experience, not least because bringing food and drink into the grounds is prohibited. Beyond that, the interpenetration of theming and consumption renders the latter a natural feature of the former, so that there are likely to be internalized motivations to spend money.

158

On the other hand, Kuenz (1993) has counselled against viewing visitors to the theme parks as consumerist zombies who unreflectively part company with their money as soon as an appropriate Disney-induced opportunity arises. Her warning is an important one and it is essential not to depict visitors as unreflective dupes. In a similar vein, Shields (1989; 1992) objects to this kind of analysis, which essentially seeks to strip away the cosmetic template of theming to reveal the base concern with trade that underpins the major malls. He argues that many visitors to West Edmonton Mall are in the role of *flâneurs*, that is strollers gazing on the fantasy worlds presented for their delectation, in the process meeting others so that a new form of community emerges from the destabilization of social relations that malls wreak on cities. For them, the mall is a liminal space which offers a break from the prosaic routines of everyday life. To see the mall as simply a clever marketing device, which is the implication of Crawford's (1992) analysis and that of Gottdiener (1986) in his examination of malls in general, is to miss the point, since people subvert the planners' goals for their own ends. A similar observation can be made about consumption in the Disney parks. However, the point that various commentators have made (and which is being made here) is that there are many aspects of the organization of consumption at the theme parks which serve to neutralize their more obvious consumerist tendencies by locking shopping into Disney narratives. Consumption becomes part of the immersion in fantasy, so that goods are purchased as symbols or signs of such narratives as childhood and nostalgia, rather than for use value. In so doing, goods are often being purchased which frequently do not directly fulfil a need that was definable prior to admission to a park. Whether this was a deliberate tactic on the part of Walt and his early associates is not at all clear, but the building of World Showcase and Disney-MGM Studios (which has 22 shops) suggests that there has been a growing realization of the commercial opportunities offered by theme park shopping. Moreover, by theming some shopping malls and even effectively turning a very small number into theme parks, retailers seem to have realized the potential that the Disney approach to consumption offers, as Crawford (1992) suggests. In recognizing the significance of Disney consumption along the lines suggested in this section, visitors are no more being regarded as passive suckers than are readers of newspaper advertisements whose aims

159

and imagery we might try to interpret. Readers may even subvert the parks' obvious commercialism as Shields (1989) suggests in relation to West Edmonton Mall, though his reservations about analyses which depict themed malls as strategies to shift shoppers' attention away from their basically commercial goals sits uneasily with his own observation that in its first year the Mall enjoyed average retails sales per square foot over twice the national figure.

There is a further level of consumption that has not been addressed – the consumption of the Disney parks as such; in other words, what is the nature of the Disney theme park experience as a holiday? This issue will be examined in the next chapter in the context of a discussion of the theme parks as indicative of postmodernism.

CONCLUSION

This section has explored a family of three motifs – the veneration of the corporation, of technological progress and of the consumer. The corporation is portrayed as a benign harbinger of the good life in the form of a plenitude of consumer goods. Technological progress is extolled and in the process worries about it are neutralized by associating it with the corporations' capacity to bring us more and more goods. Thus, consumption acts as a kind of conceptual linchpin which brings together the corporation and technological progress, and in the process perhaps reconciles us to both. Consumption also links to some of the themes that have been encountered in previous chapters, most notably, the frequent reference to the family as the context of consumption. But the chapter has also moved beyond such specific interconnections and has addressed the issue of consumerism and has shown how the notion of the narrativizing of consumption at the theme parks dovetails with the suggestion that increasingly goods and services are purchased for their symbolic rather than for their practical utility. This notion gently moves us into an area to be examined in the next chapter, namely, the suggestion that the Disney parks are sites of postmodernity, since the hailstorm of signs in which we are drenched, and which exist in plentiful supply at the parks, are emblems of the postmodern condition.

8

INTIMATING POSTMODERNITY AND THE PROBLEM OF REALITY

Postmodernism has become one of the most significant areas of theoretical analysis since the early 1980s. Summarizing this genre is no easy matter and can be compared to trying to grab hold of jelly with a clamp – it changes shape and consistency and then fragments. No attempt will be made here to summarize this stream of thought and any reader who wishes to dip into these waters would do well to examine such exemplars as Bauman (1992), Harvey (1989), and Rosenau (1992). Instead, the approach taken here will be the distinctly unpostmodernist approach of treating postmodernism as indicative of certain core themes, some of which will be examined in relation to the Disney theme parks. The status of the parks as emblems of postmodernism is not easy to define, since they variously occupy positions of cause, symptom and consequence in relation to it. That they are implicated in postmodernism is apparent through such disparate pieces of evidence as the praise heaped on them by Robert Venturi, the high priest of postmodern architecture, or the dubbing of the parks as evidence of a creeping 'hyperreality', a term strongly associated with postmodern terminology in the works of writers like Baudrillard (1983) and Eco (1986), though in the case of the former care is required in the light of his rejection of the description of himself as a postmodernist (Baudrillard, 1993a: 21–3). Thus, Mills refers to the Disney theme park as 'this most postmodern of experiences' (1990: 76) and Nelson takes the view that the parks exhibit 'the decidedly postmodernist sensibilities of eclectic style/collage, images of text, and excessive nostalgia' (1990: 61). Fjellman (1992) also associates Disney World with the postmodern world-view, while many of the writers most closely associated with postmodernist ideas often use the Disney theme parks as illustrations of their theoretical ideas (for example, Jameson: see Stephanson, 1987: 33).

The approach taken here, then, will be to focus on a small number of attributes of postmodernist thinking, rather than to attempt to encapsulate the postmodernist world-view as a whole. Perhaps this approach reflects my own ambivalence about these ideas. While I would not want to go as far as the *Independent on Sunday* journalist who pronounced the whole area of postmodernism 'irresistible but nevertheless more than slightly bonkers' (Fielding, 1992: 21), I would not want to disagree with her too much either. However, there is little doubt that post-modernist thinking has the capacity to draw to our attention features of the (post)modern world that are striking and in the process aspects of the Disney theme parks are drawn in sharper relief. I am reasonably certain that no self-respecting writer with a postmodernist predisposition would feel comfortable with the simplifying approach taken here, not *because* it simplifies but because it is doomed to failure by the very evanescence of post-modernity and of postmodernist discourse. To make matters worse, the areas to be discussed are not discrete topics, but inseparable insignia of a style of thinking and writing.

A PENCHANT FOR PASTICHE

The world of postmodernity is suffused with a sense of pastiche, sometimes in the spirit of wilful self-parody and irony. Discord-ant images are placed together to generate webs of mutually reinforcing coherence and incoherence. In architecture, for example, no blushes are spared in the plundering and placing together of the apparently incompatible (in terms of epoch, place, and / or genre). These jigsaws of taste and culture contribute to the '"degraded" landscape of schlock and kitsch' which Jameson (1991: 2) claims is a source of fascination for the postmodernist. There is a celebration of the confusion and destabilization caused by the incoherence of images and forms. One particular mani-festation of this fondness for pastiche is what Harvey (1989) refers to as 'time–space compression' in which one is faced by collages of symbols of time and place. In one of his only references to the Disney parks, Harvey writes:

The whole world's cuisine is now assembled in one place in

almost exactly the same way that the world's geographical complexity is nightly reduced to a series of images on a static television screen. This same phenomenon is exploited in entertainment palaces like Epcott [*sic*] and Disneyworld .... The general implication is that through the experience of everything from food, to culinary habits, music, television, entertainment, and cinema, it is now possible to experience the world's geography vicariously, as a simulacrum. The interweaving of simulacra in daily life brings together different worlds (of commodities) in the same space and time.

(Harvey, 1989: 300)

The significance of the reference here to a simulacrum (an image or copy of something that does not exist) will become apparent when the problem of reality is explored below, but in the meantime the importance of the idea of time-space compression should be becoming more discernible in that it refers to a common phenomenon at the Disney theme parks – the juxtaposition and mixing of diverse epochs and cultures.

Time–space compression occurs in a number of ways at the Disney theme parks. In the quotation, Harvey seems to have EPCOT's World Showcase very much in mind, with its mixing of different cuisines in 'authentic' settings, all within a relatively small space. But there is also a compression and confusion of time with these restaurants. Bistro de Paris has a decidedly early twentieth-century feel (Birnbaum, 1989), other restaurants have a timeless feel because of the impressive use of stereotypical costumes worn by the waiters and waitresses, and still others leave a much more contemporary impression. Some of the rides also exhibit the qualities depicted by Harvey. The World of Motion ride not only compresses millennia but takes in Egyptians (figuring out whether a triangular or a square or a round wheel will work best) and Italians (riding in chariots as well as the flight-obsessed Leonardo). Similar juxtapositions can be seen in the Spaceship Earth ride. A number of commentators have suggested that the visitor loses a sense of time and place at the parks. Johnson (1981) points out that the main exhibits and rides are structurally similar due to the use of similar concepts in their design, so that any sense of time and place is eroded. Again and again visitors are locked into moving cars and against a background of darkness are presented with a series of landscapes usually populated with Audio-Animatronic figures. Findlay (1992) argues that the creation of timelessness and placelessness was one of the aims of Disneyland in order to fulfil Walt's aim of creating a magical space untrammelled by the perspective of the outside world (see also Relph, 1976).

Time–space compression is substantially boosted by one of the main organizing concepts in Fjellman's (1992) book, the notion of 'decontextualization'. By this term he means the tendency for Disney Imagineers to pluck objects and their symbolic meanings (buildings, flora and fauna, historical incidents or themes) out of their context and reassemble them so that the disparate elements are presented as coherent totalities. He suggests that decontextualization makes it difficult for the visitor to maintain a coherent grasp on what is happening. This may be true, but just as, if not more, likely is the possibility that in the process new meanings are substituted, so that although conventional understandings of time and place are lost, new ones emerge and stand in for them (through a process of 'recontextualization', as Fjellman puts it). Fjellman points out that in the Jungle Cruise geography is mixed up with seamless interconnections between the Congo, Zambezi, Amazon and Irrawaddy rivers (1992: 32, 225). Time–space compression is sometimes employed in large shopping malls as the West Edmonton Mall travel publicity quoted on page 155 strongly suggests. Presumably such an environment stimulates the operation of adjacent attraction, to which Crawford (1992) refers.

The problem with firmly associating the Disneyesque principle of time–space compression with postmodernism, conceptualized either as a style of thought or a stage of society's development, is that there are clear signs of its operation in an era not normally associated with postmodernity. It is worth recalling Kasson's (1978) observations about the Midway attractions that were on show at the World's Columbian Exhibition in Chicago in 1893, some of which were quoted on pages 155–1. Kasson reveals that at Coney Island, Luna Park (which opened in 1903) was also built on such principles:

> For its opening season Luna boasted a Venetian city complete with gondoliers, a Japanese garden, an Irish village, an Eskimo village, a Dutch windmill, and a Chinese theater.

The following year, the park added a reproduction of the Durbar of Delhi and attempted to recreate its splendor.

(Kasson, 1978: 69)

But the sense of a compression of time as well as space was enhanced by shows which recreated

> such famous disasters as 'The Fall of Pompeii', simulating the eruption of Mount Vesuvius and the death of 40,000 people, the eruption of Mount Pelée and devastation of Martinique in 1902, Pennsylvania's Johnstown Flood of 1889, and Texas's Galveston Flood of 1900. For the first live disaster spectacle Luna chose a scene closer to home. In 'Fire and Flames' a four-story building was repeatedly set ablaze, the fire battled by heroic firemen while residents leaped from upper windows into safety nets below.
>
> (Kasson, 1978: 71–2)

At Hearst Castle too, the visitor finds a collage of juxtaposed artefacts which bring together and compress centuries and regions. Thus, we must be very cautious about depicting the kind of time–space compression about which Harvey (1989) writes as a postmodern phenomenon, unless we are prepared to broaden the notion of postmodernism both conceptually and temporally so that the 1893 Exhibition and Luna Park ten years later come within its purview. To do so risks giving the idea of post-modernism so much elasticity that it would cease to have much conceptual or historical value. While there is ample evidence of time–space compression at the Disney theme parks, we should be very wary of depicting the form that it takes at the parks as evidence of postmodernity or of postmodernist thinking, since in many respects it builds on traditions established in a much earlier era. However, this suggestion associates postmodernism with an epoch or era and is a viewpoint with which some writers disagree.

DEDIFFERENTIATION

Lash (1990) has drawn on a number of quintessentially post-modernist ideas to suggest that a major feature of postmodernism is *dedifferentiation*. There are a number of different ways of approaching this notion but one of its essential features is the notion of a collapse of the boundaries between institutional orders and of conceptual distinctions. Time–space compression is a feature of this notion, since it implies that the demarcations between time and space have broken down. One of the main ways in which dedifferentiation can be seen at the Disney theme parks is the lack of any clear differentiation between retailing and the features of an amusement or theme park. Crawford has remarked somewhat caustically: 'Theme park attractions are now common in shopping malls; indeed, the two forms converge – malls routinely entertain, while theme parks function as disguised supermarkets' (1992: 16). In other words, shopping and theme park amusements have become dedifferentiated in that, although we can probably still distinguish an ostensible shopping mall from an ostensible theme park, the distinction no longer matters a great deal, since for all practical purposes the boundaries between them are blurred. In the process, the roles of theme park visitor and consumer become similarly dedifferentiated.

A further area of overlap between institutional spheres is with respect to theme parks and hotels. At Disney World and Euro Disneyland most of the company's hotels are themed so that ambience, decor, staff dress and so on are suffused with a co-herent narrative. This in itself makes it difficult to know where the specifically theme park experience starts and finishes. This is of course a reaction that the Walt Disney Company is keen to create because it conveys the impression that to enjoy one of the parks to the full, visitors need to stay in one of their hotels to enjoy the magic fully. Since their Disney World hotels are often more expensive than other Orlando hotels (Sehlinger, 1994), creating this notion of the hotel as an extension of visiting a theme park has important commercial implications. However, in Las Vegas the theming of hotels is going much further and it is now be-coming extremely difficult to know whether one is visiting an hotel or a theme park. Grossman suggests that Las Vegas is close to 'becoming Disneyland on the desert' (1993: 5A). Some developers seem bent on turning Las Vegas into a destination for families, as against the more conventional clientele of singles and couples. The Luxor, opened in October 1993, boasts three interactive adventure attractions. Treasure Island, also opened in October 1993, displays sea battles in a fabricated Buccaneer Bay. MGM Grand Adventures, opened in December 1993, is a hotel and casino with its own theme park comprising twelve rides and shows which take place in nine themed streets. There is also a seven-storey recreation of the Emerald City from *The Wizard of Oz*. One *Financial Times* journalist described the MGM Grand as a challenge to relatively nearby Disneyland (Spanier, 1994). There is also the Excalibur hotel which is themed in terms of medieval preoccupations such as jousting. Assessing the new mix of hotels, Spanier writes: 'The razzle-dazzle mix of themes – cowboy, circus, medieval, South Seas, Roman, oriental, movies, space age [he might have added ancient Egypt] – might seem garish, outrageous and artificial. But it crackles with fun and energy' (1994: xi). Quite aside from the additional evidence here of time–space compression, we see a further area of dedifferentiation – of hotels and theme parks – that Disney in fact inaugurated (or at least intensified), but which the Las Vegas developers seem determined to take a few stages further. In this last case, there is a further component of dedifferentiation in the collapse of the boundaries not just between hotels and theme parks but between these and gambling casinos. The building of a theme park at Gatwick airport will further blur the boundaries between theme park, airport and shopping mall (Lloyd, 1994).

There are other indicators of dedifferentiation at the Disney parks. In the smiling, helpful 'cast member', Disney aims to create an environment in which work and play are fused, or at least this is the impression presented to the visitor. It has also been suggested that the distinction between actor and audience is broken down as the visitor becomes part of the action in a Disney universe (Apple, 1983). By placing the visitor in settings that look like movie sets (Adventureland buildings and environment for example) or in rides or attractions which derive from Disney films, such as Peter Pan's Flight, 20,000 Leagues Under the Sea, and Dumbo, the Flying Elephant, the distinction between actor and audience is less clear-cut. At Disney–MGM Studios, this effect is even more likely to be pronounced. Urry (1990) notes that a dedifferentiating characteristic of modern tourism is the tendency for entertainment and education to merge, as can be discerned in heritage centres and the like (Walsh, 1992). The Disney theme parks share in this trend in that much that goes on aims to entertain and educate. The history lessons that can be found in the Carousel of Progress or the American Adventure are obvious illustrations of this tendency. However, Rojek (1993a) has argued that there is a clear differentiation in what he calls

167

'Disney culture', a term that refers to all Disney outputs and not just the theme parks. He notes that for the visitor, work and non-work time are clearly differentiated. This was an effect intended by Walt who did not want people to be reminded of the everyday world and therefore work while in the park, hence the concealment of the outside world from view. Rojek also argues that in Disney culture, public and private space are clearly demarcated and that male and female roles are clearly distinguished. We have seen evidence of the latter in Chapter 4, in particular where it was noted that many attractions present very clear distinctions about the roles of men and women.

One area which Rojek describes as providing evidence of de-differentiation is the relationship of the Disney theme parks with the outside world. In doing so, he raises issues about the problematic nature of 'reality' in the world of Disney which will be a specific focus of attention below. Following the reflections of the French social scientist, Baudrillard (1983), Rojek argues that dedifferentiation is evident in that American society is becoming like Disneyland. He quotes Baudrillard's position:

> Disneyland is presented as imaginary in order to make us believe that the rest is real, when in fact all of Los Angeles and the America surrounding it are no longer real, but of the order of the hyperreal and simulation. It is no longer a question of a false representation of reality (ideology), but of concealing the fact that the real is no longer real.
>
> (Baudrillard, 1983: 25)

Rojek argues that the growing emphasis on the spectacular in everyday life (for example, in television presentations and the staging of events for the media) means that the distinctiveness of Disneyland as a site of the spectacular is eroded. In fact, the relationship between Disneyland and Los Angeles is a complex one. Some writers have argued the opposite of that which Baudrillard implies, in that while accepting evidence of dedifferentiation (though they most certainly do not use that term), they see Disneyland as a reflection of Los Angeles. For example, Bierman has argued that four aspects of Disneyland's design can be attributed to the Los Angeles area: 'extreme diversity in design styles, an insistence on fantasy in design, environments that are intended to be experienced in motion, and the involvement of people in the action by moving them through the areas in which it takes place' (1979: 282). Sorkin (1992) has suggested that Fantasyland, Frontierland and Tomorrowland are historic themes which can be 'read' in Los Angeles's understanding of itself. But there is no doubt that Disneyland influenced the surrounding area too. Findlay (1992) notes that Anaheim increasingly adopted a Disney approach to treating visitors to the stadium and convention centre which were built in the wake of Disneyland. A Disney-style approach to grooming, cleanliness, customer service, and vocabulary emerged. Also, Disney urban design motifs are increasingly found in a number of different contexts in the United States, not just in shopping malls, but also in main streets, neighbourhoods and even some whole towns (Warren, 1994). Such trends might be advanced further by the creation of an urban planning consultancy within Disney, though in the case of the redesign of the Seattle Center in Washington state, the company's proposals were widely derided and in the end spurned (Warren, 1994). It is clearly impossible to know where cause and effect lie in all of this, but the general point suggested by Rojek and by Baudrillard, that Disneyland's relationship with the environing area and with America in general can be characterized in terms of dedifferentiation, is compelling. The growth of theming – of malls and of hotels – can only intensify a feeling that reality is catching up with fantasy and that in the process the distinction itself between them collapses. However, although the Disney theme parks exhibit some manifestations of dedifferentiation, there are also clear indications of differentiation.

The problem of reality

A specific aspect of dedifferentiation that has preoccupied postmodernist writers is the dedifferentiation of reality and its representation. In many respects, this is the quintessential preoccupation among such writers. Walt may have been aware of the reality–fantasy elision that he was creating when he rounded on the evangelist, Billy Graham, who described Disneyland as a fantasy while being taken on a tour by Walt. In a possibly apocryphal retort, Walt is supposed to have said:

> You know the fantasy isn't here. This is very real. . . . The park is reality. The people are natural here; they're having a good time; they're communicating. This is what people

169

really are. The fantasy is – out there, outside the gates of Disneyland, where people have hatreds and people have prejudices. It's not really real.

(Quoted in Findlay, 1992: 70)

There is no doubt that people experience reality–fantasy disjunctures at Disney theme parks, as a number of commentators reveal:

'Is this really part of a movie or just another stupid show?' – Eight-year-old visitor to Disney–MGM Studios on encountering a live performance in the park.

(Nelson, 1990: 60)

There is more here [the EPCOT Center] than the entertaining prestidigitation of a wonderland or magic kingdom. It becomes a question of figuring out which side of the looking glass one is on. Three days of careful observation, for instance, were required to determine that the wading birds across the lagoon were living birds.

(Morison, 1983: 78)

Many visitors suspend daily perceptions and judgments altogether, and treat the wonderland environment as more real than real. I saw this happen one morning when walking to breakfast at my Disney Resort Hotel. Two small children were stooped over a small snake that had crawled out on to the sun-warmed path. 'Don't worry, it's rubber,' remarked their mother.

(Willis, 1993: 123)

On the All-America parade float, Cinderella, a young blond woman in a blue gown, repeated four carefully coached, robotlike movements every ten yards or so. Children asked, puzzled, 'Is that lady real?'

(Schultz, 1988: 300)

During my visit with my son and daughter, our fascination with the River Cruise's wildly attenuated distinctions between true and false – the more impressive rocks and trees, in spite of their perfection, as often as not turned out to be genuine – had drawn us back to it again, and a related curiosity sent us on still a third trip . . . to try to determine how much of the helmsman's spiel was a set piece and how much was ad-libbed.

(Wallace, 1963: 113)

At a sitting of the Indiana Jones Stunt Spectacular show, while being chased by fiendish-looking Egyptians, Indie fell and indicated 'cut'. It transpired that he had twisted his ankle and could not continue. A stand-in Indie was brought in. A little girl in front of me asked whether it was part of the show. In fact, it probably was not, since it had not occurred on previous or subsequent sittings of this show that I have attended, but the incident again points to the problem of maintaining a grip on reality (though in this case this was after all a show about the stunts involved in making a film, *Raiders of the Lost Ark*, so where reality was supposed to be in all of this is unclear).

For many visitors, there can be a very real problem of distinguishing the real and the fake, which in part is a testimony to the quality of Disney creativity, but is also a testimony to its potential to grip hold of and distort the visitor's normal perceptual cues. Lash expresses the reality problem for postmodernist writers in the following way:

> Modernism . . . had clearly differentiated and autonomized the roles of signifier, signified, and referent. Postmodernization on the contrary *problematizes* these distinctions, and especially the status and relationship of signifier and referent, or put another way, representation and reality.
>
> (1990: 12, emphasis in original)

For Lash, the pervasiveness of images which float before our eyes, but which have no obvious referent in reality, exemplifies this tendency. Bauman (1992) illustrates this kind of tendency with reference to the media, arguing that they increasingly present the world in terms of dramatic events, many of which are themselves staged for media consumption (such as the staged political rally or the visit of a politician to a hospital in the full glare of the cameras). In this way, the reality that is being represented is problematized (as Lash puts it). We no longer know what the reality is that lies behind the onrush of such images. Jameson uses the evocative phrase 'a breakdown of the signifying chain' (1991: 18) to describe the way in which images become uncoupled from their moorings in reality and become free-floating signifiers in their own right.

Baudrillard's contribution to such explorations is to emphasize the significance within modern society of 'models of a real without origin or reality: a hyperreal' (1983: 2). He draws attention to a process whereby models are fabricated which ostensibly signify a reality, but which in fact have no referent. Such a model is a simulacrum, an 'identical copy for which no original ever existed' (Jameson, 1991: 18). In the process, a hyperreality is constructed, which is forged out of simulacra which do not represent an underlying reality but merely hint at another layer of reality and which are in fact self-referential: they are what they are. They are likely to become reality in their own right: 'the real is not only what can be reproduced, but *that which is always already reproduced*. The hyperreal' (Baudrillard, 1983: 146). In fact, the simulacrum can be viewed as more real than the reality with which it exhibits a tenuous connection. As Michael Eisner put it at the opening of Disney-MGM Studios, the new theme park represents 'the Hollywood that never was and always will be' (in Birnbaum, 1989: 153). The reality/signifier distinction is dissolved, as reality is increasingly apprehended through simulacra – as hyperreality. As the quotation on page 168 specifies, 'the real is no longer real'. The hyperreal is as real as anything else and therefore becomes reality; this seems to operate with regard to the Disney theme parks:

> In both Disneyland and Disneyworld, it is clear that everything [that] can be derived from the imaginary has been caught, represented, made representable, put on display, made visual. Literally putting it on show for consumption without any metaphors is obviously a radical deterrent to the imaginary. Once again, Utopia becomes reality.
>
> (Baudrillard, 1993b: 246)

Baudrillard writes as though experiments like the Disney parks act as models for American society. He refers to Coney Island at the turn of the century, where one could find 'the craziest, the most demented architectural endeavours' (1993b: 246), which were then transplanted in Manhattan. Something similar occurs with the Disney parks: 'Just as the whole of American society is built in Disneyland's image, so the whole of American society is conducting, in real time and in the open air, the same experiment as Biosphere 2, which is therefore a fake experiment, just as Disneyland is a fake imaginary' (1993b: 249–50). Thus, the fake worlds of the Disney parks, which represent a non-existent reality, become models for American society, so that a hyperreal America is being constructed which is based on a simulacrum.

The simulacrum of the Disney parks is finally enjoined with reality, in the form of the hyperreality forged in the simulacrum's image.

Baudrillard's ideas are almost wantonly provocative and slippery, but it would be a grave mistake to dismiss what he has to say. His notions of the Disney parks as simulacra which stand for something that does not exist and of American society as catching up with the parks, signs of which have been referred to here in the Disneyfication of malls and hotels, are important for understanding the (hyper)reality of the Disney parks. Thus, when Bill Bryson writes of Euro Disneyland that it is 'the world as it should be' (1993: 16), he is in fact encapsulating Baudrillard's ideas: part model of something which does not exist; part model of something that might exist. As Eco (1986) suggests, the relentless quest for verisimilitude at the Disney parks results in admiration for the fake and stimulation of the desire for it. It does not matter that we recognize that there is fakery when we visit the park because we know that perfection has been achieved and that reality will only disappoint us.

The chief message to be drawn from this excursus into the writings of a number of writers whose work on the reality/fake distinction has been construed as exhibiting postmodernist motifs is that reality and its signifiers have become dedifferentiated. Fjellman (1992) suggests that even though people can distinguish the real from the fake, they do not greatly care about the distinction and in fact often revel in signs of artificiality. Certainly, there is much to lend credence to the idea of the theme parks as regions of hyperreality. Main Street, USA, for example, exaggerates desirable elements and eliminates negative ones to produce a model which has no basis as an entity in reality. The images of the past presented in many attractions provide iconic images which model a past that did not happen. The attention to superficial detail (such as the faces of well-known figures in Audio-Animatronic form) merely serves to conceal the unreality that lies beneath. On the other hand, there is much that is real in the Disney parks. Discovery Island has real animals. Real birds and insects (and apparently snakes) appear. There are real trees and flowers. There are real entertainers. But in the main, it is the unreal, the fabricated, that tends to be the most memorable.

Fjellman (1992) argues that the reality/fake distinction is too simplistic when applied to Disney World, arguing for a fourfold distinction between the real real, the real fake, the fake real and the fake fake. These distinctions are not easy to apprehend, but the main point to be made is that, from the point of view of writers like Baudrillard, the more crucial issue is that reality and its representation become decoupled. In effect, this means that the notion of permutations of reality and fakery proposed by Fjellman loses some of its conceptual strength, since what matters is that images float before the visitor's eyes that have an apparent origin in reality but have lost their moorings in that reality and have become a self-referential reality or hyperreality. It is this uncertainty about what constitutes reality in the Disney parks that is the source of the confusions cited by various commentators at the beginning of this section. The main consideration in this section has been to take up the suggestion that the Disney theme parks share with the postmodernist sensibility a sense of models as standing for themselves rather than for a reality that prompted them into being. It is possibly in this area that postmodernist ideas make their greatest contribution to an understanding of the nature of the Disney parks.

THE DISNEY THEME PARKS AS POST-TOURISM

This section has two main purposes. One is to relate the Disney theme-park experience to suggestions that there has been a growth of what a number of writers have called 'post-tourism', a disposition among tourists that departs from the preoccupations which they have exhibited in earlier years. This notion of 'post-tourism' is not especially central to postmodernist writings, but it has been connected to them by writers like Urry (1990), and since tourism has a fairly obvious relevance to the Disney parks, it warrants a brief discussion. Second, in addressing this topic, issues that derive from a limited number of ideas stemming from the social scientific study of tourism will be touched on and related to the Disney parks.

One of the most significant theses in the study of tourism in relatively recent years is MacCannell's (1976) discussion of the motives and quests of 'the tourist'. MacCannell portrays the modern predicament as one pervaded by alienation from and disenchantment with the world. Tourists, that is 'sightseers, mainly middle-class, who are at this moment deployed throughout the entire world in search of experience' (1976: 1), engage in tourism to come to terms with their predicament. Through tourism, people embark on a quest for authenticity, to seek meaning in foreign places in their natural, unadulterated state. However, they are invariably thwarted in their quest, since they are unable to penetrate the 'back regions' to which they travel. Instead, they are nudged into the front region where they encounter what MacCannell calls 'staged authenticity' – settings and experiences that are contrived by tourism authorities to give the semblance of authenticity. But participants invariably recognize that they have not infiltrated the real thing. In their failure to make contact with the truly authentic, tourists experience 'touristic shame' which is based on 'not being tourist enough, on a failure to see everything the way it "ought" to be seen' (1976: 10).

It is difficult to see how the Disney theme park visitor fits into this cluster of ideas, and it is precisely around this kind of problem that criticisms of MacCannell's ideas have revolved. Is it appropriate to characterize tourists as engaged in a quest for authenticity? When Schudson (1979) asked this question, his answer was bitingly simple – some do and some do not. In fact, MacCannell focuses on a particular kind of tourism and its attendant motivations; he glorifies the tourist, in spite of his attempt to have the opposite effect. MacCannell railed against Boorstin's (1961) opprobrious depiction of the tourist as a passive seeker of superficial pleasures, which was contrasted with a eulogizing portrayal of the traveller as an active seeker of real experiences. Instead, MacCannell suggested that the tourist *is* an active seeker of real experiences, but is regularly obstructed in his or her pursuit. But in presenting his stimulating revision of the nature of the tourist, MacCannell substituted a one-dimensional panegyric. As Cohen (1979), Gottlieb (1982) and others have suggested, there are in fact different types of tourist, and MacCannell's view of the tourist can be seen as either one type of tourist or as a characterization that overlaps with the different types which have been conceptually and empirically derived. Two of the five modes of tourist experiences delineated by Cohen, seem to come closer to the kind of experience represented by a Disney theme park. One is the 'recreational mode' in which tourists engage in a variety of playful experiences to restore their 'mental and physical powers' and to emerge with 'a general sense of well-being' (Cohen, 1979: 183). The other is the 'diversionary mode' which is evident in 'mere escape from the boredom and meaninglessness of routine, everyday existence, into the forgetfulness of a vacation' (ibid.: 185–6). Whereas the recreational mode also represents a break from routine, it does so in the spirit of a reaffirmation of the tourist's existence, to return refreshed; the diversionary mode is more of an escape to make everyday life tolerable. What is crucial to tourists, according to Urry (1990), is not a quest for authenticity, but that they are able to gaze on objects which are distinctively different from their normal everyday lives, and of course this is precisely the kind of encounter that the tourist industry is keen to engender.

Elements of these two modes of tourist experience can be discerned in the notion of the 'post-tourist' which has gained some currency. Feifer (1985) portrays post-tourists as self-conscious in their pursuit of a variety of diversions and as not being encumbered by lofty motives in their quest for self-realization through pleasure – however it comes. Feifer portrays the post-tourist in the following terms: 'Now he wants to behold something sacred; now something informative, to broaden him; now something beautiful, to lift him up and make him finer; and now something different, because he's bored' (1985: 269). The post-tourist 'has a humorous eye for "kitsch"' (ibid.: 270) and can be whizzed from one attraction to another without worrying about the interconnections between them or their decontexualized presentation. But above all

> the post-tourist knows that he is a tourist: not a time-traveller when he goes to stay somewhere historic; not an instant noble savage when he stays on a tropical beach; not an invisible observer when he visits a native compound. Resolutely 'realistic', he cannot evade his condition of outsider. But having embraced that condition, he can stop struggling against it.
>
> (Feifer, 1985: 271)

Thus, post-tourism is realistic and not encumbered by a conscience of higher motives, in the manner of MacCannell's tourist. Indeed, touristic shame is not likely to be significant for post-tourists in the way in which MacCannell describes it. Instead, touristic shame is likely to inhere in a failure to have fun and to be enjoined by the multiplicity of experiences placed for their delectation. The 'staging' which distresses MacCannell's tourist is part of the tourist landscape for post-tourists who revel in the quantity and quality of the fabricated artefacts and contrived experiences placed before them. Disappointment arises not from the constructed nature of the tourist experience, but when the props do not live up to expectation.

Urry (1990), Featherstone (1991) and Rojek (1993b) see the notion of post-tourism as interesting because its differences from conventional tourism (whatever that might be) signal aspects of the postmodernist world-view. Rojek identifies three key elements. First, post-tourists are not dismayed by the tendency for the tourist experience to be turned into a commodity that can be bought and sold. Instead of the tourist's contempt for commercialism, post-tourists have their tongues firmly planted in their cheeks. Second, for the post-tourist the tourist experience is an end in itself. Third, post-tourists relish being bombarded with a plethora of spectacular signs placed before them, as well as the accoutrements of tourism – 'the gift shops, the eating places, the tourist coaches and other tourists' (Rojek, 1993b: 177). In these descriptions of the world-view of post-tourists can be seen indicators of the postmodernist sensibility – the predilection for pastiche, the translation of tourism into consumption, and the barrage of signs presented to us as staged spectacles in which we are ensnared. These notions seem to offer more to an understanding of the Disney theme parks than the portrayal of tourism as revealed in the quest for authenticity. In other words, the Disney visitor is presented with a landscape which conforms much more to the perspective of the post-tourist; indeed, that landscape may well have played a prominent role in stimulating the attitude of the post-tourist.

MacCannell's ideas do not relate well to the Disney parks. We could take the view that much of what is encountered at the parks is authentic fantasy (authentic because it reflects and is consistent with the Disney version of fantasy), but this is not very helpful as an adaptation of his position. The fact that in World Showcase visitors are confronted with inauthentic buildings is irrelevant because in a sense they have gone there to marvel at their inauthenticity. But there is more to it than that, because the buildings are better than the authentic, since they are not surrounded by litter or by other buildings that might ruin the effect. These are not very promising connections, and it is significant that MacCannell (1976) makes very few references to the Disney parks. Ironically, the perspective that he railed against in his book, Boorstin's (1961) view that American tourists delight in 'pseudo-events' rather than the reality behind them, comes closer to the theme-park experience. Boorstin argued that in order to accommodate Americans' preferences, tourist authorities pander to tourists by contriving events and settings for their consumption. These pseudo-events represent the cultures and settings that the tourist seeks to avoid. They give the sense of having been to a place without the risks and inconvenience of actually doing so. MacCannell rejected these suggestions by saying that his evidence did not support the notion that 'tourists want superficial, contrived experiences' but instead yearn for authenticity (1976: 104). Yet the idea of pseudo-events, while by no means isomorphic with the attractions of the Disney parks, seems to be more congruent with the theme park experience. Boorstin viewed Disneyland as an illustration of an extreme and increasingly prominent form of pseudo-event – the tourist attraction which has no function other than being a tourist attraction.

The Disney parks provide playgrounds for the emergent post-tourist and to that extent exhibit a further aspect of postmodern taste. Through their cultivation of excitement, their presentation of soundbites of history (and the future), and their fabrication of simulacra which are better than their original referents and exhibit impossible juxtapositions, an environment is created in which 'the post-tourist emphasis on playfulness, variety and self-consciousness' (Urry, 1990: 101) can be given full rein. There is no sense of the touristic shame that suffuses MacCannell's tourist when he or she is outwitted in a vain attempt to go behind the scenes; at the Disney parks what you see is what you get and people go there knowing pretty well what they will be getting. Indeed, as many as 80 per cent of visitors have been before (Rojek, 1993b). But the Disney parks have also played an enormous role in fostering environments within which post-tourism can flourish. One writer on heritage centres has written:

> There is no doubt that the development of many heritage attractions owes a great deal to Disney, both in terms of the media employed, and the style and systems of organization developed in the Disney parks. Many heritage attractions are often considered as striving to attain the 'Disney effect' – sites of fantastic spectacle, with an emphasis on titillation, rather than education.
>
> (Walsh, 1992: 97)

Thus, while the Disney theme parks share in and provide a setting for the acting out of post-tourism, they are also in a vanguard and have prompted a huge growth in theme parks (Eyssartel and Rochette, n.d.), as well as influencing the form and character of a variety of leisure forms, such as heritage centres and museums (King, 1991; Terrell, 1991), along with hotels, casinos and shopping malls as discussed above. However, once again we have to remind ourselves not to lose historical perspective in making this kind of assessment. The Midway at the 1893 Exhibition and Coney Island's parks exhibited many attractions in which the post-tourist would have felt very comfortable. In fact, the element of playfulness, which Urry mentions in the quotation at the beginning of this paragraph, was more pronounced at Coney Island's Steeplechase Park than at the Disney parks (Kasson, 1978), but took the form of an exuberant playfulness, rather than the more reflective playfulness of the Disney parks. Thus, our assessment of the Disney parks as sites of post-tourism and hence of post-modernism has to be tempered by a recognition of their precursors in an age in which tourism was barely developed and accessible, let alone post-tourism. Equally, these reflections point to potential limitations with the idea of post-tourism, at least when it is viewed as a distinctively new approach to tourism.

FURTHER REFLECTIONS ON POSTMODERNISM

In this final and brief section, I want to address three aspects of postmodernism that do not require detailed discussion. First, postmodernist writers often reject linear notions of time and hence of progress. Harvey, for example, writes: 'Eschewing the idea of progress, postmodernism abandons all sense of historical continuity and memory' (1989: 54). Time is viewed in the postmodernist world-view as indeterminate and not associated with a notion of progress. Such notions of time are seen as constructs which limit human choice. While attractions at the Disney parks frequently distort history and give strange continuities between events, there is no doubt that, as earlier chapters have shown, attractions typically operate with a profound sense of progress and hence of linear time. There is a strong commitment to the idea of technological progress, while characterizations of the past, which invariably project us into the future too, are imbued with a sense of progress and of linear time. These tendencies can be seen in attractions like Carousel of Progress, World of Motion and Spaceship Earth, all of which, as befit their corporate sponsors, extol the contributions of the past and boost our confidence in a future which will build on them. The American Adventure projects an image of constant progress in which we learn from our mistakes, so that we can be confident in the future. Thus, the tone of the Disney parks is definitely not postmodernist in this respect.

A second postmodernist idea, which is related to the previous one and is most strongly linked to Lyotard (1984), is the notion that, in postmodern settings, what are referred to as 'meta-narratives' lose their credibility. Thus, metanarratives such as Marxism, psychoanalysis and positivism are no longer relevant because they are based on linear views of time and because they rule out the credibility of alternative schemes. Metanarratives will gradually give way to competing and equally credible micro-narratives, out of which much greater inventiveness emerges. Lyotard states: 'invention is always born of dissension. Postmodern knowledge . . . refines our sensitivity to differences and reinforces our ability to tolerate the incommensurable' (1984: xxv). Metanarratives merely undermine innovation by restricting the questioning of fundamental tenets. They generate all-inclusive accounts of the world which are incompatible with the post-modernist ethos of fragmentation and miscellany. This ethos revels in the incommensurable rather than the (as its representatives see it) artificial intellectual coherence of metanarratives which close off alternative ways of approaching problems. When the Disney parks are examined in these terms, their credentials as cathedrals of postmodernity again look unpromising. The parks are, as we have seen, chockfull of metanarratives, such as the desirability of capitalism and the corporation, of the traditional nuclear family, of self-realization through consumption, of conquest and of technological progress.

The third issue has to do with the nature of organizations under postmodernism. Some writers, most notably Clegg (1990), have sought to characterize the kind of organization that will be emblematic of postmodernity. This is a contentious intellectual pursuit since it could itself be accused of dwelling on precisely the notions of historical continuity and metanarrative from which many postmodernist thinkers shrink. Writers on postmodernism in relation to organizations typically depict them as recoiling from the emphases on rationality, strong centres of power, tough leadership, hierarchy, and structure that are viewed as character-istic of organizations under modernism (Gergen, 1992). When the views of writers such as Clegg (1990), Gergen (1992), Heydebrand (1989), and Cooke (1990) concerning the attributes of organiz-ations under postmodernity are placed together, we find that they are supposed to exhibit a greater emphasis on the following dimensions when contrasted with their counterparts under modernity: diffusion of strategic functions, empowerment, flexible skills, trust, and informality. These changes are supposed to represent a drift away from the arch-modernist emphases on control and rationality in managing modern organizations. More-over, in so far as postmodernism is indicative of a trend towards 'post-Fordism', we would expect there to be less standardization of product than under the modernist impulse of Fordism. However, as we have seen from discussions of work at the Disney parks, there is tight control of the work process through manuals, supervision and the introduction of new recruits to the Disney corporate culture. Work roles are clearly articulated and are sym-bolized by contrasting uniforms. The Disney workers collude with the technological wizardry and structures of the parks in turning out a predictable and hence standardized product for the visitor. Work routines are highly structured and rationalized to turn out a relatively homogeneous theme-park experience. Rather than a site of postmodern organization, the Disney parks are characterized by control and predictability (see Chapter 5) and by rationality in terms of both their management and their product. There is little of the informal, high-trust environment for an empowered workforce that is the focus of attention for writers touched by the postmodern world-view.

Further, while it is difficult to derive concrete information about management and work at the wider Disney organization, the discussion in Chapter 2 reveals little of the postmodernist expectations about these new forms of organization. Walt's heirs seem to have built on the centralized, rationalized approach to organization that he created, with high levels of control over the organization of work and of specialization of skill. There has continued to be a concentration of strategic functions at the upper echelons, tight control of work (such as the control over scripts and production referred to in Chapter 2), and clear differentiation of functions. However, Disney can be said to exhibit a vestige of postmodern organization in one respect suggested by Alvesson

(1990). Alvesson suggests that there is a growing concern among organizations to massage their images, and that mere success or management actions are not enough to convey impressions. He argues that this preoccupation with the organization's image rather than with its substantive performance corresponds to the fixation with images, mediated by the mass media, that is a feature of postmodernity. In this respect, Disney has almost since its inception been a postmodern organization. We saw in Chapter 1 how Walt used the popular interest in him to create the image of a happy-go-lucky organization full of satisfied workers beavering away at their craft. He was regularly depicted as uninterested in business affairs and in personal wealth, and in so doing, he and the organization came to be seen as a place of fantasy and imagination rather than operating in the realm of business and financial considerations. The Eisner–Wells era is associated with a restoration of this sense of kids having fun. Meanwhile, the theme parks heavily disguise their commercial intent. In this respect, through the manipulation of the company's image and that of the theme parks to create the impression of fun and fantasy, thereby shoving the substance of business to the sidelines, Disney has been a proto-postmodernist organization.

CONCLUSION

The aim of this chapter has been to take some of the prominent dimensions in postmodernist writing or in writing about postmodernism to determine how far the Disney parks, and to some extent the Disney organization, measure up as sites of postmodernity. The justification for this exercise has largely been in terms of the prominence of postmodernism within the social sciences and intellectual discussion in recent years and the allusion to the Disney parks as sites of postmodernism. In the event, the parks are congruent with postmodernism in some respects, such as the emphasis on pastiche and image, the idea of the post-tourist and some aspects of dedifferentiation; but not in others, such as the persistence of metanarratives and of linear views of history. The point has also been made that the existence of early indications of Disneyesque features at the 1893 Exhibition and at Coney Island render the exercise somewhat problematic, since they predate the era with which postmodernism is associated, though it has to be pointed out that some postmodernists reject the identification of postmodernity with a specific period or epoch.

In the end, the exercise is somewhat inconclusive, but that is perhaps a singularly apt conclusion from the perspective of postmodernism. But in considering these issues, a number of interesting aspects of the Disney theme parks have been brought to the fore. One of the advantages of taking a postmodernist perspective on the Disney theme parks is that it provides a framework which allows the investigator to approach them in terms which are broadly congruent with the parks' aims and ethos. In particular, the representation of the post-tourist which has been developed under the general rubric of postmodernism seems to provide a more fruitful way of understanding Disney tourism than earlier, somewhat elitist characterizations of tourists. Thus, the discussion of the parks within postmodernism has also served a pragmatic purpose, of which most postmodernists would doubtless disapprove, allowing certain areas of interest and significance to be drawn out.

9

THE BUSINESS OF FANTASY

The vast majority of the commentators whose thoughts and ideas about the Disney parks have been examined (not to mention my own contributions in this regard) have essentially entailed treating the parks as texts. Each writer has sought to unravel the parks' messages. As suggested in Chapter 4, the various writers have offered remarkably congruent accounts. This is not to say that each writer has delineated all the themes that have been covered in the preceding five chapters – this is manifestly not the case. Instead, the themes articulated and often the inferences drawn by each writer have typically overlapped with some themes and inferences associated with other authors. In spite of often quite divergent theoretical stances and projects, there is very little evidence of disagreement or incongruity between them. However, in the view of some writers the kind of textual analysis undertaken by these many writers, as well as my examination of their work and my own observations, is fatally flawed, because of its failure to take into account the perspectives of visitors to the parks and it is to this issue that I now turn.

THE AUTHORITY OF THE VISITOR

According to a viewpoint within cultural and communication studies that took root in the early 1980s, the problem with such a reliance on texts is that it fails to encapsulate the meanings attributed by audiences to the texts. This would mean that it is necessary to gain access to visitors in order to determine what consumers of the Disney theme-park experience make of the parks' texts. The ideas of Stuart Hall and the Centre for Contemporary Cultural Studies at the University of Birmingham are often presented as the chief impetus for this line of thinking. Hall (1980) argued that a text's 'preferred reading' (the meaning intended by its author or producer) may be subverted by an alternative reading (referred to as 'decoding') when it is consumed by an audience. If this occurs a 'negotiated' reading of the text might be generated in which audience members adapt the text's meaning, or an oppositional reading might be engendered which is at substantial variance with the preferred reading. Of course, the decoding by audiences may agree with the preferred reading, but the point is that without an examination of audience reception we do not know.

Morley (1980), a member of the Birmingham group, produced an influential study based on audience reactions to *Nationwide*, a British news and magazine television programme. He noted considerable diversity in the way in which the programme was interpreted and that this diversity could not be explained in terms of the differential socio-economic position of the focus groups that watched the programme and reported their reflections. Since Morley's study, there has been a veritable industry of studies of audience reactions to soap operas, news programmes, romantic fiction, rock videos, and various other sites of popular culture. The approach has been variously called 'active audience theory' (Morley, 1993), 'cultural populism' (McGuigan, 1992), and 'the new revisionism' (Curran, 1990). Its chief message is that audiences are active in the interpretation of texts and that texts are invariably 'polysemic' (that is, capable of more than one interpretation). This means that audiences can and often do engender interpretations other than those intended and that they will often differ from critics. The perspective is optimistic in tone since it views audiences as comprising 'critical, active viewers and listeners, not cultural dopes manipulated by the media' (Budd *et al.*, 1990: 170). In some of the more extreme formulations (such as Fiske, 1989), audiences come across as a resistance movement successfully resisting the ideological onslaughts of the mass media and of popular culture. Such an optimistic tone contrasted sharply with the gloomy tenor of suggestions that the media and popular culture were the instruments of a power elite which suffused people in a dominant ideology which they are incapable of resisting.

There is very little in the discussions of the Disney parks about how their messages are received. Real (1977) administered a questionnaire to Disneyland visitors, but this research sheds little light on the degree to which there is resistance and the formulation of negotiated or alternative understandings of the park and its constituents. The research method also differs greatly from the intensive, qualitative research framework within which most audience reception research has been situated. There are hints of resistance in other writings. Kuenz writes: 'It's easy to spot those who come to Disney World just to make a point of their alienation from it. There aren't many but they are there' (1993: 66). Willis (1993) suggests that people with negative views about the Disney parks can buy goods from a Disney Villains Shop, which can be found at Disney World and which stocks what she calls 'bad-guy merchandise'. However, in doing so they are buying Disney goods and are thereby fully implicated in the parks' construction of the visitor as a consumer. Sutton (1992: 284) suggests that some visitors to Disneyland experience and remember mainly negative emotions about the park. He argues that these are people 'who visit Disneyland unwillingly who are not part of a social context that embraces traditional American values'. These sets of reflections point to a small number of visitors for whom the Disney parks are less than enchanting. The implication is that they are small in number but, more importantly, there is no indication that they or anybody else decodes the parks in ways that differ from the parks' preferred reading, or more accurately, from the readings proffered by the various writers covered in this book. On the other hand, the active-audience approach raises the possibility that many visitors offer different interpretations from the commentators covered in this book or resist the messages that the commentators have decoded. However, the mere presence of an oppositional interpretation, such as that denoted by the illustrations from Willis, Kuenz, and Sutton, should not be taken to indicate that there is a variety of interpretation of the kind signalled by the active-audience approach. Rejection of the Disney messages may well be a rejection of exactly the same messages as those endorsed by those who willingly accept the Disney theme-park experience.

However, at the time of writing the ground seems to be shifting somewhat against the active-audience perspective which is being criticized on a number of grounds, of which two stand out. First, some writers have suggested that the ability of audiences to construct their own meanings of texts is much more restricted than the active-audience perspective allows for. Condit (1989) examined the accounts by two people (Jack and Jill) of an episode of the American television series *Cagney and Lacey* in which abortion was a focal ingredient. She found that Jack and Jill differed over many areas but that they 'shared a basic construction of the denotations of the text' and that there was 'nothing in their responses to suggest that they did not share a basic understanding of the story line or even of what the program was trying to convey' (Condit, 1989: 107). Condit argues that there may be a tendency for active audience researchers to exaggerate the extent and significance of alternative readings of texts. In other words, there may be limits to the polysemic qualities of texts.

A similar suggestion comes from Corner *et al.* (1990) who studied the responses of different groups to television programmes concerning the nuclear industry and nuclear energy. Each group was of a specific 'type' so that there were groups of Labour Party supporters, Conservative Party supporters, the unemployed, Friends of the Earth supporters, nuclear industry supporters, a women's discussion group, arts students, chemistry students, and so on. The potential for variety in interpretation between the groups was great. While areas of divergence between the groups could be found, there were also areas of substantial common ground. For example, the authors note that discussion groups were in agreement over the perception of one of the programmes as involving a recognition of 'uncertainty and inconclusiveness – played off against the industry's claims of near-absolute certainty' and a sub-text of 'inferences of danger, particularly through the use of visual images' (Corner *et al.*, 1990: 97–8). While the groups evaluated the messages differently, they were agreed on what the programme was attempting to convey. They agreed about the unsatisfactory nature of one of the other programmes and about the 'interpretative difficulty' of another. As with Condit's (1989) Jack and Jill, Corner *et al.* point to areas of fundamental interpretative convergence between their groups in spite of the very different stances that were held of the nuclear industry. A similar finding of fundamental convergence in interpretation was found by Barker (1993) in his examination of readers of the science fiction comic *2000 AD*.

A second criticism, which it is interesting to note has been voiced by some exponents of the active-audience perspective (e.g. Ang, 1990; Morley, 1993) as well as by its critics (for example,

McGuigan, 1992), is that the proliferation of microscopic studies of audience reactions to texts has led to a neglect of wider processes of political economy. An emphasis on the political economy of the media and cultural products fell into disfavour in the 1980s because of its association with two crimes at the level of theoretical elaboration: one crime was the postulate of a dominant ideology with the accompanying notion of the media and popular culture as organs of the ruling class; the other was the crime of economic reductionism, whereby characteristics of media texts and practices are treated as simple products of economic forces. However, a number of writers seem to be giving matters of political-economic context greater attention. Ang (1990), for example, argues that while it is appropriate to study the power of an audience to subvert the meaning of a text, the marginality of that power relative to the wider framework of power relationships within society has to be conceded. Similarly, Morley bemoans the 'neglect of all questions concerning the economic, political and ideological forces acting on the construction of texts' (1993: 15).

Just as damaging, however, is a third problem with the active-audience approach which has special reference to the present analysis of the Disney parks, namely, that the perspective can only address audiences' readings or decodings of what is actually in the text. The approach cannot readily examine audience reactions to the silences in a text, at least not without being very demanding about the kinds of analysis that audiences are expected to undertake. An audience analysis of how people respond to one of EPCOT's corporate-inspired images of history or progress might find that people respond to its messages with a pinch of salt, that they are not very serious about it, or that they offer alternative interpretations of it. But they will not be able to interpret Disney versions of conflict, of war, of minorities, of ecological problems, of dissent, of poverty, of feminism, of alternatives to capitalism, or of city life, simply because these and many other spheres are largely absent, as noted in Chapter 6. While some omissions might surface in the audience's mind, these are likely to be limited. Thus, the inability to address the many silences at the Disney parks will limit the utility of an audience reception analysis, since, as this list suggests, this is not a collection of marginally important omissions.

ECONOMIC CONSIDERATIONS

Returning to the issues of political economy, the various writers covered in this book have provided in relation to the Disney theme parks the germs of an approach of the kind advocated by Ang (1990), Morley (1993) and McGuigan (1992) – an implicit political economy approach. It does not seem too far-fetched to see many of the themes delineated in previous chapters in terms of Disney's relationship with other corporations and its status as a media conglomerate in its own right. The extolling of the corporation, of consumerism, of technological progress, and of individualism has much to do with the propagation of ideals that are in Disney's self-interest and that of the companies with which it is associated. This includes companies which act as sponsors of exhibits and attractions (General Electric, AT&T, American Express, Coca-Cola, Exxon, General Motors, etc.) but also companies which act as sponsors or partners of the parks in general (such as American Express, IBM and French Telecom at Euro Disneyland). Equally, these themes represent a world-view that is likely to be consistent with the predominantly middle-class clientele that the parks serve. For them, a diet of such themes confirms their world-view and their commitments. That these are messages that can be discerned in the Disney parks would be less significant were it not for the fact that they are owned by a huge media conglomerate which is able to pump out outputs in a variety of different media that reinforce and are reinforced by the themes noted in the theme parks. For Debord (1994 [1967]), the link between what he calls 'the spectacle' and its economic location is inescapable. He wrote, for example: 'The language of the spectacle is composed of *signs* of the dominant organization of production' (1994: 13). But as has been noted in Chapters 1 and 2, the realm of the economic and of business are continually muffled in the world of Disney.

The themes that have been described in this and earlier chapters receive reinforcement from other Disney media. Consumption, individualism and a eulogizing of the middle class can be found in Disney comics (Andrae, 1988; Dorfman and Mattelart, 1975). Writing about different Disney outputs, Giroux, in line with many of the writers discussed in earlier chapters, refers to them as presenting 'a notion of choice that is attached to the proliferation of commodities' and 'a cultural universe that is largely conservative in its values, colonial in its production of racial differences, and middle class in its portrayal of family values' (1994: 87). Many of these themes are repeated in Giroux's analysis of Touchstone Pictures films and in particular of *Pretty Woman*, the fairytale story of a prostitute who is saved by a wealthy businessman:

> The pervasive symbol of ideological unification through which Disney defines its view of capitalism, gender, and national identity is the family. In this case, the white, nuclear, middle-class family becomes the ethical referent for linking consumerism, gender roles, motherhood, and class chivalry.
>
> (Giroux, 1994: 98)

As Schiller observes, it is the 'panoply of cultural means *together*' (1989: 151 – original emphasis) that is critical to the capacity of large media conglomerates to present a world-view which bolsters and reinforces their position in the modern economic system and that system itself. How far audiences are actively able to inscribe their own interpretations into media texts when they receive a common message from the different products of a media conglomerate (and in all probability from other media conglomerates too) has to be questioned. It is not the single media text that is crucial, as implied by proponents of the active-audience approach, but the extent to which mutually reinforcing messages are capable of succumbing to the supposed guerrilla tactics of audiences. Moreover, in getting across the larger political-economic themes associated with capitalism, corporations, consumerism and so on, Disney's technical wizardry and capacity to present *the* view has to be acknowledged. It has long been recognized that Walt's versions of fairy-tale classics became in most people's minds the way in which they conceptualized those classics in the future. The point was made well in a BBC1 television programme *Disney: The Fairy Tale Years* in which Glen Keane, Supervising Animator for *Beauty and the Beast*, remarked about the responsibility of developing Disney characters:

> The intimidating thing about it, when you're going to do a Disney character, a Disney heroine, a Disney something that's classic like a fairy-tale character, the Disney version becomes the definitive version. Nobody remembers what Snow White and the Seven Dwarfs looked like before Disney's

version of them. And now kids will grow up thinking *that* is Beast, but he wasn't that way for quite a while.[1]

Thus, the power of the Disney text has much to do with its technical mastery in presenting apparently definitive accounts of its subject matter.

A further role of the Disney world-view is that it delivers audiences unto corporations for advertising their goods.[2] A number of writers have noted the various tie-ins between films and consumer products (deCordova, 1994; Eckert, 1978; Wasko *et al.*, 1993). Wasko *et al.* have noted the growing use of 'product placements' in Hollywood movies, whereby products appear in films and represent a covert form of advertising for which corporations pay. According to Wasko *et al.*, Disney is one of five movie companies known to be heavily involved in product placement activity: in *Pretty Woman*, there were 18 brand-name references. The sponsors and various companies that associate themselves with the Disney theme parks are similarly having audiences created for their products, not necessarily in the sense of an audience for specific products (though this too occurs, as in Future World's World in Motion and in the speciality shops in World Showcase) but for their corporate identities, hence the remark quoted on page 145 of the General Electric executive who praised Disney's ability to present the company 'dramatically, memorably, and favorably to the public' (Wallace, 1985: 43). Indeed, companies are happy to associate themselves with Disney because of its generally revered status within US culture, hence their preparedness in the early years of the Eisner–Wells era to spend vast sums on new EPCOT pavilions ($92 million by Metropolitan Life for the Wonders of Life) and to renegotiate existing agreements with respect to both pavilions and partnership agreements, such as Delta's replacement of the then ailing Eastern Airlines as official Disney World carrier, a ten-year agreement worth $40 million to Disney (Grover, 1991: 78).

Such interconnections with other corporations takes place against a backcloth of motifs at the Disney theme parks which are highly supportive of the system within which the corporations operate. Thus, there seems to be a definite association between the heavy presence of corporations at the Disney theme parks and the motifs of consumerism, the value of corporations, individualism, capitalism, and so on, that the various commentators have gleaned

191

from their analyses. These motifs, moreover, reinforce the world-view of the white, middle-class visitors who represent their clientele. Similarly, Zukin points out that Disney World relies on 'explicit ties between culture and economy and between middle-class consumers and global corporations' (1991: 273). Nor can these associations be readily dismissed as a clinical paranoia or as a type of conspiracy theory, since it is difficult to find in the parks motifs that are inconsistent with such associations. In other words, there is little to suggest that values *inimical* to consumer-ism, individualism, capitalism, corporations, and the white middle class are being portrayed. Problems stemming from corporate activity are sometimes acknowledged (as in The Land), but are depicted as being solved; blacks and native Americans appear as symbols rather than as representatives of beliefs; and working-class labour is all but ignored. This is not to say that there is a total coherence in the Disney world-view. Two inconsistencies have been hinted at in the book. One is that there is a deliberate cultivation of nostalgia which is coupled with a panegyric to the past. Since nostalgia is often laced with melancholy and a sense of loss (Turner, 1987), it is difficult to see how the past can simul-taneously be extolled as it certainly is at the parks. If the past is so great, there would have to be something wrong by implication with the present, but the commitment to the status quo in the parks strikes a positive note about the present as well. In part, the tension is overcome by sanitizing the past, but it is never fully reconciled.

A second tension is between the commitment to individualism and to the corporation. Corporations can be viewed as antipath-etic to individualism since they seek to subsume individual action within a system. It is the corporation that is working on our behalf to solve the ecological problems of the past that The Land identifies, not individuals. It is corporations that are the business heroes of modern and future capitalism, not individuals. It is corporations that are developing wondrous technologies, not individuals. And as Zukin (1991) observes, even progress becomes a corporate product. In fact, the vision of Disney World is distinctly anti-individualist. As one writer puts it: 'competitors and parasites (which is to say, other free-entrepreneurs) are kept miles away' (Harrington, 1979: 37), a posture which is em-blematic of the quest for control identified in Chapter 5. Walt's life-story may be a paean to individualism, an Horatio Alger story of overcoming all odds to achieve success, in which he repeatedly sought to cede as little control as possible to others after his misfortune with Oswald the Lucky Rabbit, but it also represents a story of the building of a corporation which, through its control over copyrights, land and contracts, celebrates an individualism that it keeps at bay.

These reflections raise the political-economic context of the Disney parks in order to show how a concentration on the audience reception of their varied attractions would occlude forces which engender a distinctive set of themes and messages which have been the subject of Part II. Since these themes and messages are consistent with other Disney media and, if Schiller (1989) is to be believed, with other media conglomerates, it is the reception of these messages in total and in tandem which is crucial, not simply those of the parks *per se*. These reflections about political economy differ from the largely discredited 'dominant ideology' thesis[3] in that their purpose is not to suggest that the Disney world-view provides the tools whereby a dominant social stratum legitimates itself, but that there is a clear association between the interests of the company and its corporate sponsors at the parks, the white middle class who are its typical clientele, and the Disney world-view, as represented in the themes that have been articulated in this book. Themes which are consistent with the interests of corporations and the white middle class tend to be given particular integrity, while those which are inimical to their interests are either ignored or are conveyed as having less integrity.

Nor are these connections indicative of economic reductionism, since the wider political-economic factors that have been identified are presented as merely restricting the range of variation in the setting of the themes discussed here. The political-economic context constrains but does not determine the forms that the themes comprise.[4] Indeed, there are many attractions which have not been touched on in this book or have been mentioned only fleetingly, since they are not specifically indicative of these motifs. Peter Pan's Flight and 20,000 Leagues Under the Sea, for example, do not connect with many of the points made by commentators on the parks and in fact are barely mentioned. These attractions do relate to Disney films and merchandise, and hence are implicated in the points that have been made about consumerism and the inter-referential character of Disney outputs, but they are much less entangled with the loftier speculations which lock Disney motifs into a political-economic context. In a way, this makes those messages which have been addressed in this book more effective, because the heady brew of fantasy, fun and message makes the distortions of history, the intimations of racism or sexism, the preference for some social forms (such as the conventional nuclear family or the corporation), the celebration of consumption and so on all the more difficult to notice when imbibed on the hoof, scurrying from one attraction to another armed with guide and camcorder. And it is right that visitors are not weighed down with concerns about how to interpret the parks as texts in the manner of the many commentators covered in this book (not to mention the author himself). It is this political-economic context, which, right from the early days, Disney has sought to suppress. In depicting Walt as a dreamer unconcerned with financial gain and disinterested in business as such, in portraying work as play for animators whistling while they worked or theme-park employees as hosts, in presenting senior executives as children having fun, in giving narratives to consumption at the theme parks so that it becomes part of the fun and fantasy, and in many other ways, the significance of that political-economic context is dissembled. As a result, the significance of the Disney enterprise as the business of fantasy is typically concealed.

However, the messages that the Disney theme parks provide are constantly changing. Unlike traditional texts, the parks are constantly undergoing change. This means that many of the observations made in this book will change, while some of the wider arguments about the foundation of Disney fantasy in business may also change, and therefore some reinterpretation may prove necessary. Doubtless, I shall go again – purely for fieldwork purposes, of course.

NOTES

1 THE LIFE OF WALT DISNEY

1 Walt certainly approved of his daughter's efforts, as can be seen when he wrote:

> No doubt you have been reading Diane's series in the Post about her Dad. . . . We are really proud of her pitching herself into this assignment and doing what we think is a good job. It required a lot of work and research on her part, but I think she really enjoyed it.
>
> (Letter to his sister Ruth, 5 December 1955, private source)

2 Interestingly, Custen (1992) has found that these motifs also appeared in Hollywood biographical films at around the same time as the period covered by Lowenthal's (1944) research.
3 'The testimony of Walter E. Disney Before the House Committee on Un-American Activities', in Peary and Peary (eds) (1980): 95.
4 The well-known palaeontologist, Gould, has noted how Mickey's appearance changed over the years, so that he 'assumed an ever more childlike appearance as the ratty character of *Steamboat Willie* became the cute and inoffensive host of the Magic Kingdom' (1979: 32).

2 DISNEY AFTER WALT

1 Mintzberg (1991) notes that this is a common problem among entre-preneurial organizations led by a strong charismatic leader.
2 There is some evidence to suggest that this pattern – of a strong, charismatic leader whose flights of fancy are restrained by a partner who also allows the former a more prominent role in line with his/her charismatic credentials – occurs in many other organizations. Jermier has suggested, for example, that the 'shielding of the charismatic heroine from business and other more mundane matters may be instrumental in the success of the Body Shop' (1993: 229). An analysis of British business pairings that is broadly along these lines can be found in Olins (1993), while Toth (1981) has attempted a more sociological analysis of this phenomenon. The implication is that not

only did Roy restrain Walt's excesses (something which Walt frequently acknowledged), but that he also allowed Walt's image to be unsullied with the world of business affairs so that Walt could ostensibly concentrate on the more creative aspects of the company's work and the promotion of its efforts. This strategy further reinforced Walt's capacity to present himself to the world as relatively unconcerned with matters of business, which was referred to in the previous chapter.

4 A FAMILY PILGRIMAGE

1 This and many other quotations can be found in 'The wisdom of Walt Disney', *Wisdom*, 32 (December), 1959.

5 CONTROL AND PREDICTABILITY

1 The design of a new display of the Crown Jewels prompted three Tower of London officials to fly to Disney World to study its approach to the control of crowd flow ('Disney jewel in crown', *The Times*, 16 February 1994: 3).

6 BACK TO THE FUTURE

1 'Disneyland: the fun and fantasy of the Magic Kingdom of Walt Disney', *Wisdom*, 32 (December), 1959: 72. This article comprises a detailed description of Disneyland in Walt's own words, with some introductory matter by an anonymous author.
2 While waiting in a queue at Innoventions the person in front of me complained that he was disappointed with the exhibits because he felt that they were unremarkable and that he was encountering little that was new. This had surprised him because this new area of EPCOT had been much heralded by Disney executives. It turned out that my informant worked for Disney, albeit in a different part of Disney World.
3 'Disneyland: The fun and fantasy of the Magic Kingdom of Walt Disney', *Wisdom*, 32 (December), 1959: 72.

9 THE BUSINESS OF FANTASY

1 In a television programme entitled *Disney: the Fairy Tale Years* in BBC1's *Omnibus* series. It was shown on 22 September 1992.
2 Chaney takes this kind of suggestion even further when he suggests that 'the activity of leisure can be defined as the mobilisation of audiences for popular culture' (1993: 163).
3 This thesis has been shown wanting on a number of grounds – see Abercrombie *et al.* (1980).
4 I have found Murdock's (1989a, 1989b) arguments especially helpful in this connection.

BIBLIOGRAPHY

Abercrombie, N., Hill, S., and Turner, B.S. (1980) *The Dominant Ideology Thesis*, London: Allen & Unwin.

Adamson, J. (1975) *Tex Avery: King of Cartoons*, New York: Da Capo.

Adler, S. (1983) 'Snow White for the defense: why Disney doesn't lose', *American Lawyer*, March: 32–5.

Aldridge, A. (1994) 'The construction of rational consumption in *Which?* magazine: the more blobs the better?' *Sociology*, 28: 899–912.

Alexander, G. (1994) 'Power play in the magic kingdom', *The Sunday Times* (Section 3), 28 August: 5.

Alexander, J. (1953a) 'The amazing story of Walt Disney: Part 1', *Saturday Evening Post*, 31 October: 24–5, 80, 84–6, 90, 92.

—— (1953b) 'The amazing story of Walt Disney: Part 2', *Saturday Evening Post*, 7 November: 26–7, 99–100.

Allan, R. (1985) 'Alice in Disneyland', *Sight and Sound*, Spring: 136–8.

Allen, H. and Denning, M. (1993) 'The cartoonists' front', *South Atlantic Quarterly*, 92: 89–117.

Alvesson, M. (1990) 'Organization: from substance to image?', *Organization Studies*, 11: 373–94.

Andrae, T. (1988) 'Of mouse and the man', in *Walt Disney's Mickey Mouse in Color*, New York: Pantheon.

Ang, I. (1990) 'Culture and communication: toward an ethnographic critique of media consumption in the transnational media system', *European Journal of Communication*, 5: 239–60.

Anon. (1932) 'Mickey Mouse's fourth birthday finds organization world-wide', *Motion Picture Herald*, 1 October: 42–3, 51.

—— (1934) 'The big bad wolf', *Fortune*, November: 88–95, 142–8.

—— (1948) 'The mighty mouse', *Time*, 25 October: 33.

—— (1950) 'Money from mice', *Newsweek*, 13 February: 84–9.

—— (1954) 'Father Goose', *Time*, 27 December: 30–4.

—— (1962) 'The wide world of Disney', *Newsweek*, 31 December: 48–51.

—— (1965) 'Disney's live-action profits', *Business Week*, 2 July: 78–82.

—— (1967) 'Disney without Walt', *Forbes*, 1 July: 39–40.

Apple, M. (1983) 'Uncle Walt', *Esquire*, December: 164–8.

Arlidge, J. (1992) 'Disney casts recruits for European venture', *Independent*, 7 January: 3.

Bailey, A. (1982) *Walt Disney's World of Fantasy*, New York: Everest House.
Barker, M. (1989) *Comics: Ideology, Power and the Critics*, Manchester: Manchester University Press.
—— (1993) 'Seeing how far you can see: on being a "fan" of *2,000AD*', in D. Buckingham (ed.), *Reading Audiences: Young People and the Media*, Manchester: Manchester University Press.
Barley, S.R., Meyer, G.W., and Gash, D.C. (1988) 'Cultures of culture: practitioners and the pragmatics of normative control', *Administrative Science Quarterly*, 33: 24–60.
Barrier, M. (1974) 'Of mice, wabbits, ducks and men: the Hollywood cartoon', *AFI Report*, 5: 18–26.
—— (1979) '"Building a better mouse": fifty years of Disney animation', *Funnyworld*, 20: 6–15.
Bass, B.M. (1985) *Leadership and Performance Beyond Expectations*, New York: Free Press.
Baudrillard, J. (1983) *Simulations*, New York: Semiotext(e).
—— (1993a) 'I don't belong to the club, to the Seraglio: interview with Mike Gane and Monique Arnaud', in M. Gane (ed.), *Baudrillard Live: Selected Interviews*, London: Routledge.
—— (1993b) 'Hyperreal America', *Economy and Society*, 22: 243–52.
Bauman, Z. (1992) *Intimations of Postmodernity*, London: Routledge.
Beard, R. (1982) *Walt Disney's Epcot Center*, New York: Harry N. Abrams.
Bendazzi, G. (1994) *Cartoons: One Hundred Years of Cinema Animation*, London: John Libbey.
Bierman, J.H. (1976) 'The Walt Disney robot dramas', *Yale Review*, 66: 223–36.
—— (1979) 'Disneyland and the "Los Angelization" of the arts', in M. Matlaw (ed.), *American Popular Entertainment*, Westport, Conn.: Greenwood Press.
Biggart, N.W. (1989) *Charismatic Capitalism: Direct Selling Organizations in America*, Chicago: University of Chicago Press.
Billig, M. (1994) 'Sod Baudrillard! Or ideology critique in Disney World', in H.W. Simons and M. Billig (eds), *After Postmodernism: Reconstructing Ideology Critique*, London: Sage.
Birmingham, S. (1964) 'The greatest one-man show on earth: Walt Disney', *McCall's*, 91: 98–101, 121.
Birnbaum, S. (1989) *Walt Disney World: The Official Guide*, New York: Avon Books.
Blake, P. (1972) 'Walt Disney World', *Architectural Forum*, 136: 24–41.
Blocklyn, P.L. (1988) 'Making magic: the Disney approach to people management', *Personnel*, 65: 28–35.
Boehme, L.R. (1975) 'The Magic Kingdom: is it really magic?', *American Opinion*, May: 13–20, 85–90.
Boorstin, D.J. (1961) *The Image: A Guide to Pseudo-events in America*, New York: Harper & Row.
Boyer, P.J. (1991) 'Katzenberg's seven-year itch', *Vanity Fair*, November: 64–79.
Bragdon, C. (1934) 'Mickey Mouse and what he means', *Scribner's*, July: 40–3.

Bright, R. (1987) *Disneyland: Inside Story*, New York: Harry N. Abrams.

Bristol, G.T. (1938) 'Snow White: inanimate characters become a new force in merchandising', *Dun's Review*, April: 13–17.

Brophy, P. (1991) 'The animation of sound', in A. Cholodenko (ed.), *The Illusion of Life: Essays on Animation*, Sydney: Power.

Bryman, A. (1992) *Charisma and Leadership in Organizations*, London: Sage.

—— (1993) 'Charismatic leadership in business organizations', *Leadership Quarterly*, 4: 289–304.

Bryson, B. (1993) 'Of mice and millions', *Observer Magazine*, 28 March: 16–23.

Budd, M., Entman, R.M., and Steinman, C. (1990) 'The affirmative character of U.S. cultural studies', *Critical Studies in Mass Communication*, 7: 169–84.

Bukatman, S. (1991) 'There's always Tomorrowland: Disney and the hypercinematic experience', *October*, 57: 55–78.

Cabarga, L. (1988) *The Fleischer Story*, New York: DaCapo.

Calás, M.B. (1993) 'Deconstructing charismatic leadership', *Leadership Quarterly*, 4: 305–28.

Carlzon, J. (1987) *Moments of Truth*, New York: Ballinger.

Carr, H. (1931) 'The only unpaid movie star', *American*, March: 55–7, 122–5.

Chamberlain, M. (1981) 'How the world of Disney is building for the future', *Marketing Week*, 11 December: 28–37.

Chaney, D. (1990) 'Subtopia in Gateshead: the MetroCentre as a cultural form', *Theory, Culture and Society*, 7: 49–68.

—— (1993) *Fictions of Collective Life: Public Drama in Late Modern Culture*, London: Routledge.

Chase, M. and Shaw, C. (1989) 'The dimensions of nostalgia', in C. Shaw and M. Chase (eds), *The Imagined Past: History and Nostalgia*, Manchester: Manchester University Press.

Churchill, D.W. (1934) 'Now Mickey Mouse enters art's temple', *New York Times Magazine*, 3 June: 13, 21.

—— (1938) 'Disney's philosophy', *New York Times Magazine*, 6 March: 9, 23.

Clegg, S. (1990) *Modern Organizations: Organization Studies in the Postmodern World*, London: Sage.

Cohen, E. (1979) 'A phenomenology of tourist experiences', *Sociology*, 13: 179–201.

—— (1988) 'Traditions in the qualitative sociology of tourism', *Annals of Tourism Research*, 15: 29–46.

Condit, C.M. (1989) 'The rhetorical limits of polysemy', *Critical Studies in Mass Communication*, 6: 103–22.

Conger, J.A. (1989) *The Charismatic Leader: Beyond the Mystique of Exceptional Leadership*, San Francisco: Jossey-Bass.

—— (1993) 'Max Weber's conceptualization of charismatic authority: its influence on organizational research', *Leadership Quarterly*, 4: 277–88.

Cooke, P. (1990) *Back to the Future: Modernity, Postmodernity, and Locality*, London: Unwin Hyman.

Corner, J., Richardson, K., and Fenton, N. (1990) *Nuclear Reactions: Form and Response in Public Issue Television*, London: John Libbey.

Cox, G.D. (1989) 'Don't mess with the Mouse', *National Law Journal*, 11, 31 July: 1, 26–7.

Crafton, D. (1982) *Before Mickey: The Animated Film, 1989–1928*, Cambridge, Mass.: MIT Press.

Crawford, M. (1992) 'The world in a shopping mall', in M. Sorkin (ed.), *Variations on a Theme Park: The New American City and the End of Public Space*, New York: Noonday.

Culhane, J. (1976) 'The old Disney magic', *New York Times Magazine*, 1 August: 11, 32–6.

Culhane, S. (1986) *Talking Animals and Other People*, New York: St Martin's Press.

Curran, J. (1990) 'The new revisionism in mass communication research: a reappraisal', *European Journal of Communication*, 5: 135–64.

Custen, G.F. (1992) *Bio/Pics: How Hollywood Constructed Public History*, New Brunswick, N.J.: Rutgers University Press.

Davidson, B. (1964) 'The fantastic Walt Disney', *Saturday Evening Post*, 7 November: 66–74.

Davis, S.O. (1980) 'Wish upon a falling star at Disney', *New York Times Magazine*, 16 November: 144–52.

Deal, T.E. and Kennedy, A.A. (1982) *Corporate Cultures*, Reading, Mass.: Addison-Wesley.

Debord, G. (1994) *The Society of the Spectacle* (1967), New York: Zone Books.

deCordova, R. (1994) 'The Mickey in Macy's window: childhood, consumerism, and Disney animation', in E. Smoodin (ed.), *Disney Discourse*, New York: Routledge.

Dennett, A.S. (1989) 'A postmodern look at EPCOT's American Adventure', *Journal of American Culture*, 12: 47–53.

De Roos, R. (1963) 'The magic worlds of Walt Disney', *National Geographic*, August: 159–207.

Dickson, E.J. (1993) 'Who's afraid of the big bad mouse?', *The Sunday Times Magazine*, 28 March: 30–4.

Disney, R. (1969) 'My unforgettable brother, Walt Disney', *Reader's Digest*, March: 133–9.

Disney, W. (1931) 'Mickey Mouse: how he was born', *Windsor Magazine*, October: 641–5.

—— (1934) 'The life story of Mickey Mouse', *Windsor Magazine*, January: 259–63.

—— (1941) 'Growing pains', *American Cinematographer*, March: 106–7, 139–42.

Doctorow, E.L. (1972) *The Book of Daniel*, London: Macmillan.

Dorfman, A. and Mattelart, A. (1975) *How to Read Donald Duck: Imperialist Ideology in the Disney Comic*, New York: International General.

Eckert, C. (1978) 'The Carole Lombard in Macy's window', *Quarterly Review of Film Studies*, 3: 1–22.

Eco, U. (1986) *Travels in Hyperreality*, London: Pan.

Eddy, D. (1955) 'The amazing secret of Walt Disney', *American*, August: 28–9, 110–15.

Edwards, R. (1979) *Contested Terrain: The Transformation of the Workplace in the Twentieth Century*, London: Heinemann.

Eisen, A. (1975) 'Two Disney artists', *Crimmer's: The Harvard Journal of Pictorial Fiction*, Winter: 35–44.

Eisman, R. (1993) 'Disney magic', *Incentive*, September: 45–56.

Eliot, M. (1993) *Walt Disney: Hollywood's Dark Prince*, New York: Birch Lane.

Elliott, H. (1994) 'Disney goes for older generation', *The Times*, 3 May: 5.

Ewen, S. (1988) *All Consuming Images: The Politics of Style in Contemporary Culture*, New York: Basic Books.

Eyssartel, A.-M. and Rochette, B. (n.d.) *Des mondes inventés: les parcs à thèmes*, Paris: Les Éditions de la Villette.

Featherstone, M. (1991) *Consumer Culture and Postmodernism*, London: Sage.

Feifer, M. (1985) *Going Places*, London: Macmillan.

Feild, R.D. (1942) *The Art of Walt Disney*, New York: Macmillan.

Fessier, M. (1967) 'Legacy of a last tycoon', *Los Angeles Times West*, 12 November: 16–23.

Fielding, H. (1992) 'Teach yourself post-modernism', *Independent on Sunday*, 15 November: 21.

Finch, C. (1973) *The Art of Walt Disney: From Mickey Mouse to the Magic Kingdoms*, New York: Harry N. Abrams.

Findlay, J.M. (1992) *Magic Lands: Western Cityscapes and American Culture after 1940*, Bekeley, Cal.: University of California Press.

Fiske, J. (1989) *Understanding Popular Culture*, London: Unwin Hyman.

Fjellman, S.M. (1992) *Vinyl Leaves: Walt Disney World and America*, Boulder, Col.: Westview Press.

Fleischer, R. (1993) *Just Tell Me When to Cry: Encounters with the Greats, Near-Greats and Ingrates of Hollywood*, New York: Carroll & Graf.

Flower, J. (1991) *Prince of the Magic Kingdom: Michael Eisner and the Re-making of Disney*, New York: John Wiley.

Ford, B. (1989) *Walt Disney*, New York: Walker.

Ford, G. (1975) 'Warner Brothers', *Film Comment*, 11: 10–16, 93, 96.

Forgacs, D. (1992) 'Disney animation and the business of childhood', *Screen*, 33: 361–74.

Francaviglia, R.V. (1981) 'Main Street USA: a comparison/contrast of streetscapes in Disneyland and Walt Disney World', *Journal of Popular Culture*, 15: 141–56.

France, V.A. (1991) *Window on Main Street*, Nashua, N.H.: Laughter Publications.

Freedland, J. (1994) 'Mighty mouse in magic kingdom', *Guardian*, 31 January: 8–9.

Fushaho, A. (1988) 'Disneyland's dreamlike success', *Japan Quarterly*, 35: 58–62.

Gaines, J. (1993) '"You don't necessarily have to be charismatic . . .": an interview with Anita Roddick and reflections on charismatic processes in The Body Shop International', *Leadership Quarterly*, 4: 347–59.

Galbraith, J.K. (1992) *The Culture of Contentment*, New York: Houghton Mifflin.

Garfield, B. (1991) 'How I spent (and spent and spent) my Disney vacation', *Washington Post*, 7 July: B5.

201

Gergen, K.J. (1992) 'Organization theory in the postmodern era', in M. Reed and M. Hughes (eds), *Rethinking Organization: New Directions in Organization Theory and Analysis*, London: Sage.

Gindin, R. (1984) 'The mystique of training at Disney World', *Restaurant Business*, 10 February: 242.

Giroux, H.A. (1994) 'Beyond the politics of innocence: memory and pedagogy in the "Wonderful World of Disney"', *Socialist Review*, 23: 79–107.

Goff, N. (1979) 'Disney: all gassed up and ready to go', *Financial World*, 1 September: 14–18.

Goldberger, P. (1972) 'Mickey Mouse teaches the architects', *New York Times Magazine*, 22 October: 40–1, 92–9.

Gomery, D. (1994) 'Disney's business history: a reinterpretation', in E. Smoodin (ed.), *Disney Discourse*, New York: Routledge.

Gordon, M. (1958) 'Walt's profit formula: dream, diversify – and never miss an angle', *Wall Street Journal*, 4 February: 1, 12.

Gottdiener, M. (1982) 'Disneyland: a Utopian urban space', *Urban Life*, 11: 139–62.

—— (1986) 'Recapturing the center: a semiotic analysis of shopping malls', in M. Gottdiener and A.P. Lagopolous (eds), *The City and the Sign*, New York: Columbia University Press.

Gottlieb, A. (1982) 'Americans' vacations', *Annals of Tourism Research*, 9: 165–87.

Gould, S.J. (1979) 'Mickey Mouse meets Konrad Lorenz', *Natural History*, 88: 30–6.

Greene, K. and Greene, R. (1991) *The Man Behind the Magic: The Story of Walt Disney*, New York: Viking.

Grossman, C.L. (1993) 'Vegas deals new hand of family fun', *USA Today* (International Edition), 11 August: 5A.

Grover, R. (1991) *The Disney Touch: How a Daring Management Team Revived an Entertainment Empire*, Homewood, Ill.: Irwin.

—— (1994) 'Jeffrey Katzenberg: no more Mr Tough Guy?', *Business Week*, 31 January: 46–7.

Haden-Guest, A. (1973) *The Paradise Program: Travels through Muzak, Hilton, Coca-Cola, Texaco, Walt Disney and other World Empires*, New York: Morrow.

Halas, J. and Manvell, R. (1959), *The Technique of Film Animation*, London: Focal Press.

Halevy, J. (1958) 'Disneyland and Las Vegas', *The Nation*, 7 June: 510–13.

Hall, S. (1980) 'Encoding/decoding', in S. Hall, D. Hobson, A. Lowe, and P. Willis (eds), *Culture, Media, Language*, London: Hutchinson.

Hand, D.D. (n.d.) *Memoirs: David Dodd Hand*, privately printed.

Harmetz, A. (1985) 'The man re-animating Disney', *New York Times Magazine*, 29 December: 13–18, 3, 37, 42–3.

Harrington, M. (1979) 'To the Disney station: corporate socialism in the Magic Kingdom', *Harper's*, January: 35–44, 86.

Harvey, D. (1989) *The Condition of Postmodernity*, London: Basil Blackwell.

Hayes, T.C. (1984) 'Trouble stalks the Magic Kingdom', *New York Times*, 17 June: 1, 12.

Heydebrand, W.V. (1989) 'New organizational forms', *Work and Occupations*, 16: 323–57.

Holleran, A. (1992) 'The mouse and the virgin', in *Fodor's 93: Walt Disney World*, New York: Fodor's.

Holliss, R. and Sibley, B. (1988) *The Disney Studio Story*, New York: Crown.

Hollister, P. (1940) 'Genius at work: Walt Disney', *Atlantic Monthly*, December: 689–701.

Horton, J.O. and Crew, S.R. (1989) 'Afro-Americans and museums: towards a policy of inclusion', in W. Leon and R. Rosenzweig (eds), *History Museums in the United States*, Urbana, Ill.: University of Illinois Press.

Howell, J.M. and Avolio, B.J. (1992) 'The ethics of charismatic leadership: submission or liberation?', *The Executive*, 6: 43–54.

Hulett, S. (1992) 'Walt Disney's *Pinnochio*', in *1992 Screen Cartoonists Annual*.

Hunt, P. and Frankenberg, R. (1990) 'It's a small world: Disneyland, the family and the multiple re-presentations of American childhood', in A. James and A. Prout (eds), *Constructing and Reconstructing Childhood: Contemporary Issues in the Sociological Study of Childhood*, London: Falmer.

Iacocca, L. (1984) *Iacocca: An Autobiography*, New York: Bantam.

Jackson, K.M. (1993) *Walt Disney: A Bio-bibliography*, Westport, Conn.: Greenwood.

Jackson, T. (1994) 'Disney seeks solutions to the park's midlife and identity crises', *Tampa Tribune* (Business and Finance section), 8 August: 8–9.

Jacobs, L. (1939) *The Rise of the American Film: A Critical History*, New York: Harcourt, Brace.

Jacobson, G. and Hillkirk, J. (1986) *Xerox: American Samurai*, New York: Collier.

Jameson, F. (1991) *Postmodernism, or, The Cultural Logic of Late Capitalism*, London: Verso.

Jenkins, I. (1992) 'French turn on "fascism" at Disney', *The Sunday Times* (section 3), 16 February: 6.

Jermier, J.M. (1993) 'Introduction – charismatic leadership: neo-Weberian perspectives', *Leadership Quarterly*, 4: 217–33.

Johnson, D.M. (1981) 'Disney World as structure and symbol: re-creation of the American experience', *Journal of Popular Culture*, 15: 157–65.

Jones, C. (1991) 'What's up, down under?', in A. Cholodenko (ed.), *The Illusion of Life: Essays in Animation*, Sydney: Power.

Kapsis, R.E. (1989) 'Reputation building and the film art world: the case of Alfred Hitchcock', *Sociological Quarterly*, 30: 15–35.

Kasindorf, J. (1991) 'Mickey Mouse time at Disney', *New York*, 7 October: 32–42.

Kasson, J.F. (1978) *Amusing the Million: Coney Island at the Turn of the Century*, New York: Hill & Wang.

Keat, R., Whiteley, N. and Abercrombie, N. (1994) 'Introduction', in R. Keat, N. Whiteley, and N. Abercrombie (eds), *The Authority of the Consumer*, London: Routledge.

King, M.J. (1981) 'Disneyland and Walt Disney World: traditional values in futuristic form', *Journal of Popular Culture*, 15: 116–40.

—— (1983) 'McDonald's and Disney', in M. Fishwick (ed.), *Ronald Revisited: The World of Ronald McDonald*, Bowling Green, Ohio: Bowling Green University Popular Press.

—— (1991) 'The theme park experience: what museums can learn from Mickey Mouse', *The Futurist*, November-December: 24–31.

King, P. (1986) 'The marketing challenge: backstage at Walt Disney World', *Food Management*, July: 74–8, 142–8.

Kinney, J. (1988) *Walt Disney and Assorted Other Characters: An Unauthorized Account of the Early Years at Disney's*, New York: Harmony.

Klein, N.M. (1993) *Seven Minutes: The Life and Death of the American Animated Cartoon*, London: Verso.

Kottak, C.P. (1982) 'Anthropological analysis of mass enculturation', in C.P. Kottak (ed.), *Researching American Culture*, Ann Arbor, Mich.: University of Michigan Press.

Kotter, J. and Heskett, J.L. (1992) *Corporate Culture and Performance*, New York: Free Press.

Kuenz, J. (1993) 'It's a small world after all: Disney and the pleasures of identification', *South Atlantic Quarterly*, 92: 63–88.

Lang, G.E. and Lang, K. (1988) 'Recognition and renown', *American Journal of Sociology*, 94: 79–109.

Langer, M. (1992) 'The Disney–Fleischer dilemma: product differentiation and technological innovation', *Screen*, 33: 343–60.

Langley, W. (1993) 'Euro-dismal', *The Sunday Times*, 22 August: 9.

Lash, S. (1990) *Sociology of Postmodernism*, London: Routledge.

Lawrence, E.A. (1986) 'In the Mick of time: reflections on Disney's ageless mouse', *Journal of Popular Culture*, 20: 65–72.

Leerhsen, C. (1989) 'How Disney does it', *Newsweek*, 3 April: 14–20.

Lenburg, J. (1993) *The Great Cartoon Directors*, New York: Da Capo.

Lennon, P. (1993) 'Priest who took Mickey for a ride', *Guardian* (section 2), 25 October: 2–3.

Leyda, J. (1942) 'The dimensions of Disney', *Saturday Review*, 6 June: 5.

Lloyd, C. (1994) 'Airport rides ready for take-off', *The Sunday Times* (section 3), 10 July: 10.

Long, K.H. (1994) 'Quiet region debates value of theme park', *Tampa Tribune* (Travel section), 31 July: 1.

Lowenthal, D. (1985) *The Past is a Foreign Country*, Cambridge: Cambridge University Press.

—— (1989) 'Nostalgia tells it like it wasn't', in C. Shaw and M. Chase (eds), *The Imagined Past: History and Nostalgia*, Manchester: Manchester University Press.

Lowenthal, L. (1944) 'Biographies in popular magazines', in P.F. Lazarsfeld and F. Stanton (eds), *Radio Research: 1942–1943*, New York: Duell, Sloan & Pearce.

Lutz, E.G. (1920) *Animated Cartoons: How They Are Made, Their Origin and Development*, New York: Scribner.

Lyotard, J.-F. (1984) *The Postmodern Condition: A Report on Knowledge*, Manchester: Manchester University Press.

MacCannell, D. (1976) *The Tourist: A New Theory of the Leisure Class*, New York: Schocken.
—— (1992) *Empty Meeting Grounds: The Tourist Papers*, London: Routledge.
McDonald, J. (1966) 'Now the bankers come to Disney', *Fortune*, May: 138–41, 223–4.
McGuigan, J. (1992) *Cultural Populism*, London: Routledge.
Maltin, L. (1973) *The Disney Films*, New York: Crown.
—— (1987) *Of Mice and Magic: A History of American Animated Cartoons*, revised edition, New York: Plume.
Mann, A. (1934) 'Mickey Mouse's financial career', *Harper's*, 168: 714–21.
Marin, L. (1984) *Utopics: Spatial Play*, London: Macmillan.
Marling, S. (1993) *American Affair*, London: Boxtree.
Martin, J. (1992) *Cultures in Organizations: Three Perspectives*, New York: Oxford University Press.
Massie, J. (1992) 'How we got here', *1992 Screen Cartoonists Annual*.
Masters, K. (1994) 'A house divided', *Vanity Fair*, 57 (November): 122–8, 156–60.
Mechling, E.W. and Mechling, J. (1981) 'The sale of two cities: a semiotic comparison of Disneyland with Marriott's Great Adventure', *Journal of Popular Culture*, 15: 166–79.
Medved, M. (1993) 'Still wishing on a star', *The Sunday Times*, 8 August: 24–5.
Merritt, R. and Kaufman, J.B. (1992) *Walt in Wonderland: The Silent Films of Walt Disney*, Perdenone: Edizioni Biblioteca dell'Imagine.
Meyer, M. (1994) 'Of mice and men', *Newsweek*, 5 September: 40–7.
Miller, D. Disney (1956) *The Story of Walt Disney*, New York: Dell.
Mills, S.F. (1990) 'Disney and the promotion of synthetic worlds', *American Studies International*, 28: 66–79.
Mintzberg, H. (1991) 'The entrepreneurial organization', in H. Mintzberg and J.B. Quine (eds), *The Strategy Process: Concepts, Contexts, Cases*, Englewood Cliffs, N.J.: Prentice-Hall.
Mooney, J. (1994) 'Disney on the edge?', *Empire*, November: 78–84.
Moore, A. (1980) 'Walt Disney World: bounded ritual space and the playful pilgrimage center', *Anthropological Quarterly*, 53: 207–18.
Morison, E.E. (1983) 'What went wrong with Disney's world's fair', *American Heritage*, 35: 70–9.
Morley, D. (1980) *The 'Nationwide' Audience*, London: British Film Institute.
—— (1993) 'Active audience theory', *Journal of Communication*, 43: 13–19.
Mosley, L. (1986) *The Real Walt Disney: A Biography*, London: Grafton.
Mulkay, M. and Chaplin, E. (1982) 'Aesthetics and artistic career', *Sociological Quarterly*, 23: 117–38.
Murdock, G. (1989a) 'Cultural studies: missing links', *Critical Studies in Mass Communication*, 6: 436–40.
—— (1989b) 'Critical inquiry and audience activity', in R. Dervin, L. Grossberg, B.J. O'Keefe, and E. Wartella, *Rethinking Communication, vol. 2: Paradigm Exemplars*, Newbury Park, Cal.: Sage.
Nadler, D.A. and Tushman, M.L. (1990) 'Beyond the charismatic leader: leadership and organizational change', *California Management Review*, 32: 77–97.

BIBLIOGRAPHY

Natale, R. (1986) 'Prince of the Magic Kingdom: Michael Eisner re-animates Disney', *California Business*, December: 18–23.

Neff, R. (1990) 'In Japan, they're Goofy about Disney', *Business Week*, 12 March: 39.

Nelson, S. (1986) 'Walt Disney's EPCOT and the world's fair performance tradition', *Drama Review*, 30: 106–46.

—— (1990) 'Reel life performance: the Disney–MGM Studios', *Drama Review*, 24: 60–78.

Nye, R.B. (1981) 'Eight ways of looking at an amusement park', *Journal of Popular Culture*, 15: 63–75.

Olins, R. (1993) 'Dynamic duos – or terrible twins?', *The Sunday Times* (section 3), 30 May: 8.

Peary, D. and Peary, G. (eds) (1980) *The American Animated Cartoon: A Critical Anthology*, New York: Dutton.

Peters, T. and Austin, N. (1985) *A Passion for Excellence*, New York: Random House.

Peters, T. and Waterman, R. (1982) *In Search of Excellence: Lessons from America's Best-run Companies*, New York: Harper & Row.

Potts, M. and Behr, P. (1987) *The Leading Edge: CEOs who Turned Their Companies Around*, New York: McGraw-Hill.

Reader, I. (1993a) 'Introduction', in I. Reader and T. Walter (eds), *Pilgrimage in Popular Culture*, London: Macmillan.

Reader, I. (1993b) 'Conclusions', in I. Reader and T. Walter (eds), *Pilgrimage in Popular Culture*, London: Macmillan.

Real, M.R. (1977) *Mass-mediated Culture*, Englewood Cliffs, N.J.: Prentice-Hall.

Relph, E. (1976) *Place and Placelessness*, London: Pion.

Ritzer, G. (1993) *The McDonaldization of Society*, Thousand Oaks, Cal.: Pine Forge.

Roberts, E.A. (1994) 'History is different from Disneyhistory', *Tampa Tribune* (Commentary section), 31 July: 1.

Robertson, R. (1990) 'After nostalgia? Wilful nostalgia and the phases of globalization', in B.S. Turner (ed.), *Theories of Modernity and Post-modernity*, London: Sage.

Rojek, C. (1993a) 'Disney culture', *Leisure Studies*, 12: 121–35.

—— (1993b) *Ways of Escape: Modern Transformations in Leisure and Travel*, London: Macmillan.

Rose, F. (1989) *West of Eden: The End of Innocence at Apple Computer*, London: Business Books.

—— (1990) 'Taking care of business', *Premiere*, November: 104–12.

Rosenau, P.M. (1992) *Post-modernism and the Social Sciences: Insights, Inroads, and Intrusions*, Princeton, N.J.: Princeton University Press.

Ross, I. (1982) 'Disney gambles on tomorrow', *Fortune*, 4 October: 62–8.

Rowe, C. and Koetter, F. (1978) *Collage City*, Cambridge, Mass.: MIT Press.

Rugare, S. (1991) 'The advent of America at EPCOT Center', in R. Diprose and R. Ferrell (eds), *Cartographies: Structuralism and the Mapping of Bodies and Spaces*, North Sydney, Australia: Allen & Unwin.

Sayers, F.C. (1965) 'Walt Disney accused', *Horn Book*, December: 602–11.

Sayle, M. (1983) 'Of mice and yen', *Harper's*, August: 36–45.

Schein, E.H. (1985) *Organizational Culture and Leadership*, San Francisco: Jossey-Bass.

Schickel, R. (1986) *The Disney Version: The Life, Times, Art and Commerce of Walt Disney*, revised edition, London: Pavilion.

Schiller, H.I. (1973) *The Mind Managers*, Boston, Mass.: Beacon.

—— (1989) *Culture, Inc.: The Corporate Takeover of Public Expression*, New York: Oxford University Press.

Schudson, M. (1979) 'Review essay: On tourism and modern culture', *American Journal of Sociology*, 84: 1249–58.

Schultz, J. (1988) 'The fabulous presumption of Disney World: Magic Kingdom in the wilderness', *Georgia Review*, 42: 275–312.

Sehlinger, B. (1994) *The Unofficial Guide to Walt Disney World*, New York: Prentice Hall.

Seldes, G. (1931) 'Mickey Mouse maker', *New Yorker*, 19 December: 23–7.

—— (1937) 'No art, Mr Disney?', *Esquire*, September: 91, 171–2.

Sertl, W.J. (1989) 'Hollywood divine: Disney–MGM Studios in Orlando', *Travel and Leisure*, 19: 140–6, 192–6.

Shearer, L. (1972) 'How Disney sells happiness', *Parade*, March 26: 4–6.

Shields, R. (1989) 'Social spacialization and the built environment: the West Edmonton Mall', *Environment and Planning D: Society and Space*, 7: 147–64.

—— (1991) *Places on the Margin: Alternative Geographies of Modernity*, London: Routledge.

—— (1992) 'The individual, consumption cultures and the fate of community', in R. Shields (ed.), *Lifestyle Shopping: The Subject of Consumption*, London: Routledge.

Simons, C. (1990) 'Business and leisure', *Landscape Architecture*, 80: 42–5.

Smith, R.C. and Eisenberg, E.M. (1987) 'Conflict at Disneyland: a root-metaphor analysis', *Communication Monographs*, 54: 367–80.

Smoodin, E. (1993) *Animating Culture: Hollywood Cartoons from the Sound Era*, Oxford: Roundhouse.

Snyder, N.H., Dowd, J.J., and Houghton, D.M. (1994) *Vision, Values and Courage: Leadership for Quality Management*, New York: Free Press.

Solomon, C. (1989) *Enchanted Drawings: The History of Animation*, New York: Alfred A. Knopf.

—— (1990) 'The new toon boom', *Los Angeles Times Calendar*, 19 August: 8–9, 94–5.

—— (1993) 'Disney's daughter attacks book', *Los Angeles Times*, 17 July: F14.

Sorkin, M. (1992) 'See you in Disneyland', in M. Sorkin (ed.), *Variations on a Theme Park: The New American City and the End of Public Space*, New York: Noonday.

Spanier, D. (1994) 'Poker with the plastic pirates', *The Financial Times*, 22 January: xi.

Stanley, L. (1993) 'On auto/biography in sociology', *Sociology*, 27: 41–52.

Starobinski, J. (1966) 'The idea of nostalgia', *Diogenes*, 54: 81–103.

Stephanson, A. (1987) 'Regarding postmodernism – a conversation with Fredric Jameson', *Social Text*, 17: 29–54.

Susman, W. (1989) 'Did success spoil the United States?: dual representations on postwar America', in L. May (ed.), *America: Culture and Politics in the Age of Cold War*, Chicago: University of Chicago Press.

Sutton, R.I. (1992) 'Feelings about a Disneyland visit: photography and the reconstruction of bygone emotions', *Journal of Management Inquiry*, 1: 278–87.

Taylor, J. (1987) *Storming the Magic Kingdom: Wall Street, the Raiders and the Battle for Disney*, New York: Viking.

Terrell, J. (1991) 'Disneyland and the future of museum anthropology', *American Anthropologist*, 93: 149–53.

Tester, K. (1993) *The Life and Times of Post-modernity*, London: Routledge.

Thomas, B. (1976) *Walt Disney: An American Original*, New York: Simon & Schuster.

—— (1991) *Disney's Art of Animation from Mickey Mouse to Beauty and the Beast*, New York: Hyperion.

Thomas, F. and Johnston, O. (1981) *Disney Animation: The Illusion of Life*, New York: Abbeville.

Thomas, M. (1969) 'The men who followed Mickey Mouse', *Dun's Review*, 94: 34–8.

Tichy, N.M. and Devanna, M.A. (1986) *The Transformational Leader*, New York: John Wiley.

Tietyen, D. (1990) *The Musical World of Walt Disney*, Milwaukee, Wis.: Hal Leonard.

Toth, M.A. (1981) *The Theory of the Two Charismas*, Washington D.C.: University Press of America.

Toufexis, A. (1985) 'No Mickey Mousing around', *Time*, 11 March: 40.

Turner, B.S. (1987) 'A note on nostalgia', *Theory, Culture and Society*, 4: 147–56.

Turner, R. (1991) 'Hollywood blues as Disney stumbles', *The Sunday Times*, 17 November: 7.

Turner, V. and Turner, E. (1978) *Image and Pilgrimage in Christian Culture*, New York: Columbia University Press.

Urry, J. (1990) *The Tourist Gaze: Leisure and Travel in Contemporary Societies*, London: Sage.

Van Maanen, J. (1991) 'The smile factory: work at Disneyland', in P.J. Frost, L.F. Moore, M.R. Louis, C.C. Lundberg and J. Martin (eds), *Reframing Organizational Culture*, Newbury Park, Cal.: Sage.

—— and Kunda, G. (1989) '"Real feelings": emotional expression and organizational culture', *Research in Organizational Behavior*, 11: 43–103.

Wakefield, N. (1990) *Postmodernism: The Twilight of the Real*, London: Pluto.

Waldrep, S. (1993) 'The contemporary future of tomorrow', *South Atlantic Quarterly*, 92: 139–55.

Wallace, I. (1949) 'Mickey Mouse and how he grew', *Collier's*, 9 April: 20–36.

Wallace, K. (1963) 'The engineering of ease', *New Yorker*, 7 September: 104–29.

Wallace, M. (1981) 'Visiting the past: history museums in the United States', *Radical History Review*, 25: 63–96.

—— (1985) 'Mickey Mouse history: portraying the past at Disney World', *Radical History Review*, 32: 33–57.

Waller, G.A. (1980) 'Mickey, Walt and film criticism from *Steamboat Willie* to *Bambi*', in D. Peary and G. Peary (eds), *The American Animated Cartoon: A Critical Anthology*, New York: Dutton.

Walsh, K. (1992) *The Representation of the Past: Museums and Heritage in the Post-modern World*, London: Routledge.

Wanger, W. (1943) 'Mickey Icarus, 1943', *Saturday Review*, 4 September: 18–19.

Warde, A. (1994) 'Consumers, identity and belonging: reflections on some theses of Zygmunt Bauman', in R. Keat, N. Whiteley, and N. Abercrombie (eds), *The Authority of the Consumer*, London: Routledge.

Warren, S. (1994) 'Disneyfication of the metropolis: popular resistance in Seattle', *Journal of Urban Affairs*, 16: 89–107.

Wasko, J., Phillips, M., and Purdie, C. (1993) 'Hollywood meets Madison Avenue: the commercialization of US films', *Media, Culture and Society*, 15: 271–93.

Wasserman, A. (1983) 'Un and loathing at EPCOT', *Industrial Design Magazine*, March/April: 34–9.

Weber, B. (1969) 'The Disney troika', *California Business*, 20 October: 7, 18–19.

Weber, M. (1968) *Economy and Society* (1925), 3 vols, eds G. Roth and C. Wittich, New York: Bedminster.

Weinstein, R.M. (1992) 'Disneyland and Coney Island: reflections on the evolution of the modern amusement park', *Journal of Popular Culture*, 26: 131–64.

Welsh, T. (1994) 'Best and worst corporate reputations', *Fortune*, 7 February: 32–6.

Westley, F.R. and Mintzberg, H, (1989) 'Visionary leadership and strategic management', *Strategic Management Journal*, 10: 17–32.

Wiener, J. (1993) 'Murdered ink', *The Nation*, 256: 743–50.

Willis, S. (1993) 'Disney World: public use/private state', *South Atlantic Quarterly*, 92: 119–37.

Wilson, A. (1992) *The Culture of Nature: North American Landscape from Disney to the Exxon Valdez*, Cambridge, Mass.: Basil Blackwell.

Wolf, J.C. (1979) 'Disney World: America's vision of Utopia', *Alternative Futures*, 2: 72–7.

Yoshimoto, M. (1994) 'Images of empire: Tokyo Disneyland and Japanese cultural imperialism', in E. Smoodin (ed.), *Disney Discourse*, New York: Routledge.

Zehnder, L.E. (1975) *Florida's Disney World*, Tallahassee, Fla.: Peninsular Publishing.

Zukin, S. (1990) 'Socio-spatial prototypes of a new organization of consumption: the role of real cultural capital', *Sociology*, 24: 37–56.

—— (1991) *Landscapes of Power: From Detroit to Disney World*, Berkeley, Cal.: University of California Press.

AUTHOR INDEX

SUBJECT INDEX

Disney theme park attractions are designated 'attraction' in brackets. EPCOT Center pavilions are designated 'pavilion' in brackets.

214